# COMPLETE METHOD
## TROMBONE EUPHONIUM
### ARBAN

# J. B. Arban

# Complete Method

## for Trombone & Euphonium

## Joseph Alessi & Dr. Brian Bowman

Jean Baptiste Arban
(1825 - 1889)

**ARBAN COMPLETE METHOD
FOR TROMBONE & EUPHONIUM
BY JOSEPH ALESSI & DR. BRIAN BOWMAN**
Encore Music Publishers
PO BOX 212
MAPLE CITY MI 49664-0212
www.EncoreMuPub.com

Copyright © 2015 Encore Music Publishers
International Copyright Secured. All Rights Reserved.
Printed in U.S.A.

No part of this work covered by the copyrights hereon may be reproduced, stored in a retrieval system or transmitted in any form or by any means, electronic, mechanical, photocopying, recording, scanning or otherwise, except as permitted under Sections 107 or 108 of the 1976 United States Copyright Act, without written permission of the publisher.
ISMN M-800004-01-8

# Table of Contents

| | |
|---|---:|
| The Arban Brothers | 4 |
| Report | 5 |
| Biography of Mr. Joseph Alessi | 6 |
| Biography of Dr. Brian Bowman | 7 |
| Preface by Mr. Joseph Alessi | 8 |
| Preface by Dr. Brian Bowman | 9 |
| First Studies | 13 |
| Studies on Syncopation | 29 |
| Studies on Dotted Eighth and Sixteenth Notes | 32 |
| Studies on the Slur | 43 |
| Scale Studies Major | 64 |
| Scale Studies Minor | 87 |
| Scale Studies Chromatic | 88 |
| Ornamentation | 100 |
| Gruppetto | 109 |
| Double Appoggiatura | 116 |
| Simple Appoggiatura | 119 |
| Grace Note | 121 |
| Portamento | 123 |
| Trill | 125 |
| Mordant | 134 |
| Intervals | 138 |
| Octaves and Tenths | 147 |
| Triplets | 148 |
| Studies in Sixteenth Notes | 154 |
| Perfect Major and Minor Chords | 160 |
| Dominant Seventh Chords | 167 |
| Diminished Seventh Chords | 168 |
| Cadenzas | 171 |
| Multiple Tonguing (Triple) | 174 |
| Multiple Tonguing (Double) | 197 |
| Arban's Comments from the Original Edition | 214 |
| The Art of Phrasing | 215 |
| Duets | 281 |
| Characteristic Studies | 322 |
| Solos | 347 |
| Euphonium Fingering Charts | 394 |

# THE ARBAN BROTHERS
from
*My Musical Life and Recollections*
by
# Jule Riviere 1893

It was while in garrison at Lyons that I made the acquaintance of the Arban brothers, who, in their different ways, were all remarkable men. Louis, the eldest, was the aeronaut of the day, and his ascents in 1842-43 created quite a sensation, till, like most balloonists, he went up never to be heard of again. This fatal ascent took place from a square in Madrid.

The second brother, Charles, was proprietor of a grand casino in Lyons, called *la Rotonde*, where concerts and balls were held all the year round. In addition to this onerous occupation Charles Arban managed to superintend a large manufactory of fireworks bearing his name, besides also finding time for certain ingenious inventions, one of which was a flying machine, that however, if I remember rightly, went no higher than the chimney pots when the experiment was tried in the gardens of la Rotonde.

The lion's share of ability, however, in the Arban family fell to Jean Baptiste, who developed talent at a very early age, and became at once a remarkable performer on the cornet-a-pistons. I well remember Jean Baptiste Arban's appointment as cornet solo in the picked band that went out to St. Helene on board the *Belle-Poule*, under the command of the Prince di Joinville, to bring back the remains of Napoleon I for sepulchre in the Invalides.

This clever cornet player was also a particularly affable man, and instances of his good nature were constantly occurring. One that came within my own experience is worthy of passing mention, for it happened on the first day of our acquaintance, when no laws, written or unwritten could have called for the gracious concession he made to play a cornet solo at a concert I was giving on a summer afternoon at the Salle St. Barbe. Arban, who was in his sailor's dress had neither cornet nor music with him, but I had no sooner made the suggestion for him to oblige us with something than he was ready to mount the platform with an instrument borrowed from the band, and to play the *Carnival de Venice* with variations, which he did in marvelous style. Our friendship, which was sealed from that day, lasted for nearly half a century, till, in fact, the day of his death in 1889.

Arban was always acknowledged to be one of the best cornet players in France. This was clearly the opinion of Jullien, who engaged him in conjunction with Koenig, as the two soloists in his orchestra, when he was in the zenith of his popularity in London. Koenig excelled in slow movements, but when what is called tonguing was wanted Arban had no equal.

On his return to Paris he was appointed professor of the cornet class at the Conservatoire, a post he held till his death. Besides being a very fine player, Arban was also a composer of some note, his musical achievements consisting of cornet solos, studies, etc.; whilst to him the musical world is indebted for a book called Arban's *Cornet Tutor*, which is still considered the best that has ever been published.

As conductor also of the *Paris Bals de l'Opera* Arban will long be remembered, for this is a post he filled for years, till in fact the winter of 1889, when he caught the chill which killed him.

Arban, who had never been an extravagant man, amassed a comfortable fortune, which on his death went to his only daughter. Many were the projects he formed as we used to sit chatting together, of ending his days on the shores of the Mediterranean we both loved so well. And with this object in view he bought land enough to build two villas upon in Monte Carlo, occupying his leisure in superintending the construction of the houses; but, as I have said, he died in harness in the capital.

# REPORT

*The Committee of Musical Studies of the Conservatory on Mr. Arban's Cornet Method*

The Committee of musical studies has examined the work submitted to them by Mr. Arban. This work, the extent of which is considerable, is based upon excellent principles, and contains every instruction calculated to produce a good performer on the cornet.

This work is, to a certain extent, a résumé of the knowledge acquired by the author during his long experience as both professor and performer, and may be termed a written embodiment of the information resulting from his musical career.

The various kinds of articulation, the tonguing, the staccati, and so forth, are seriously considered, ingeniously analyzed, and successfully resolved, the numerous lessons which the author devotes to each of these points are deserving of special mention.

In the copious series of instructions, wherein all other musical questions are discussed, we observe a profound appreciation of difficulties, and a thorough tact in overcoming them. The latter part of this work contains a long succession of studies as interesting in subject as in form, and concludes with a collection of solos, which are, as it were, the embodiment of application of the previous lessons; in these studies, in these solos, shine forth the qualities, at once brilliant and solid, of which the author has so often given proof.

For this reason the committee, rendering due homage to the Method of which Mr. Arban is the author, unhesitatingly approve it, and adopt it unreservedly for instruction at the Conservatory.

Signed:

Auber, Meyerbeer, Kastner, A. Thomas, Reber, Razin, Benoist, Dauverné, Vogt, Prumier, Emile Perrin,
Edouard Monnais, *Imperial Commissioner*
A. De Beauchesne, *Secretary*

**JOSEPH ALESSI** was appointed Principal Trombonist of the New York Philharmonic in 1985. Mr. Alessi began musical studies in his native California with his father, Joseph Alessi, Sr. He has performed with the San Francisco Ballet Orchestra and was a soloist with the San Francisco Symphony before continuing his musical training at Philadelphia's Curtis Institute of Music. Prior to joining the New York Philharmonic, he was second trombone of the Philadelphia Orchestra for four seasons and principal trombone of L'Orchestre Symphonique de Montreal for one season.

Mr. Alessi is an active soloist, recitalist, and chamber music performer. In April 1990, he made his solo debut with the New York Philharmonic, performing Creston's *Fantasy for Trombone*, and in 1992 premiered Christopher Rouse's Pulitzer Prize-winning *Trombone Concerto* with the Orchestra, which commissioned the work for its 150th Anniversary Celebration. He has been a guest artist with the Lincoln Symphony, the Colorado Symphony Orchestra, the Santa Barbara Symphony, the New Japan Philharmonic, the Orchestra of Teatro Bellini in Catania Sicily, the Mannheim National Theater Orchestra, and the National Repertory Orchestra and has appeared in recitals at colleges and universities throughout the United States.

Mr. Alessi has also participated in numerous festivals, including the Festivale Musica di Camera in Protogruaro, Italy, the Cabrillo Music Festival, Swiss Brass Week, and the Lieksa Brass Week in Finland. He was featured in the 1997 International Trombone Festival in Feldkirch, Austria, and the International Meeting of Brass Instruments in Lille, France. He is a founding member of the Summit Brass ensemble at the Rafael Mendez Brass Institute in Tempe, Arizona.

Currently on the faculty of the Juilliard School, Mr. Alessi has taught at Temple University in Philadelphia and the Grand Teton Music Festival in Wyoming. His students now occupy posts with many major symphony orchestras throughout the United States.

**Dr. Brian Bowman** is one of the foremost euphonium soloists in the world today. His history of euphonium firsts is impressive:

• First euphonium recital in New York's Carnegie Recital Hall 1976 • First euphoniumist to serve as president of the Tubists Universal Brotherhood Association (now I.T.E.A.) • First euphonium concert tour of Japan • First Guest Euphonium Artist-Falcone International Euphonium Competition • First euphonium master class at the Paris Conservatory Superior of Music, France • Master teacher at the first Deutsche Tubaforum workshop to include the euphonium, tenor horn and baritone, Hammelburg, Germany 1991.

Dr. Brian L. Bowman enjoys a distinguished career as a soloist, clinician, recording artist, educator and administrator. Dr. Bowman has held the principal euphonium position—in addition to being a featured soloist—in each of the bands he has been associated with: The University of Michigan Symphony Band, The United States Navy Band, The United States Bicentennial Band, The United States Air Force Band and the River City Brass Band.

In addition to his live performances, Dr. Bowman can be heard on over 35 service band recordings and his six solo albums. Currently Professor of Music (Euphonium) in the College of Music at The University of North Texas, Dr. Bowman has also served on the music faculty of eight other universities. In 1989 he was named the British Magazines Euphonium Player of the Year, and in 1995 was given the Lifetime Achievement Award from the Tubists Universal Brotherhood Association. He is the only living euphoniumist to be included in the book Twentieth-Century Brass Soloists by Michael Meckna.

Dr. Bowman has contributed significantly to the body of literature available for euphonium performers today. Not only have composers written new works at Bowman's specific request, but also many works have resulted merely from the composer being acquainted with Bowman and having heard his performance capabilities. Of the seven new euphonium works commissioned by the Tubists Universal Brotherhood Association since it's inception in 1974, Bowman has premiered four. A major thrust of Bowman's career has been working to generate quality new compositions for his beloved instrument.

# PREFACE
## by Mr. Joseph Alessi

All athletes have daily routines which they rely upon religiously in the most stressful and competitive moments of their careers. In my teaching experience, I have found that adding a routine or a group of repetitive exercises can greatly increase students' productivity and consistency from day to day. The pupils who had not experienced these regimens before—and who do now—all see immediate improvement in their playing. I believe the Arban book to be perhaps the greatest staple in a brass-player's routine.

I owe my introduction to the Arban book to my father and my first teacher, Joseph Alessi Sr. He had the opportunity to study with another creator of a fine basic fundamental study book, Max Schlossberg. Fundamentals is what the Arban book is all about. Too often I hear students trying to learn difficult pieces without respecting fundamental approaches. The Arban *Method* offers these basics and progressively introduces the *daily diet* of brass playing. The book is filled with exercises on long tones, attacks using immediate air, the lip slur—one of the most fundamental understandings a brass player can embrace—flexibility, intervals, theory and chord structure, rapid tonguing, and the fabulous characteristic studies. Each one of Arban's sections can be part of a fantastic journey into a small piece of the total puzzle.

I mentioned theory here because daily studying of pages 161-171 was invaluable to me for music theory and harmony tests. Arban's references to a wide array of arpeggios and chordal structures were very important to me at a young age. Upon closer examination of the Arban book, you will find that a good percentage of this book is geared towards the euphonium player. However, at a young age, I was not aware of this point, and I concentrated on practicing most of these exercises as if they were designed for the trombonist. This helped tremendously in my quest to have command of the instrument. If you are looking to have great technique—especially the kind that will allow you to play difficult solos, i.e. *Creston Fantasy*, the Pryor repertoire, or any other *pyrotechnic* solos—the Arban book should be included in your daily routine. I cannot begin to say enough about this wonderful collection of exercises by Arban. I will add only a few short thoughts to what is contained therein: Use a metronome often when exploring this book. Also, attempt to learn these exercises so that they become *second nature*. When the difficulty factor ceases, it allows your brain to completely direct its attention to musical thoughts and creativity. Like a juggler who can keep four or five objects in the air and can simultaneously carry on an unrelated conversation, learn Arban inside out.

# PREFACE

*by Dr. Brian Bowman*

The *Arban's Complete Conservatory Method* for Trumpet has been the most widely used brass text for over a century. Although written almost one hundred-fifty years ago, it still is the most comprehensive and complete text covering all aspects of technical development. This material is especially valuable for the euphonium/baritone horn student as it covers many aspects of technical development appropriate for valved brass instruments.

While numerous editions have been prepared in treble clef, there has been no complete bass clef edition available for the low brass player. Especially valuable in this newly prepared edition is the inclusion of sections heretofore unavailable in bass clef including the melodic *Art of Phrasing* studies. Care has been taken to eliminate the note errors and other mistakes prevalent in other bass clef editions.

In the original edition of *Arban's Complete Conservatory Method* Arban wrote a preface, which is paraphrased below:

It may appear somewhat strange to undertake the defense of the cornet {euphonium} at a time when this instrument has given proofs of its excellence, both in the orchestra {band, brass band} and solo performance, where it is no less indispensable to the composer, and no less liked by the public than the flute, the clarinet, and even the violin; where, in short, it has definitely won for itself the elevated position to which the beauty of its tone, the perfection of its mechanism and the immensity of its resources, so justly entitle it.

But this was not always the case; the cornet {euphonium} was far less successful when it first appeared; and, indeed, not many years ago, the masses treated the instrument with supreme indifference, while that time-honored antagonist—routine—contested its qualities, and strove hard to prohibit their application. This Phenomenon, however, is of never-failing recurrence at the birth of every new invention, however excellent it may be, and of this fact the appearance of the saxhorn and the saxophone, instruments of still more recent date than the cornet, gave a new and striking proof.

The first musicians who played the cornet {euphonium} were, for the most part, either horn or trumpet players. Each imparted to his performance the peculiarities resulting from his tastes, his abilities and his habits, and I need scarcely add that the kind of execution which resulted from so many incomplete and heterogeneous elements was deficient in the extreme, and, for a long while, presented the lamentable spectacle of imperfections and failures of the most painful description.

Gradually, however, matters assumed a more favorable aspect. Executants really worthy of the name of artists began to make their appearance. However, regardless of the brilliant accomplishments of such performers, they could not deny the faults of their original training, viz., the total lack of qualifications necessary for ensemble playing, and decided musicianly tendencies. Some excited admiration for their extreme agility; others were applauded for the expression with which they played; one was remarkable for lip; and other for the high tone to which he ascended; others for the brilliancy and volume of their tone. In my opinion, it was the reign of specialists, but it does not appear that a singly one of the players then in vogue ever thought of realizing or of obtaining the sum total of qualities which alone can constitute a great artist.

This, then, is the point upon which I wish to insist, and to which I wish to call particular attention. At the present time, the incompleteness of the old school of performers is unanimously acknowledged, as is also the insufficiency of the instruction. That which is required is methodical execution and methodical instruction. In a word, it is necessary that the cornet, as well as the flute, the clarinet, the violin, and the voice, should possess the pure style and the grand method of which a few professors, the Conservatory in particular, have conserved the precious secret and the salutary traditions.

This is the aim which I have incessantly kept in view throughout my long career: and if a numerous series of brilliant successes obtained in the presence of the most competent judges and the most critical audiences, give me the right to believe that I have, at any rate, approached the desired end, I shall not be laying myself open to the charge of presumption, in confidently entering upon the delicate mission of transmitting to others the results of my own thorough studies and assiduous practice. I have long been a professor, and this work is to a certain extent merely the résumé of a long experience, which each day has brought nearer to perfection.

My explanations will be found as short and clear as possible, for I wish to instruct and not to terrify the student. Long pages of text are not always read, and it is highly advantageous to replace the latter by exercises and examples. This is the wealth which I consider cannot be too lavishly accumulated; this is the source which can never be too plentifully drawn from. This, however, will be perceived from the extent of the present volume, in which, in my opinion, will be found the solution of all difficulties and of all problems.

I have endeavored throughout to compose studies of a melodic nature, and in general to render the study of the instrument as agreeable as possible. In a word, I have endeavored to lead the pupil, without discouragement, to the highest limits of execution, sentiment and style, destined to characterize the new school.

*J. B. Arban*

It is interesting to note that many of Mr. Arban's observations are still relevant today. Before this edition, students with the bass clef versions would have to consult the treble clef editions for sections missing and to correct note errors. It is hoped that the appropriate preparation and practice of this edition will prepare the euphonium player for every technical challenge.

Great appreciation for this edition should be given to Wesley Jacobs, principal tubist of the Detroit Symphony Orchestra and Publisher of this volume. Without his work this edition would not be possible.

# Fingering Charts

Fingering charts for non-compensating and compensating baritones and euphoniums appear on page 394 of this book.

# Fingering

To assure accurate and rhythmic technique, press the fingers down quickly. Many technical problems can be avoided by snapping the fingers down quickly. The fingers should be placed on the valve buttons in a gentle curve with the thumb placed opposite the fingers. Avoid letting the fingers slide over the valves so that the second joint of the finger is over the valve button.

# Slide Matters

It is important to have your slide in good working order to avoid any stress when maneuvering the handslide. Dents, alignment, and corrosion can all contribute to a sluggish slide. Hold the slide with the first two fingers and the thumb. The third finger should ride on the underside of the lower slide. The first two fingers and the thumb should always be in contact with the slide brace. When the slide is being extended, the thumb should act like a drive train—initiating the movement—and the first two fingers should act like the brakes. The reverse is true when retracting the slide—the thumb being the brakes and the two fingers being the drive train. The wrist and arm act together as one unit, thus avoiding excessive movement with the wrist which leads to sloppy slide technique and glissy slide movements.

# Tools of Practice

Every serious student should have some additional practice equipment to aid his/her development:

- A mirror is essential to help give the player an idea of embouchure activity and to watch for excess movement—especially while tonguing. It may be a small mirror that fits on the music stand or a larger one mounted on a wall or door. Furthermore, watching oneself in a mirror while practicing solo performances can help eliminate any visual peculiarities that might be distracting during performance.

- A metronome is crucial to developing a sense of pulse and rhythmic stability. Using a metronome to assure rhythmic precision and consistency is the surest way to develop accuracy and speed in performance.

- Electronic tuners will help the player check intonation and can be invaluable in training the ear to hear pitch correctly.

- A recording device is an essential practice tool in the practice studio for checking rhythm and pitch. It is not necessary to spend a lot of money on this valuable device, but the machine should have two essential features; a built-in speaker for instant playback and feedback, and it must be a machine that is capable of playing back the same pitch at which you recorded. When practicing tuning, try recording a low $B^b$. Sustain this note for as long as possible, take a deep breath and repeat it several times. Play this note back on the recording device, preferably through a quality sound system. On your instrument, play other notes on top of this recorded drone note thus producing various intervals. This will teach you exactly where to place your perfect $4^{ths}$, $5^{ths}$ and other intervals. Tuning on your instrument by this method then becomes strictly a matter of listening for intervals, as it should be.

# BASIC MECHANICS

## MR. ALESSI

A good brass player spends many hours in front of a mirror watching and listening. A good rule to follow is to form the embouchure so that all the muscles around the aperture are working in unison. Picture a fireman's net—the center being the aperture of your embouchure. Around this net are eight firemen pulling out from the center to keep the net taut. Think of your muscles working in this same way to preserve the stability and openness of the aperture. Keep a close eye on the area just below the bottom lip, the goal being to have as little movement as possible and to maintain a flat chin. In addition, try to form your embouchure away from the mouthpiece and the instrument. A good brass player knows how to do this.

It is important to study inhalation and exhalation. Developing both embouchure and air together is a winning combination. Breathe through the corners of your mouth and try to form the embouchure as you inhale, always keeping the mouthpiece in contact with the lips. This will avoid excessive movement after the tone is initiated. Try to breathe in the most natural way starting the inhalation from near the belt line. Feel this sensation by lying on the floor on your back and breathing normally. I often think conceptually of breathing—away from the instrument—and try to think of that concept again when my instrument is in my hands. Breathe as you would in a doctor's office when the stethoscope has been placed on your chest. Try closing your eyes and imagining this scenario. Notice that when you breathe in this manner, your mouth is formed perfectly naturally. It is held very simply and without tension.

# First Studies

## Mr. Alessi

TONE CLONING—In these initial exercises (1-8), there are several points and goals to keep in mind:

- Breathe naturally

- *Clone* each note so all the notes are the same style and tone quality.

- Avoid excessive embouchure movement.

- Blow through all the notes and, in general, play with a longer style and a firm attack.

- Take a brief rest at every double bar.

## Dr. Bowman

Most students do not begin playing with the Arban's book as their first text. These first studies can be used to improve tone quality, intonation and especially articulation control and clarity at any level of performance. *The sign of a really fine performer is the consistency of everything done technically!* This means that each note has the same clear, clean beginning articulation and tone quality.

One of the best uses of this first section is to help develop clarity of articulation. Using a mirror to check embouchure stability is often very useful. Most articulation clarity problems are not just tonguing problems, but a lack of coordination of the tongue, breath and embouchure. Be sure to work for complete independence of the tongue from the embouchure and the jaw. Pitfalls to avoid would be excess movement of the jaw and the lips. While watching in the mirror play the exercise keeping the embouchure firm and not *chewing* or *kissing* each note with excessive embouchure and jaw motion. Begin each tongue with the embouchure in place rather than letting the articulation form the embouchure. At the same time avoid getting a rigid or stiff embouchure that is not flexible. Listening to your sound is the best aid for improving all aspects of performance. Indications of tonguing/articulation problems include a scooping of the beginning of each sound, a delay in the release of the air and a fuzzy beginning to the sound.

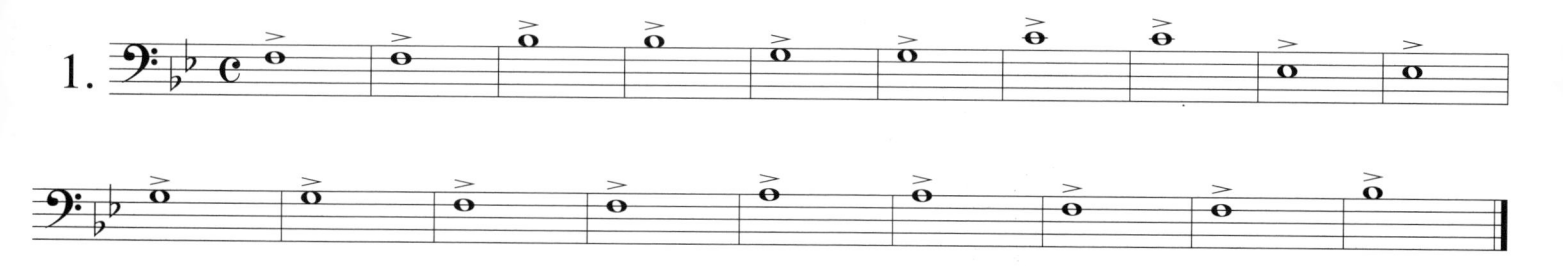

*FUNDAMENTALS* Arban • 13

14 • Arban FUNDAMENTALS

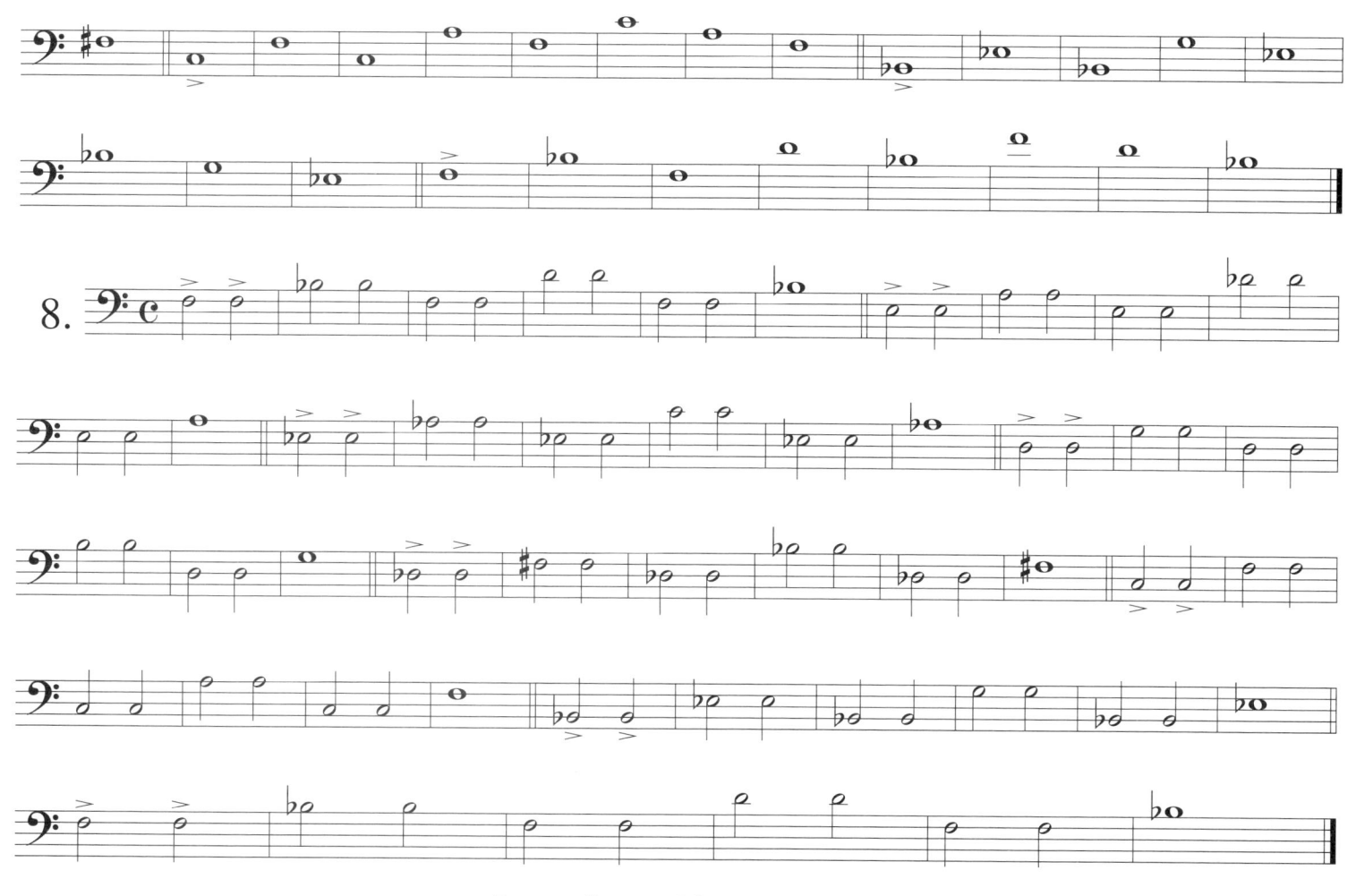

### Etudes 9 and 10—Mr. Alessi

Practice these exercises slurred. The goal is to use natural slurs when possible. Perform these exercises slowly, attempting to have the smoothest possible slide connections. Listen to what happens while traveling to and from notes. Is the sound clean and smooth? Try to move the slide as late as possible without affecting your air flow. Separate air flow and slide movements so that these functions work independently. When breathing, repeat the preceding note so as not to miss any connections.

*FUNDAMENTALS Arban • 15*

16 • Arban FUNDAMENTALS

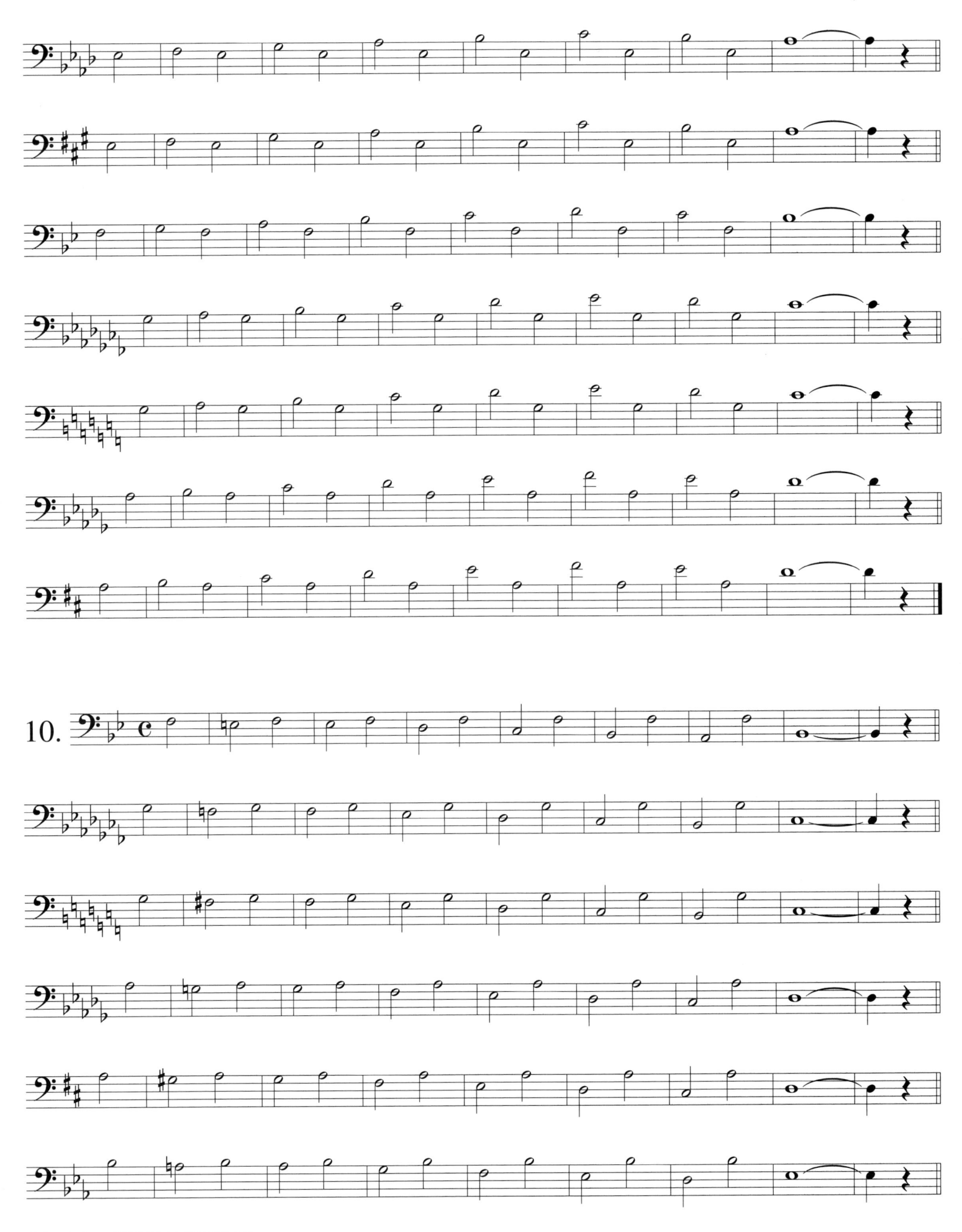

## Etudes 11-27—Mr. Alessi

Once again, it is important to *clone* every note, and attack each note firmly. When breathing, try not to lose any time against the metronome. Learn how to breathe quickly through the corners of your mouth. Conceal your breathing for the recording and play it back to hear if any breaths are noticeable (similar to how a magician practices in order to conceal hand movements from the public).

FUNDAMENTALS Arban • 17

18 • Arban FUNDAMENTALS

FUNDAMENTALS Arban • 19

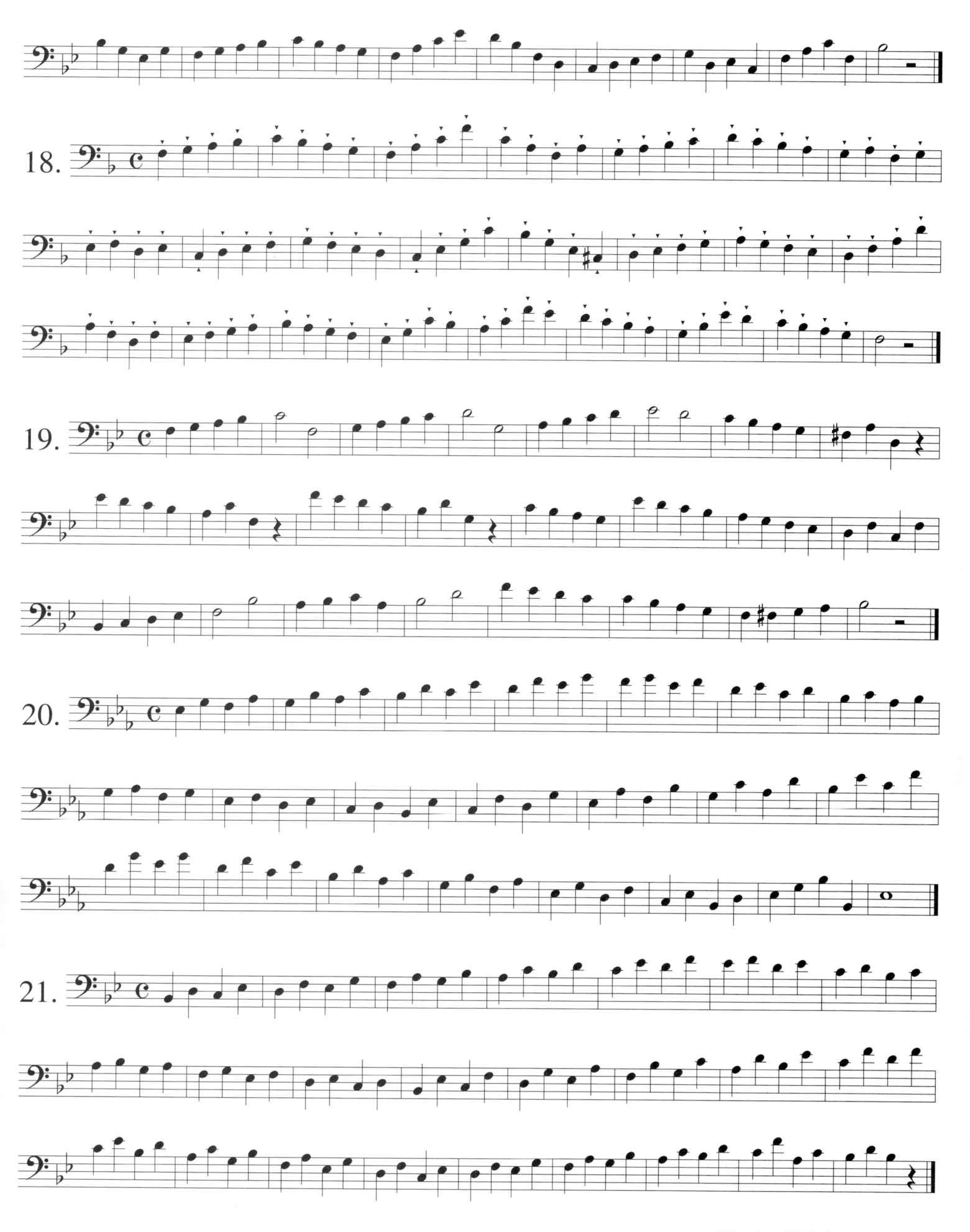

20 • Arban FUNDAMENTALS

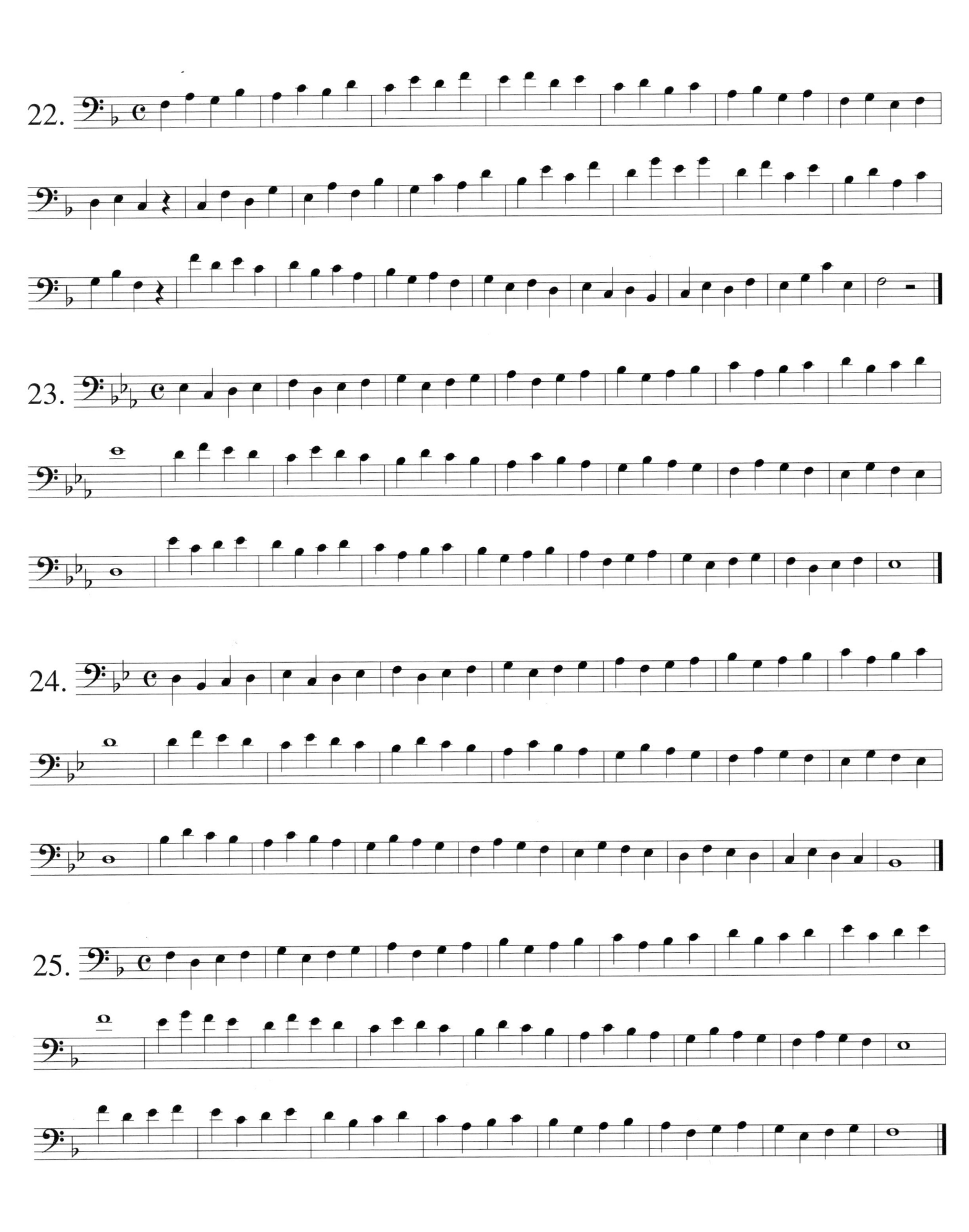

*FUNDAMENTALS Arban • 21*

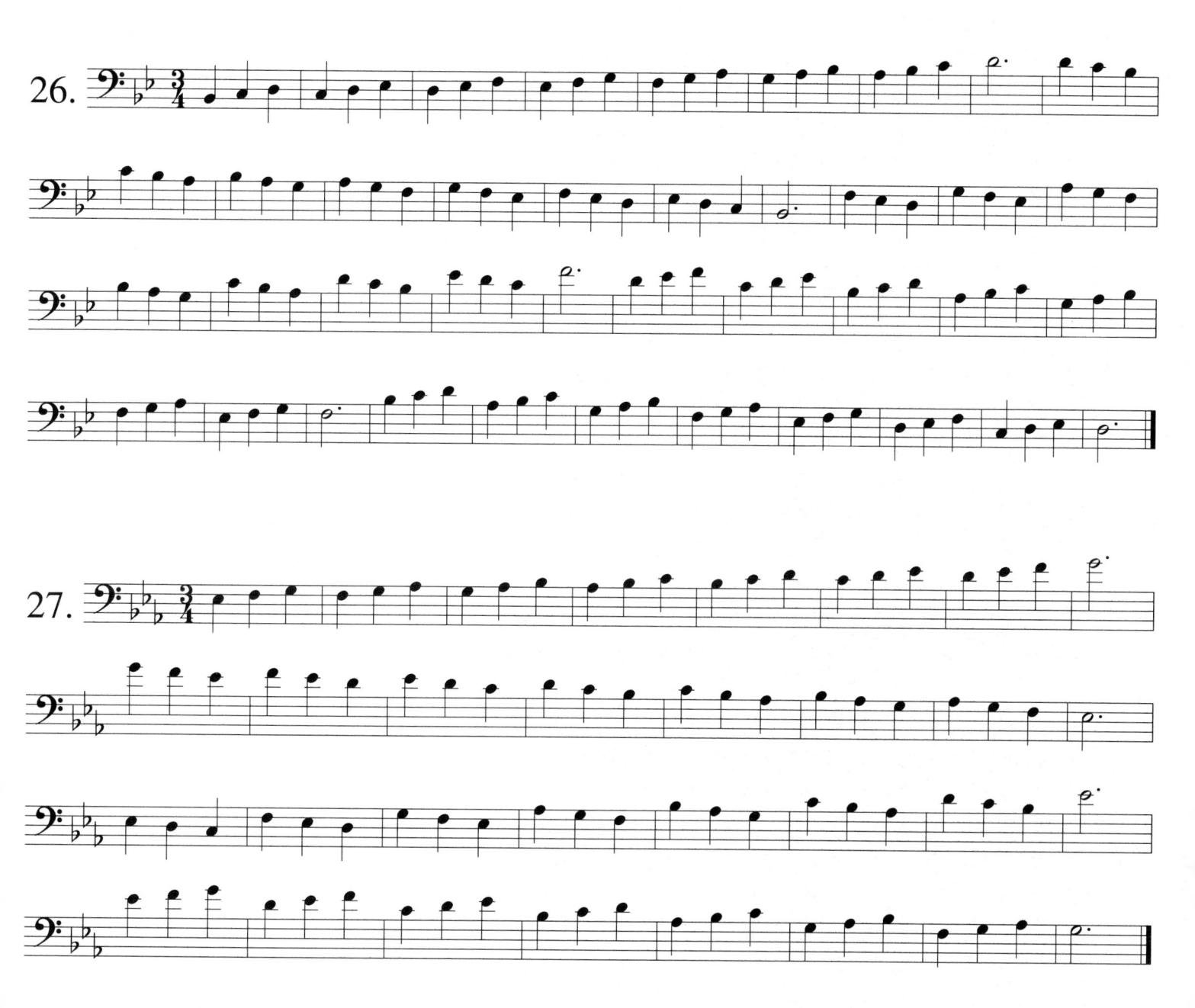

## Exercises 28-45—Mr. Alessi

Suggested tempo ♩= 96

The goal for these exercises should be to coordinate the tongue, slide and air so that all three of these functions are happening at the same time. For separated playing, remember to hold the slide firmly with no break of the wrist. Before attempting the suggested tempo marking, try the following exercise: Play number 28 at half the speed. Play with clear breaks between the notes. At the end of each note, move your slide quickly to the next position—ahead of the attack for the note to which you are moving. This will teach you the feeling and timing of the slide movement for this style of playing.

Continue now at the suggested tempo with the same feeling of timing and slide movement. Strive for even attacks with a broad style of playing. For more advanced studies, play these exercises in tenor clef adding one flat and also down one octave from that which is written. Use 6th position for low *C* and utilize 4th position for *d1* when surrounded by *c1* and *Eb1*.

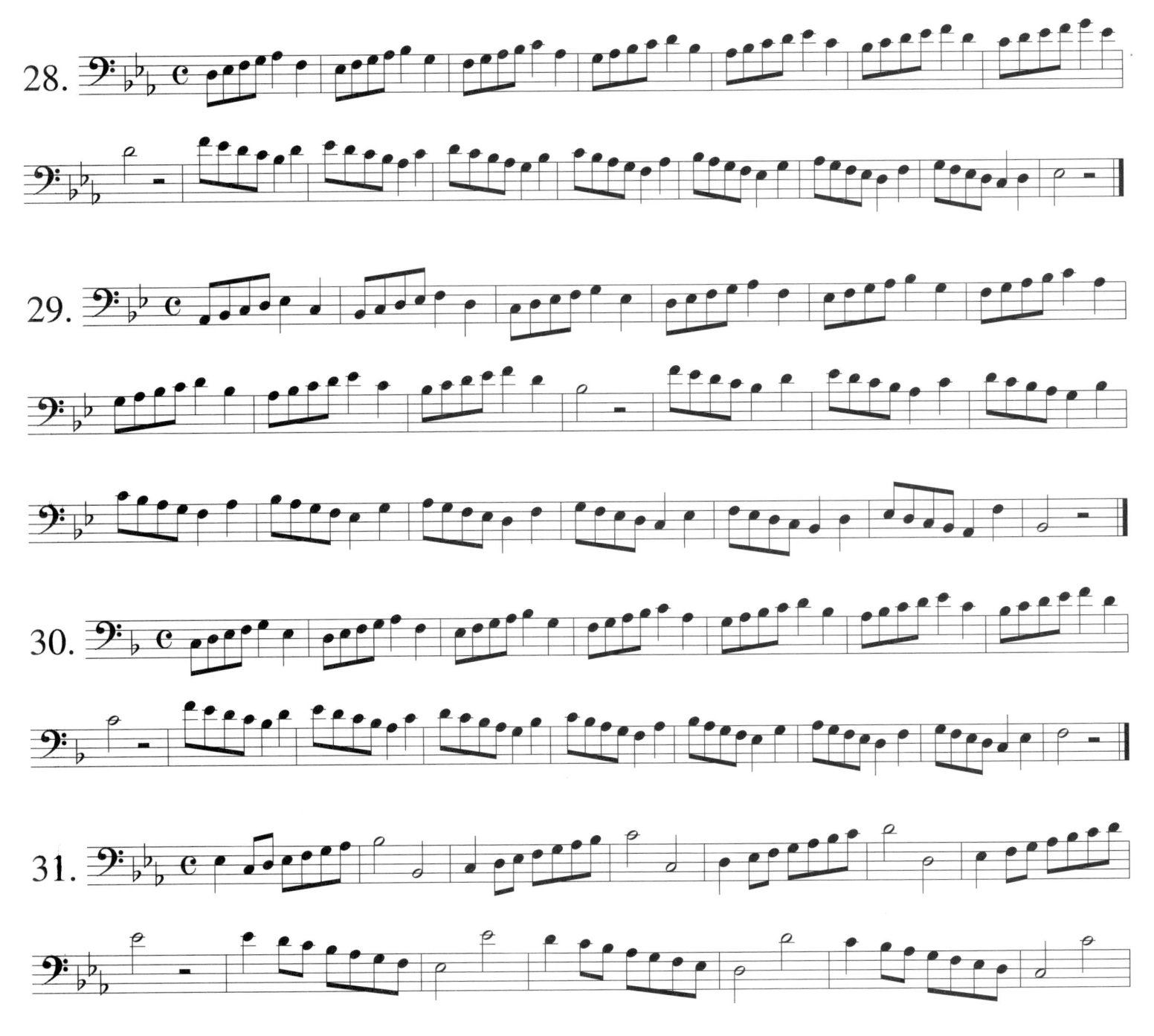

22 • Arban FUNDAMENTALS

*32.*

*33.*

*34.*

*35.*

24 • Arban FUNDAMENTALS

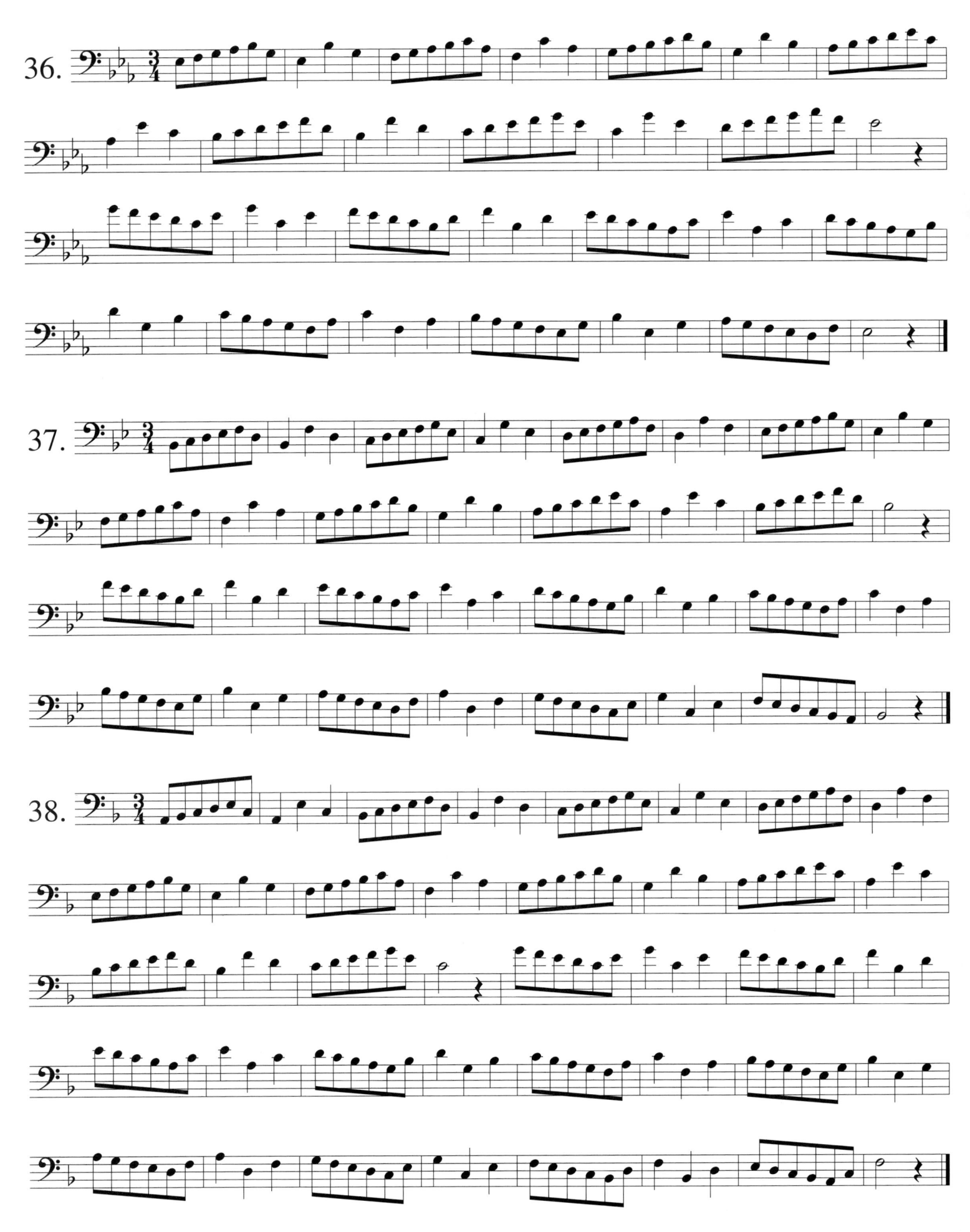

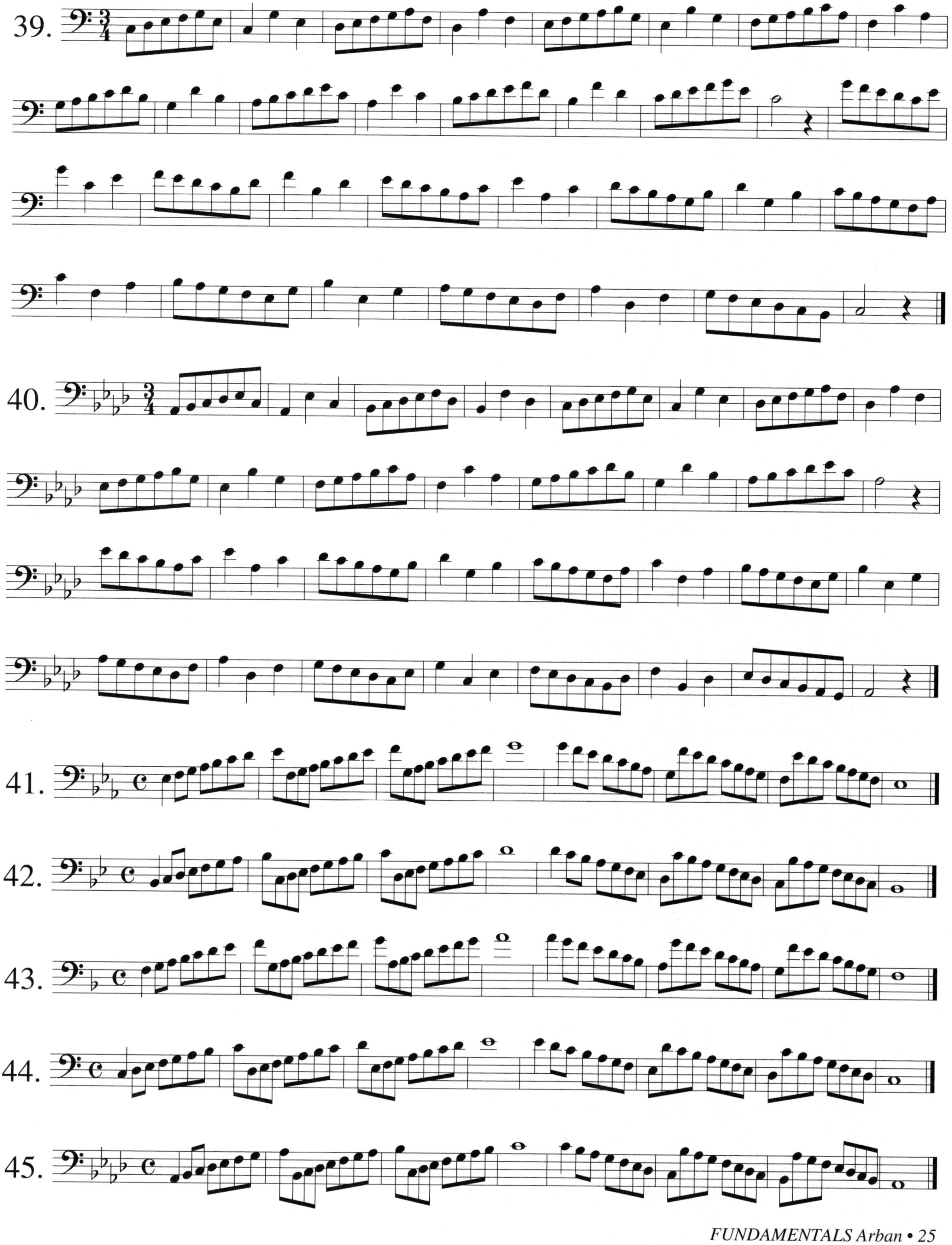
39.
40.
41.
42.
43.
44.
45.

## Intonation in Chord Patterns and Endurance 46—Mr. Alessi

There are many goals to keep in mind when practicing number 46. I would like to bring to your intention the importance of knowing your music theory and how it relates to tuning. Notice how this exercise proceeds through the circle of fourths. Here is a brief analysis of the first 8 measures: Measures 1-2: I chord; Measures 3-4: dominant seventh chord of B♭ major or F7; Measures 5-6: I chord in first inversion with and added dominant seventh of E♭ major; Measure 7: 1st inversion E♭ major; Measure 8: B♭ chord again which becomes the dominant of the new key on the second line, E♭ major.

The point of this is to know where to place the intonation of major thirds (generally lower) as well as to know how to tune the dominant seventh chord (by lowering the pitch of the 7th) as it resolves to the major third of the 1st inversion chord.

The other goal is to play the entire exercise without stopping always remembering to strive for the same sound and attack. Suggested tempo: ♩ = 120.

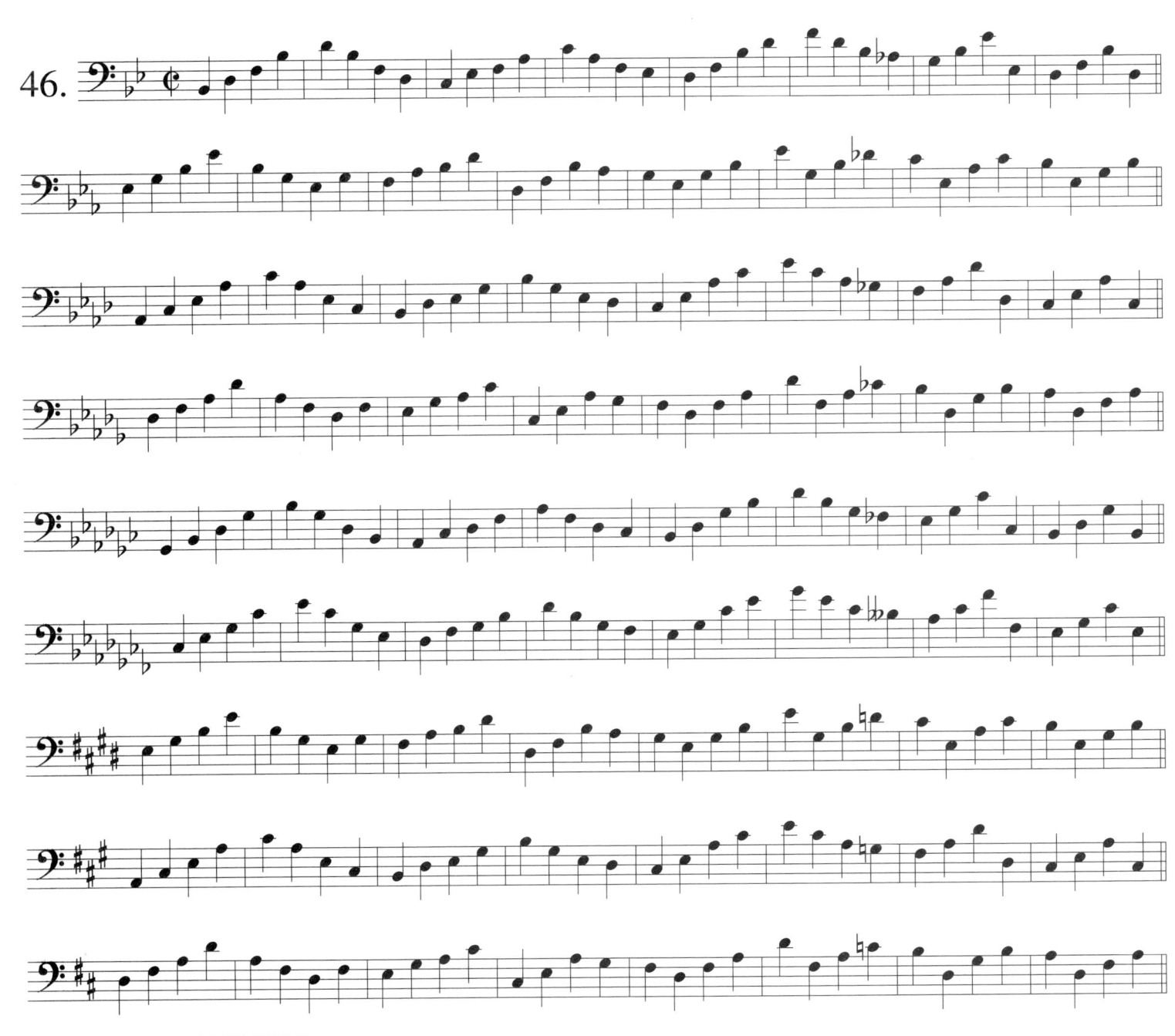

INTERVALS 47-50—MR. ALESSI

- Play equal and even-sounding (full sounding) eighth notes. Don't play too *pecky* or short.
- In number 47, listen to the 2nd, 3rd and 4th beats of every other bar for an even-sounding scale as it descends to the downbeat.
- Hold the slide firmly with no breaking of the wrist.
- In number 48, be careful not to *splat* the lower note. Keep the lower note full-sounding.

It is very important as the intervals widen, to think syllabically from note to note. Think *TAH* and *TEE* when executing the interval of an octave—the lower being *TAH*. For a low $B^b$, I prefer to think of the syllable *TOE*.

Remember to keep the same anchor point on the bottom lip—*don't let the mouthpiece travel up on your face when executing a wide ascending interval.* Be careful not to pounce on or *splat* the lower notes.

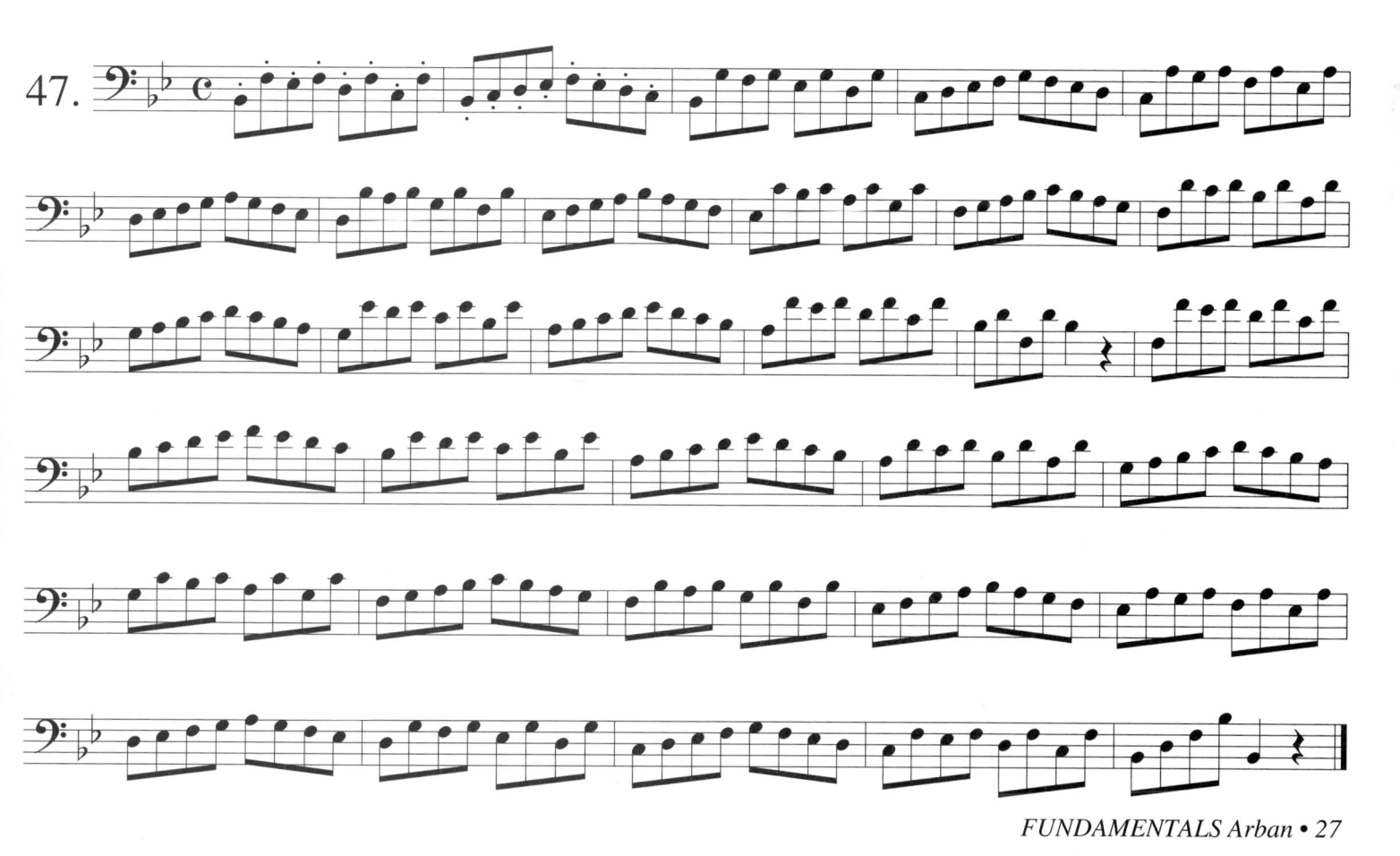

28 • Arban STUDIES ON SYNCOPATION

# Studies on Syncopation

### Etudes 1-12—Dr. Bowman

The two basic rules for syncopation are: *Separate* and *Accent*. In usual practice and interpretation this means to separate the shorter notes and accent the longer ones. Be certain that all of the shorter notes in these exercises are the same length. Avoid the pitfall of playing the last note of the measure too long—instead make it the same length as the first note of the measure. In accenting the longer notes use more of a breath accent than a stronger articulation. A basic rule of playing these exercises—as well as many sections of this book—is to play the longer notes fuller and louder and the shorter notes softer, within the chosen dynamic.

### Etudes 1-12—Mr. Alessi

Two additional points to remember when playing syncopation:

**Feel a strong beat in response to every accented long note played.** For example, in measure one if you are counting four beats to the bar, it is important to feel a strong *beat-three* in response to the attack of the *F* half note. If you continue this process the rhythm is *glued* together in many respects. When feeling this strong response, try to hear it as a percussion instrument. (i.e. a cymbal or bass drum) thus creating a *band in your head*.

**Move the slide rhythmically.** Often we do not think of a slide movement in this way. As an exercise, tongue each note and move the slide very accurately without making any tone. In a way, mime the entire exercise to enhance coordination between the tongue, slide and air. Of course, when doing any exercise in this book, always remember to use a metronome. In general, breathe towards the end of each bar after the final longer note value. Phrase every two, four, or eight bars.

30 • Arban STUDIES ON SYNCOPATION

STUDIES ON SYNCOPATION Arban

## Studies on Dotted Eighth and Sixteenth Notes

### Etudes 13-18—Dr. Bowman

This rhythm is often played as a triplet rather than a duple. Be certain to subdivide each beat into the lowest value note and make the ratio rhythmically correct—three-to-one in the dotted figures. Avoid cutting the dotted note short or putting a rest in between the dotted note and the shorter note.

### Etudes 13-18—Mr. Alessi

The dotted eighth followed by a sixteenth is one of the most important rhythms to learn correctly. It is frequently performed incorrectly. The common mistake is performing this rhythm as a triplet. To prevent this from happening think eighths while playing (with the emphasis on eighths 2, 4, 6, and 8 in common time). Hear these emphasized beats in your head as you would hear a percussion instrument. This will help prevent the tendency to play the rhythm as a triplet. Accent slightly the sixteenth or *kick it* to play in the correct marked style. Sustain the dotted eighth as a violinist would play it with a full-bow.

32 • Arban STUDIES ON DOTTED EIGHTH AND SIXTEENTH NOTES

**Allegro moderato**

14.

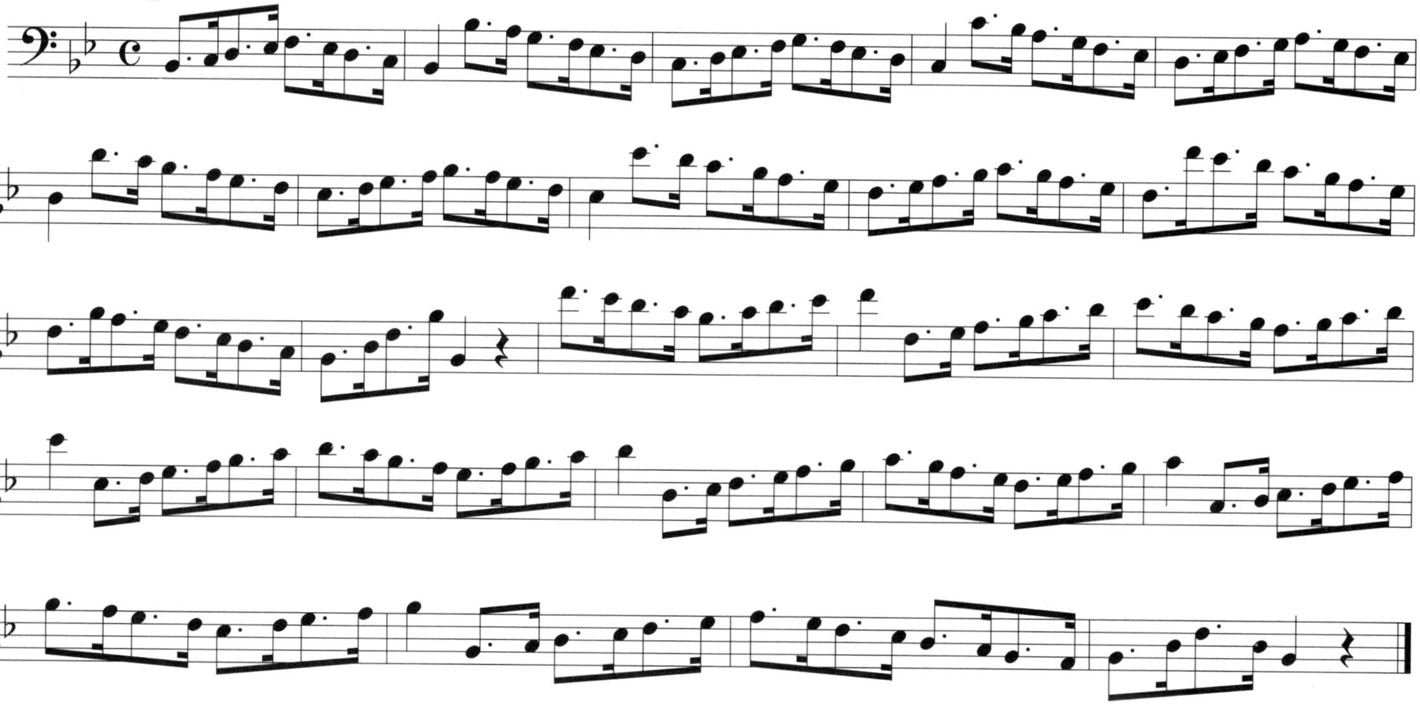

**Allegro**

15.

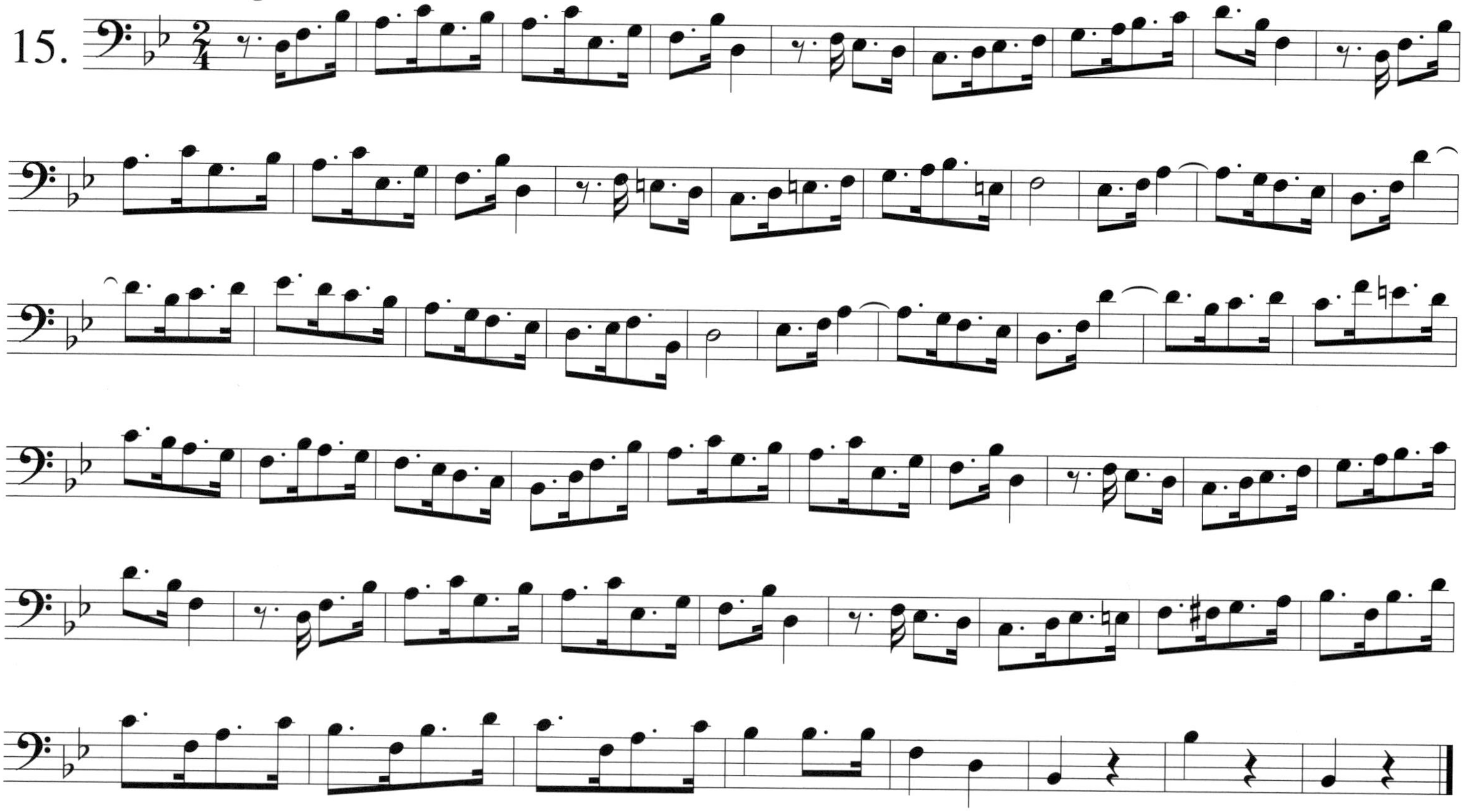

34 • Arban STUDIES ON DOTTED EIGHTH AND SIXTEENTH NOTES

### Articulation and Style 19-38
### Dr. Bowman

These studies are excellent for developing articulation speed and clarity and at the same time learning basic principles of style. The most important aid to correct style is to determine what notes are melodically grouped together. As an example, in #19, the first four notes comprise the first basic statement and belong together. The fifth note really leads across the bar line and is a pickup to the first four-note figure in the second measure. This pattern is repeated many times throughout the exercise. Determining the musical tendencies in each exercise will be essential to the musical development offered by this section.

Generally, play the eighth notes shorter than the sixteenth notes and make the eighth notes all the same length. Don't be hampered by playing from bar line to bar line—learn to play musically over the bar lines.

### Mr. Alessi

These are some of my favorite exercises. Play the sixteenth notes evenly. Think of all the exercises (19-27) in 4/8 time. Move the tongue with air, not the reverse. To help develop this *tongue with air* concept, adjust the *air to tongue mixture* making sure not to use too much tongue. Think *dah dah* when executing repeated sixteenths. For more advanced players, perform exercises 19-38 without interruption. Make a segue from one exercise to the next, aiming for consistent tone and articulation. This is excellent training for embouchure and air.

STUDIES ON DOTTED EIGHTH AND SIXTEENTH NOTES Arban • 35

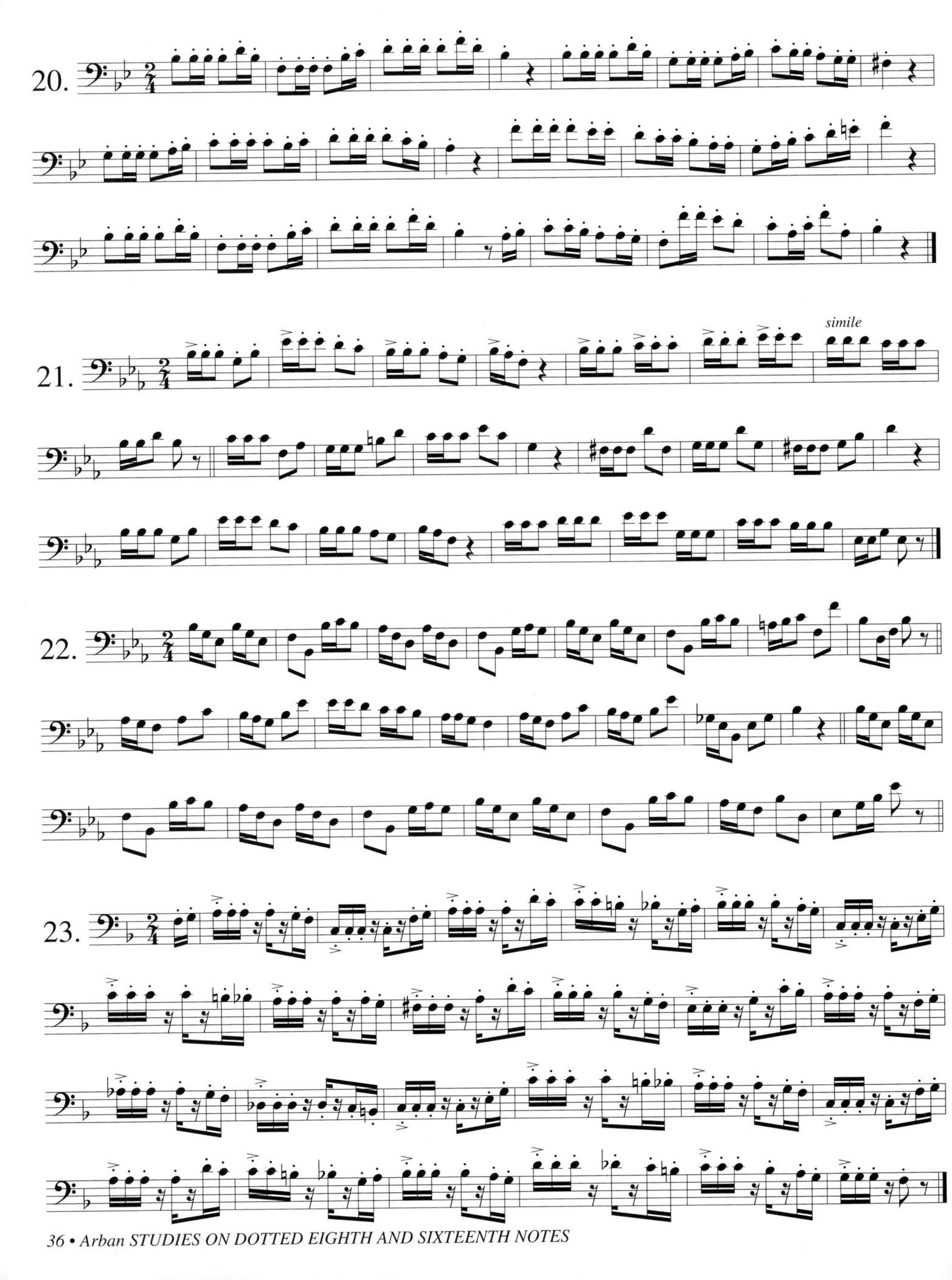

36 • Arban STUDIES ON DOTTED EIGHTH AND SIXTEENTH NOTES

STUDIES ON DOTTED EIGHTH AND SIXTEENTH NOTES Arban • 37

38 • Arban STUDIES ON DOTTED EIGHTH AND SIXTEENTH NOTES

STUDIES ON DOTTED EIGHTH AND SIXTEENTH NOTES Arban • 39

40 • Arban STUDIES ON DOTTED EIGHTH AND SIXTEENTH NOTES

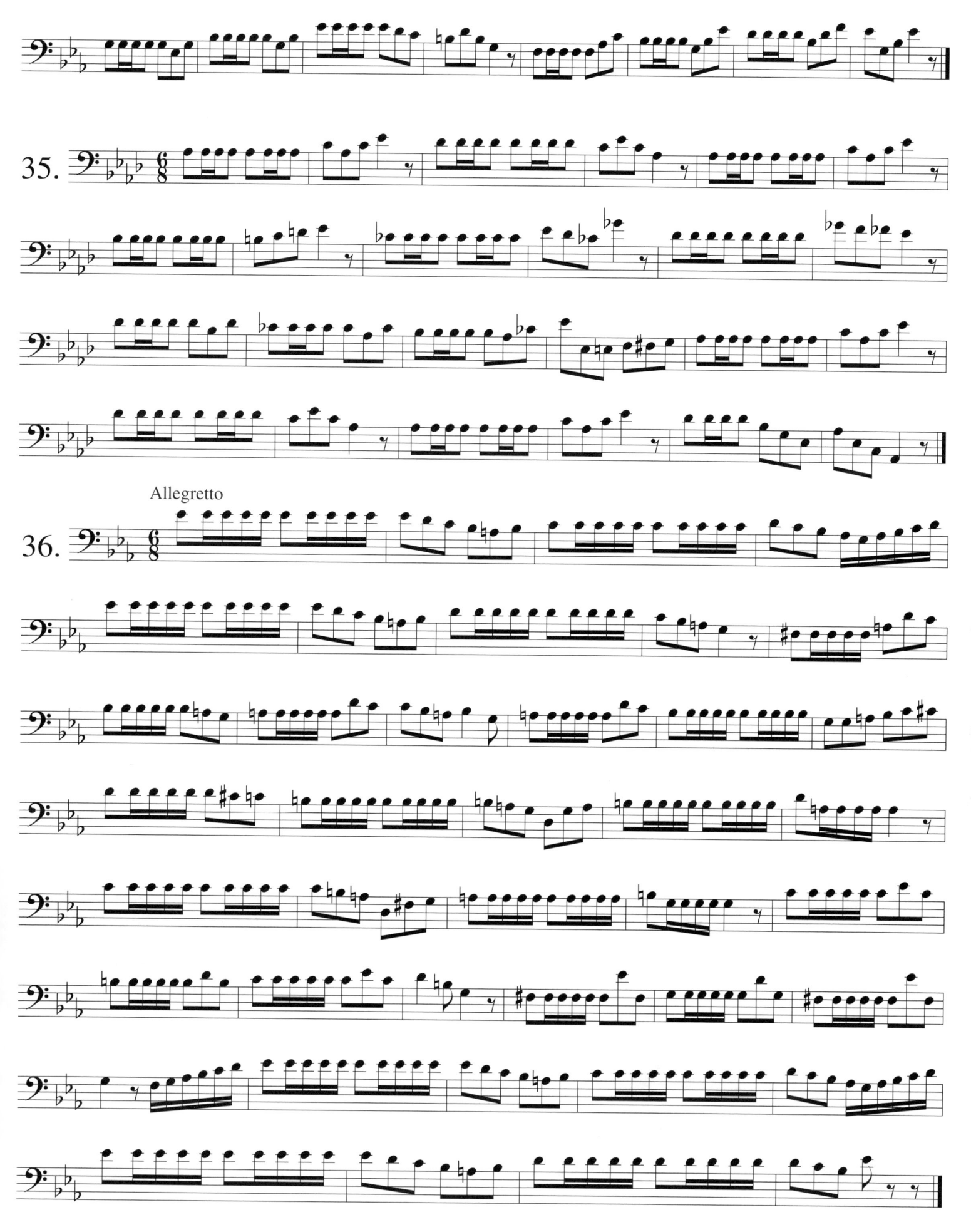

*STUDIES ON DOTTED EIGHTH AND SIXTEENTH NOTES* Arban

42 • Arban STUDIES ON DOTTED EIGHTH AND SIXTEENTH NOTES

# STUDIES ON THE SLUR

### STUDIES 1-15—DR. BOWMAN

Most students are aware of lip slur and flexibility exercises. These first exercises can be used as legato and intonation exercises. Exercises #1-15 are excellent for listening to intonation. An electronic tuner can be used to check the ear accuracy and develop interval memory. Exercise #15 is an excellent test of lip flexibility and breath control.

### STUDIES 1-2—MR. ALESSI

#### SLIDE MOVEMENTS IN HALF STEPS—STUDIES 1-2

For the trombonist, it is most important to realize that the half-step slide-movement from 1st position to 2nd position can sound more *glissy* than when moving the slide from 1st position to 4th position. Perhaps this happens because we are moving the slide the distance of only one position and believe it is fine to relax the wrist and mind. Therefore, take great care in executing these most basic half step movements, moving the slide later rather than sooner.

### STUDIES 3-16—MR. ALESSI

#### BLOWING THROUGH THE BOTTOM NOTE—STUDIES 3-16

One of the most fundamental concepts for brass players is the importance of blowing through the bottom note when executing ascending natural slurs. Think of a diver preparing to dive off a spring-loaded diving board. The diver's first motion is to flex the muscles and go down, which creates tension in the springboard. This tension will propel the diver up and off the board. This is exactly what I think of when breathing and blowing for these ascending natural slurs. This concept—along with thinking vowels in this manner; *ah* for the bottom note and *ee* for the top—is a winning combination for clean natural slurs. Execute this section in an unhurried tempo, using natural slurs when possible, striving for clean slurs with no imperfections. Please note that when ascending and moving the slide out, be careful to adjust the speed of air in order not to *bump* the top note causing a rough slur.

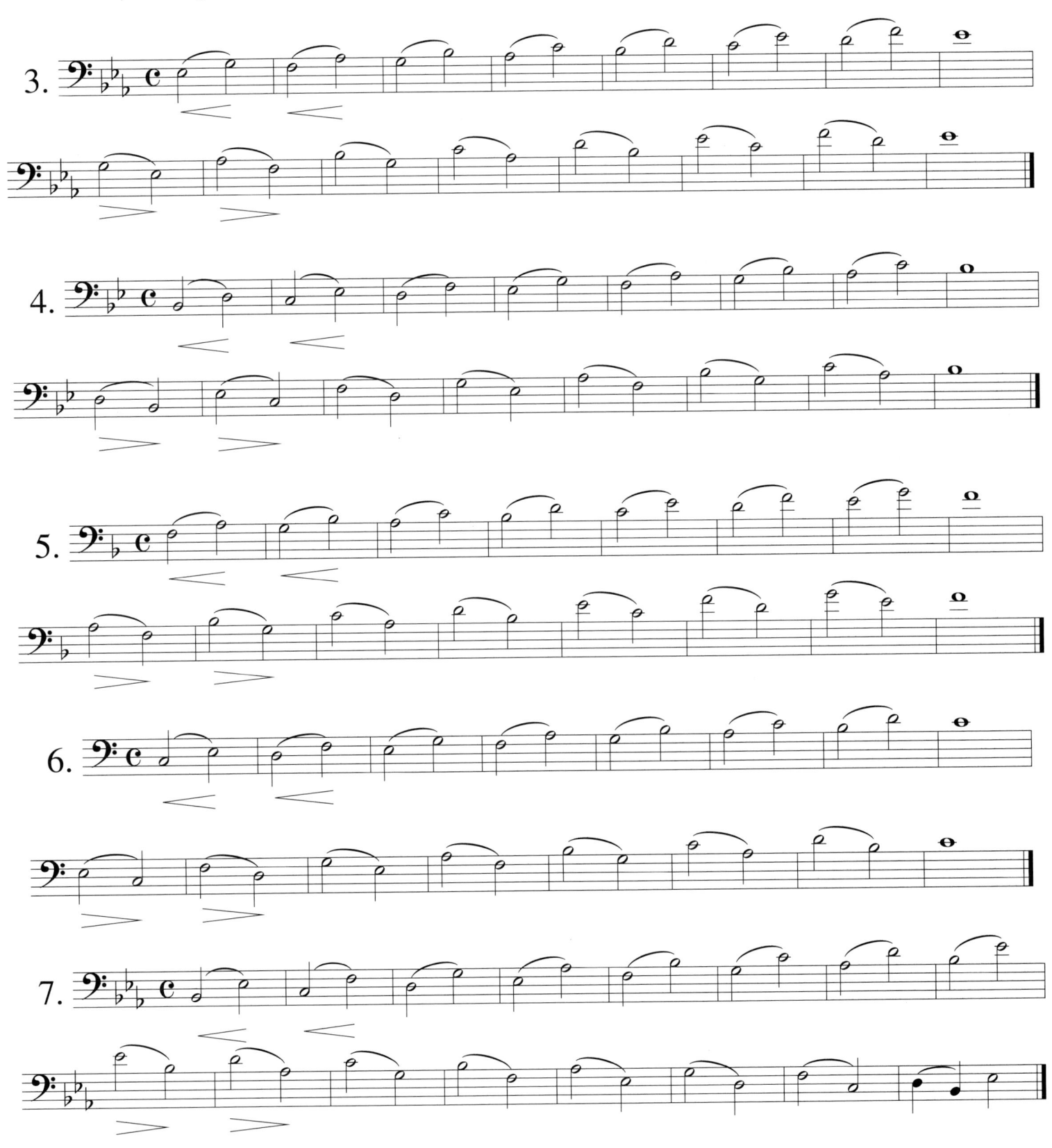

THE SLUR Arban • 45

46 • Arban THE SLUR

### Studies 16-30—Dr. Bowman

While performing exercises #16-30 be sure to take deep breaths and keep a steady flow of air through the slurs. When notes *stick,* or the slur is not smooth, try playing the interval on the mouthpiece alone (buzzing) and play a glissando between the *sticking* notes to assure that the lips are vibrating. Use this technique whenever there are response problems in legato slurs or lip slurs. Using the alternate fingerings for some of the notes will adversely affect intonation. Learn to play all fingerings in tune and with a good sound.

### Studies 16-36—Mr. Alessi

Flexibility is the key to limbered slurs, coordinated embouchure and correcting uneven eighth notes or a *limp* in your rhythm. When executing the constant triplets, sixteenths, and sextuplets, there are several points to keep in mind:
- Breathe on the bar line with a short auxiliary *sip* breath so as not to upset the rhythm.
- If necessary, pulsate downbeats to stay coordinated with the metronome (advanced players can disregard this suggestion).
- Think *ah-ee-ah-ee-ah-ee-ah-ee* for all these exercises, especially for the faster rhythms.
- Select a tempo so that you can execute the faster rhythms. Don't play these studies too quickly. The suggested tempo for exercises 31-36 is ♪=120.

For exercises 31-36 the goal is to be aware of ascending natural slurs when moving the slide out. In other words, be aware of *against the grain* slurs. Listen for any roughness or *bumps* when executing this type of slur. To avoid these problems, slow the air a bit and try not to *jam* air into the upper note.

*THE SLUR* Arban • 47

48 • Arban THE SLUR

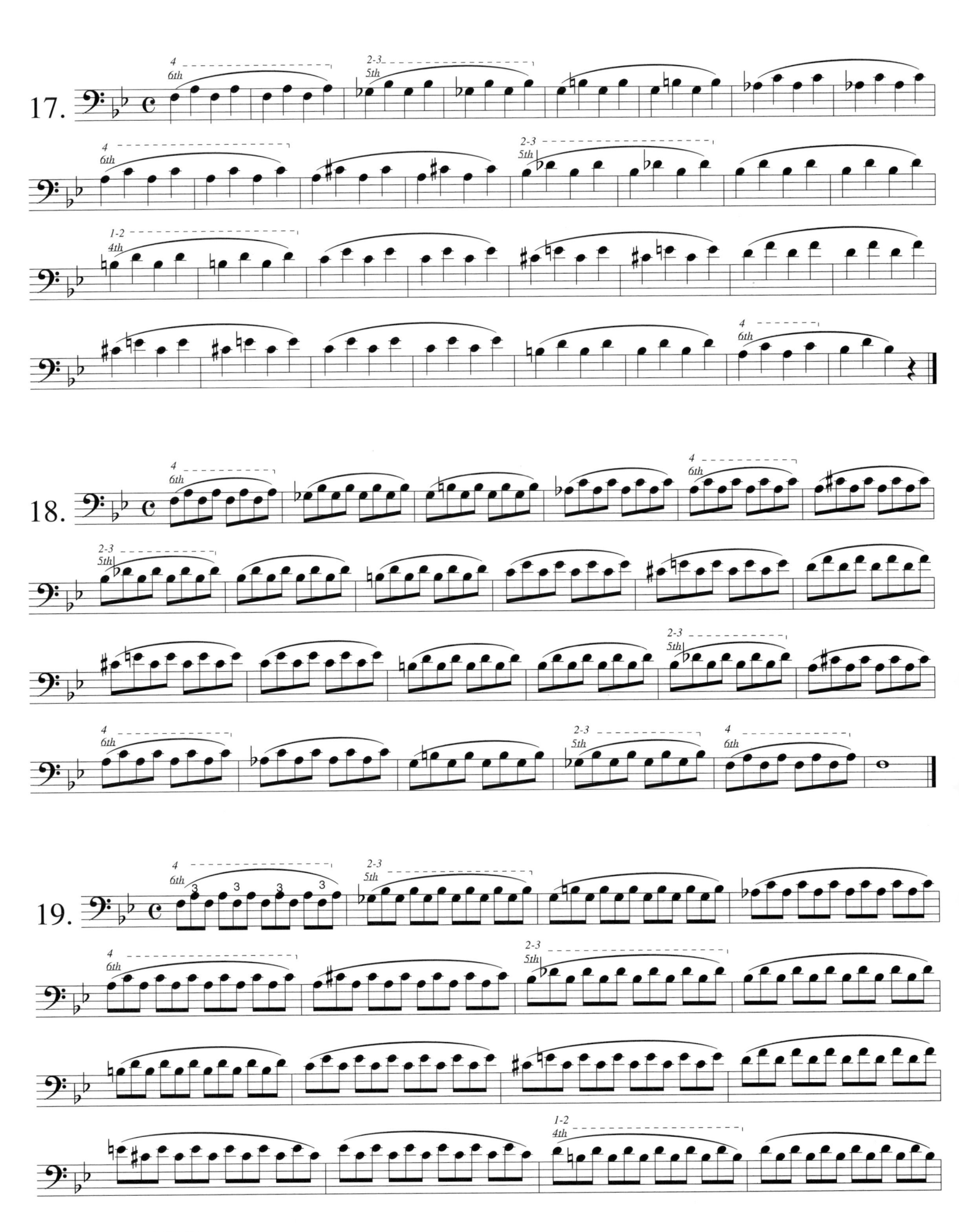

*THE SLUR Arban • 49*

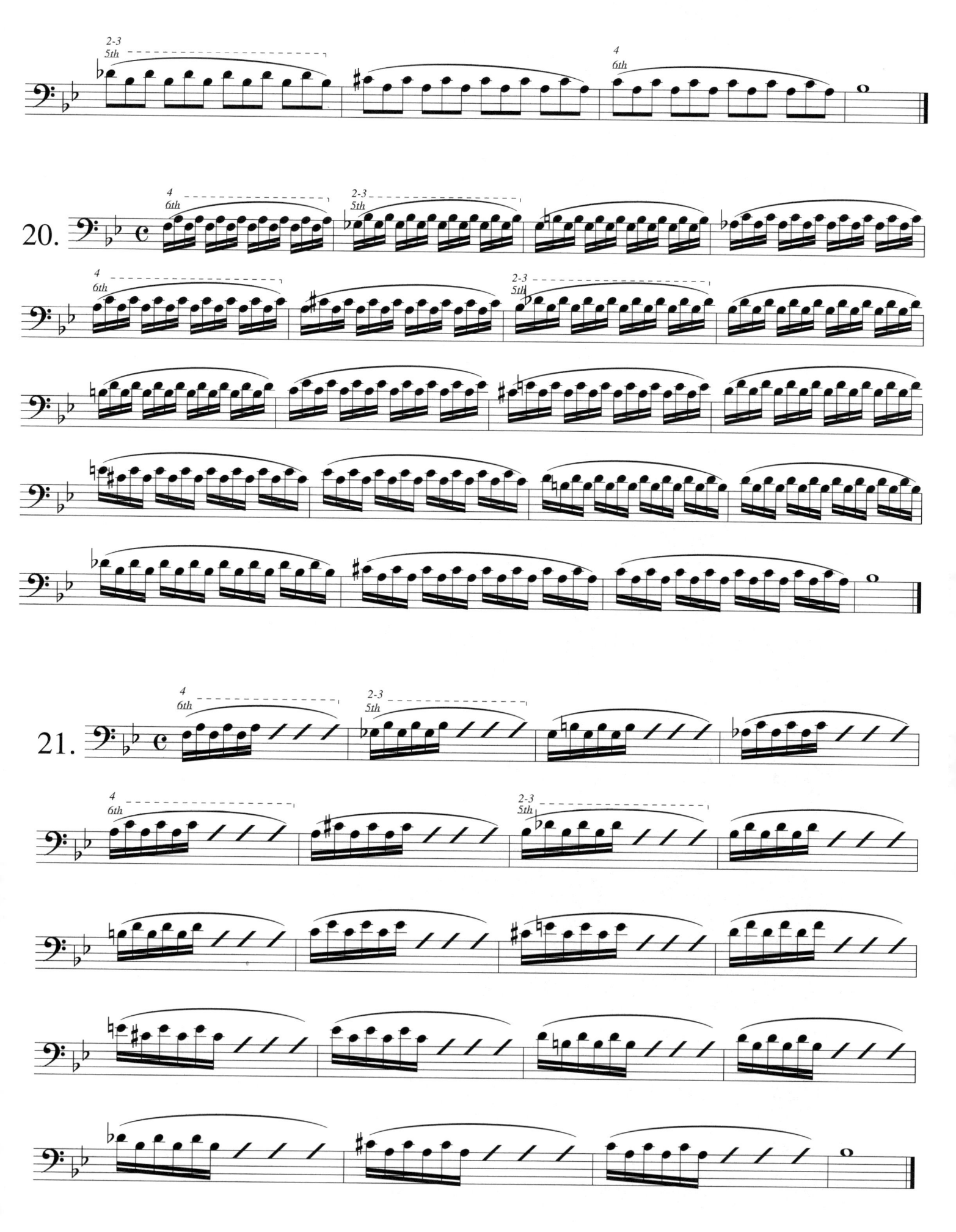

**22.**

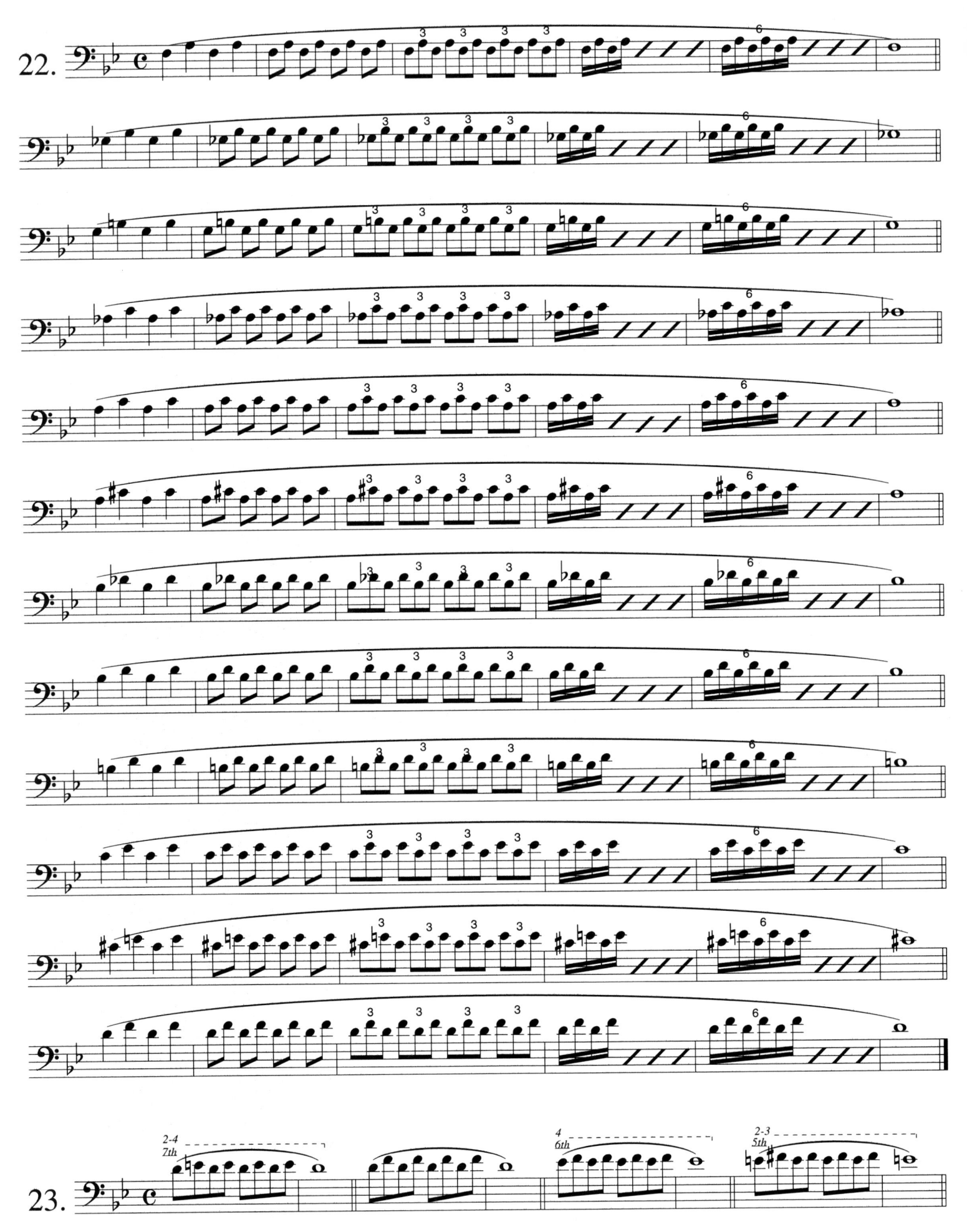

**23.**

50 • Arban THE SLUR

1-2 4th
2-3 5th
1-2 4th
1 3rd
Allegro
24.
3
3
3
3
4 6th
2-3 5th
4 6th
2-3 5th
2-4 7th
4 6th
2-3 5th
4 6th
2-3 5th
4 6th
2-4 7th
4 6th
Allegro
25.
4 6th
2-3 5th
4 6th
2-3 5th
2-4 7th
4 6th
2-3 5th
4 6th
2-3 5th
4 6th
2-4 7th
4 6th

52 • Arban THE SLUR

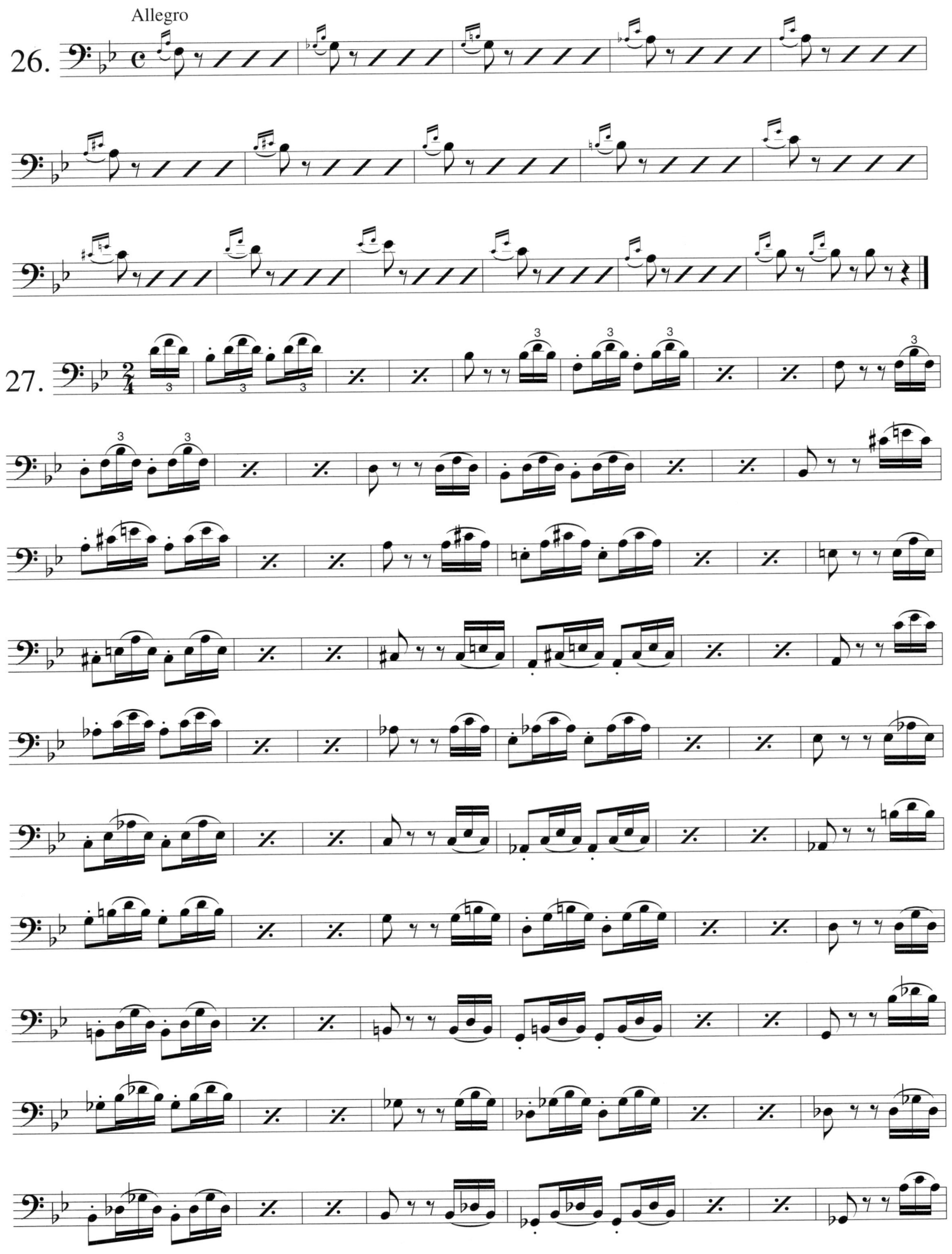

*THE SLUR* Arban • 53

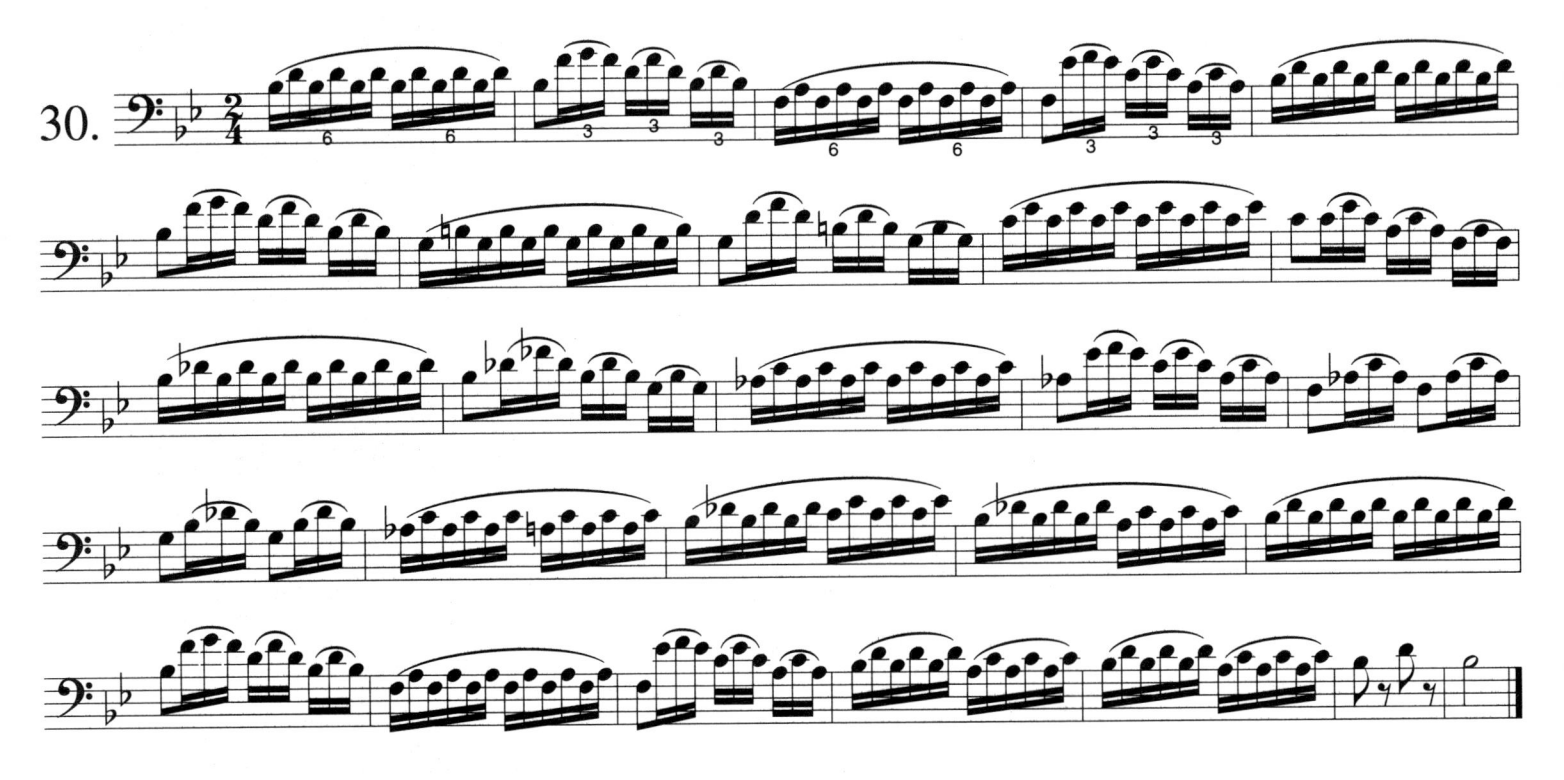

STUDIES 31-69—DR. BOWMAN

Exercises #31-69 combine lip slurs with fingering challenges to help develop coordination. Remember to push the fingers down all the way quickly and in rhythm.

54 • Arban THE SLUR

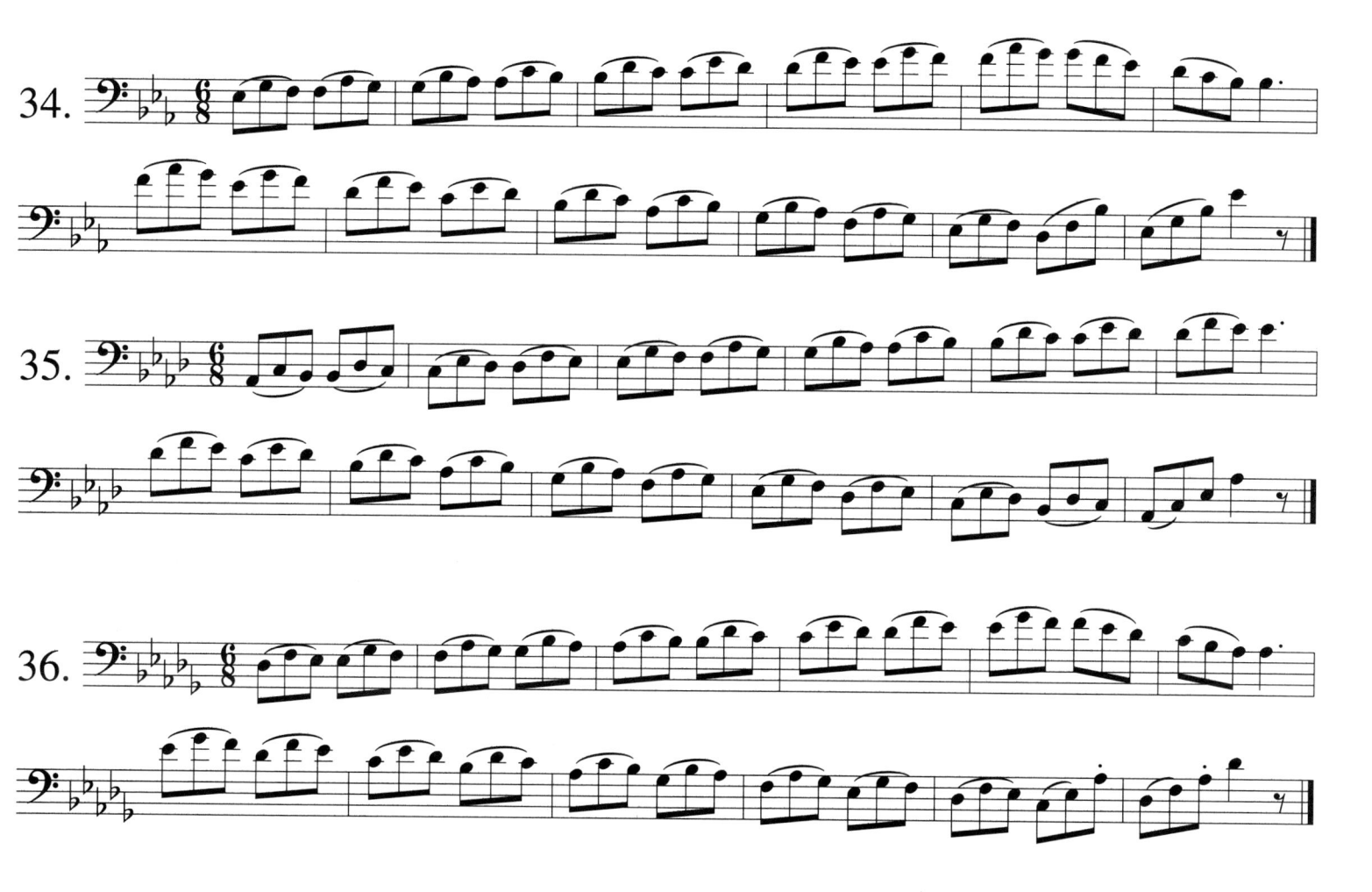

## Studies 37-54—Mr. Alessi

A common mistake when playing the two-note slur is to *clip* the second note, causing an uneven slur. To avoid this problem:

- Mentally draw a line over the second note and think the syllables *tah-hah* as you play. This will insure even rhythm.

- Think 4/8 meter for all of the 2/4 exercises to ensure evenness.

- Use natural slurs when possible.

Exercises 55-60 can be omitted for the trombonist if desired. They are mainly designed for the euphonium player.

*THE SLUR Arban • 55*

56 • Arban THE SLUR

THE SLUR Arban • 57

58 • Arban THE SLUR

*THE SLUR* Arban • 59

### Studies 61-69—Mr. Alessi

#### Grace Notes—Studies 61-67

For trombonists, it is important to play these exercises in a moderate tempo. Stylistically, don't rush the grace note and try not to *clip* the note after the grace. The goal is to make the natural slurred grace sound like the legato-tongued grace. Keep the air moving.

#### Articulated Arpeggios—Studies 68-69

- Use different vowels when ascending and descending. *OH, AH, EE.*

- Never *clip* the last slurred note.

- Blow through all notes and let the air move the tongue.

*THE SLUR* Arban • 61

Allegretto grazioso

**67.**

**68.**

62 • Arban THE SLUR

69.

# SCALE STUDIES

### STUDIES 1-69—DR. BOWMAN

Scales are essential to developing fundamental playing abilities. The development of fingering patterns and aural recognition of key centers are just two of the benefits of careful scale practice.

I recommend that the student use a metronome to assure even rhythm and consistency of tempo in each exercise. In addition, practice an equal amount of time without the metronome so that inner pulse and rhythmic stability are developed.

Avoid articulating these exercises with a short staccato articulation, especially as they increase in speed. Keep an even flow of air supporting the articulation. Practice the articulated exercises all slurred and then all articulated, keeping the same airflow for both the slurred and the articulated sections.

Dynamics can be altered to challenge the performer. Try playing one exercise *ffff* and then another *pppp* for control.

A good test for speed is to play exercise #4 with a metronome, working up to your top single tonguing speed. This pattern is appropriate to repeat in all keys. It is natural and appropriate to crescendo when ascending and decrescendo when descending.

Change the key signature of some exercises to provide more study in other keys. For example: perform the B♭ major exercises in B major—5 sharps.

### STUDIES 1-69—MR. ALESSI

Scales are fundamental to technique and to the development of good intonation. Keep in mind that speed is not essential in these studies. I have heard players perform the famous *William Tell* and *La Gazza Ladra* excerpts well technically—but with poor intonation—making the performance or audition flawed. Be extremely careful that you perform these scales with accurate intonation, rather than just playing in the vicinity of the pitch. Let the air move the tongue and think the syllable *dah*. Playing with a slightly firm wrist will prevent messy slide movements that cause pitch problems. Always subdivide into eighth notes, and think of playing a crescendo for the ascending lines. When practicing scales that are all-slurred, I suggest using a legato tongue for every note. For extended study play these exercises in all keys and different registers, i.e. tenor clef, and bass clef down an octave.

*Trombonists may omit numbers, 16, 22, 28, 34, 41, 49, 55, 61, 67, 68.

64 • Arban SCALES

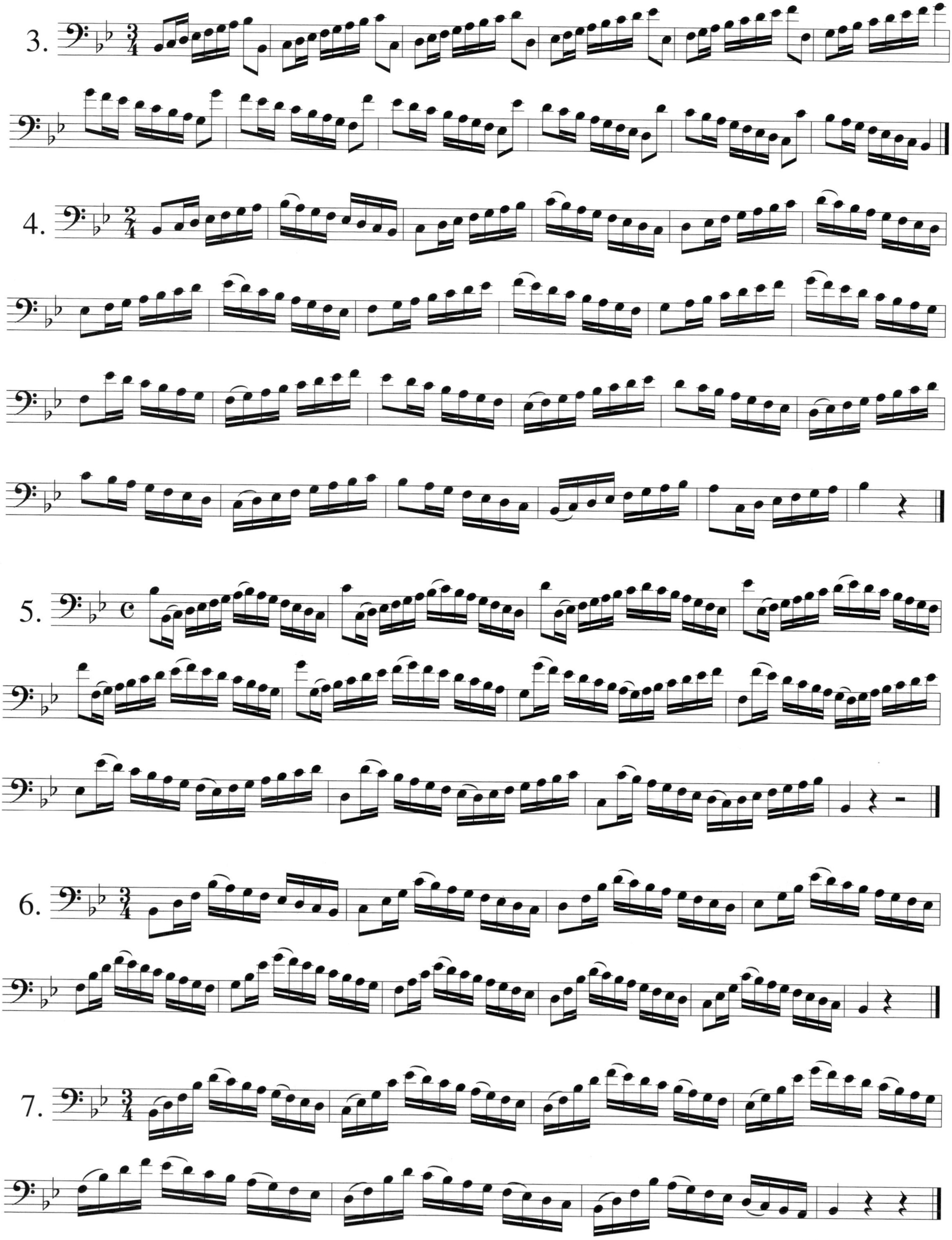
3.
4.
5.
6.
7.

66 • Arban SCALES

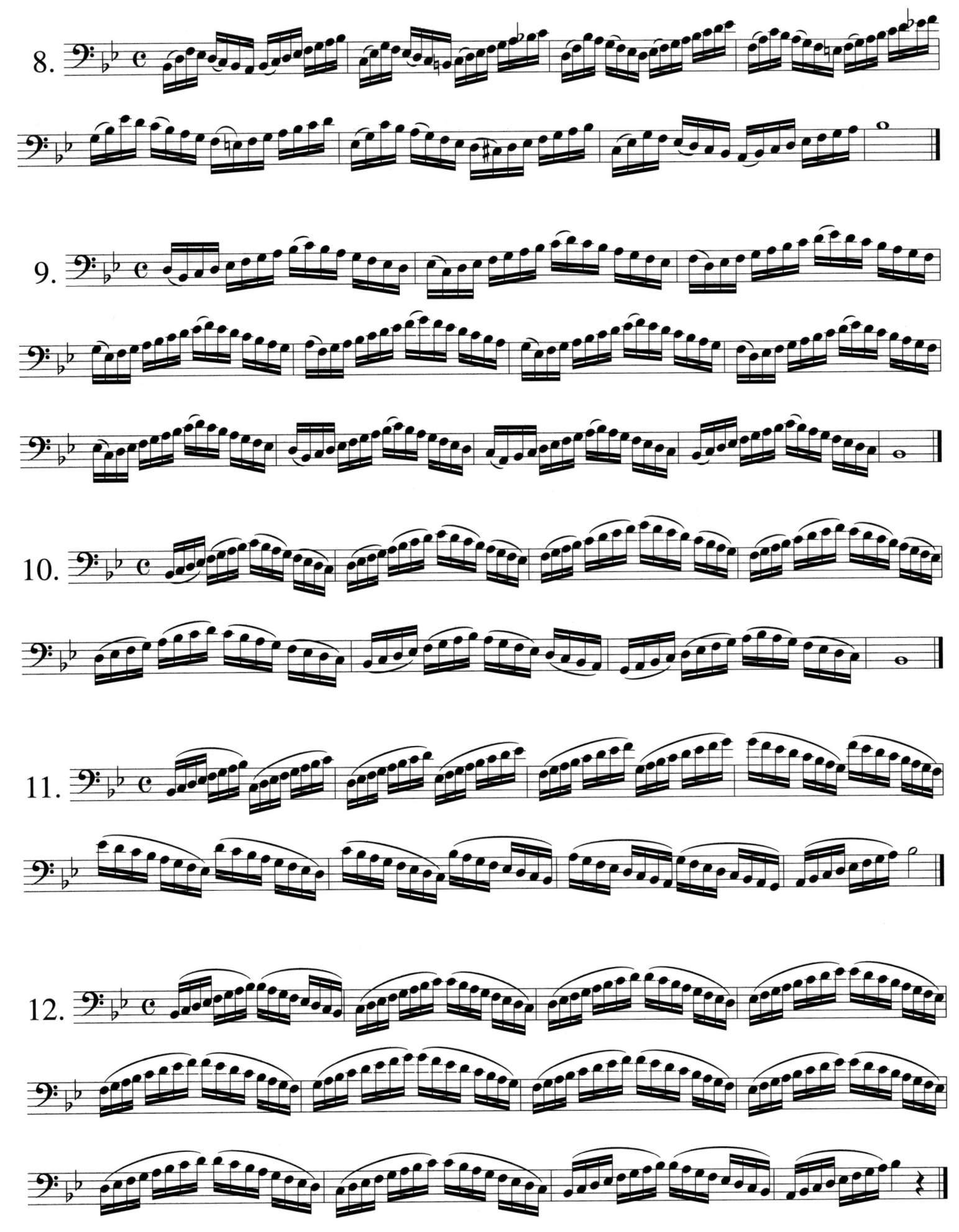

SCALES Arban • 67

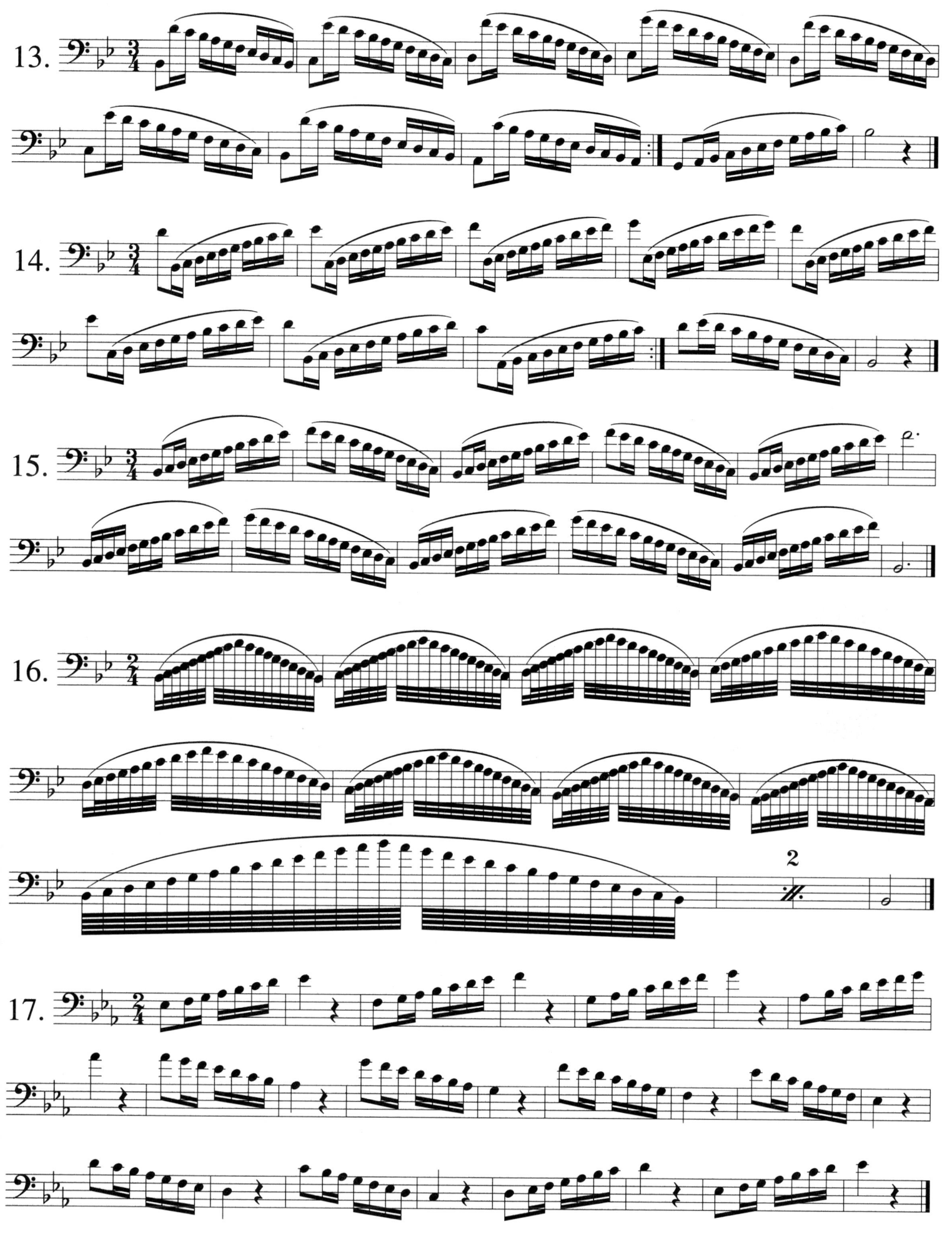

68 • Arban SCALES

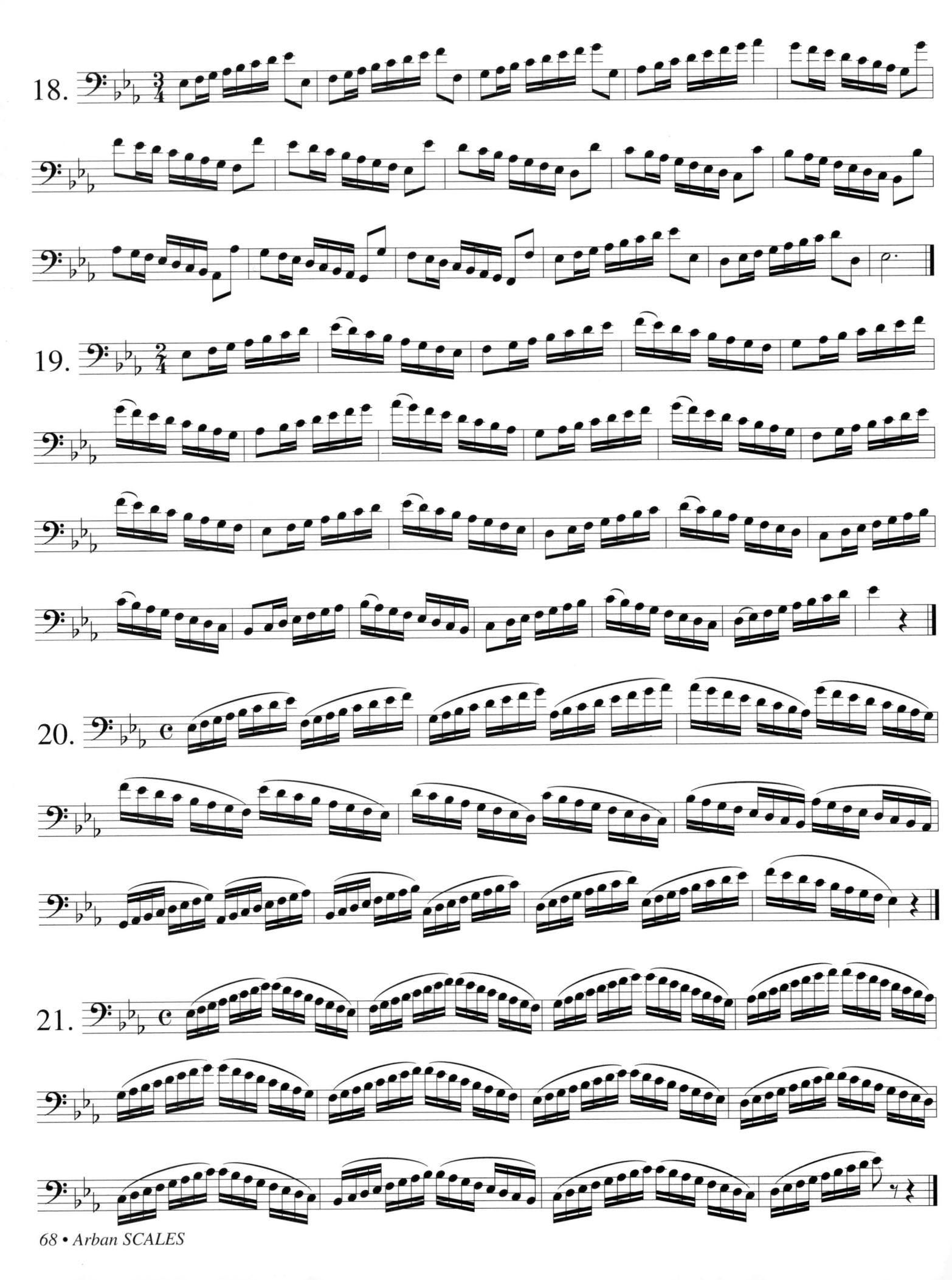

SCALES Arban • 69

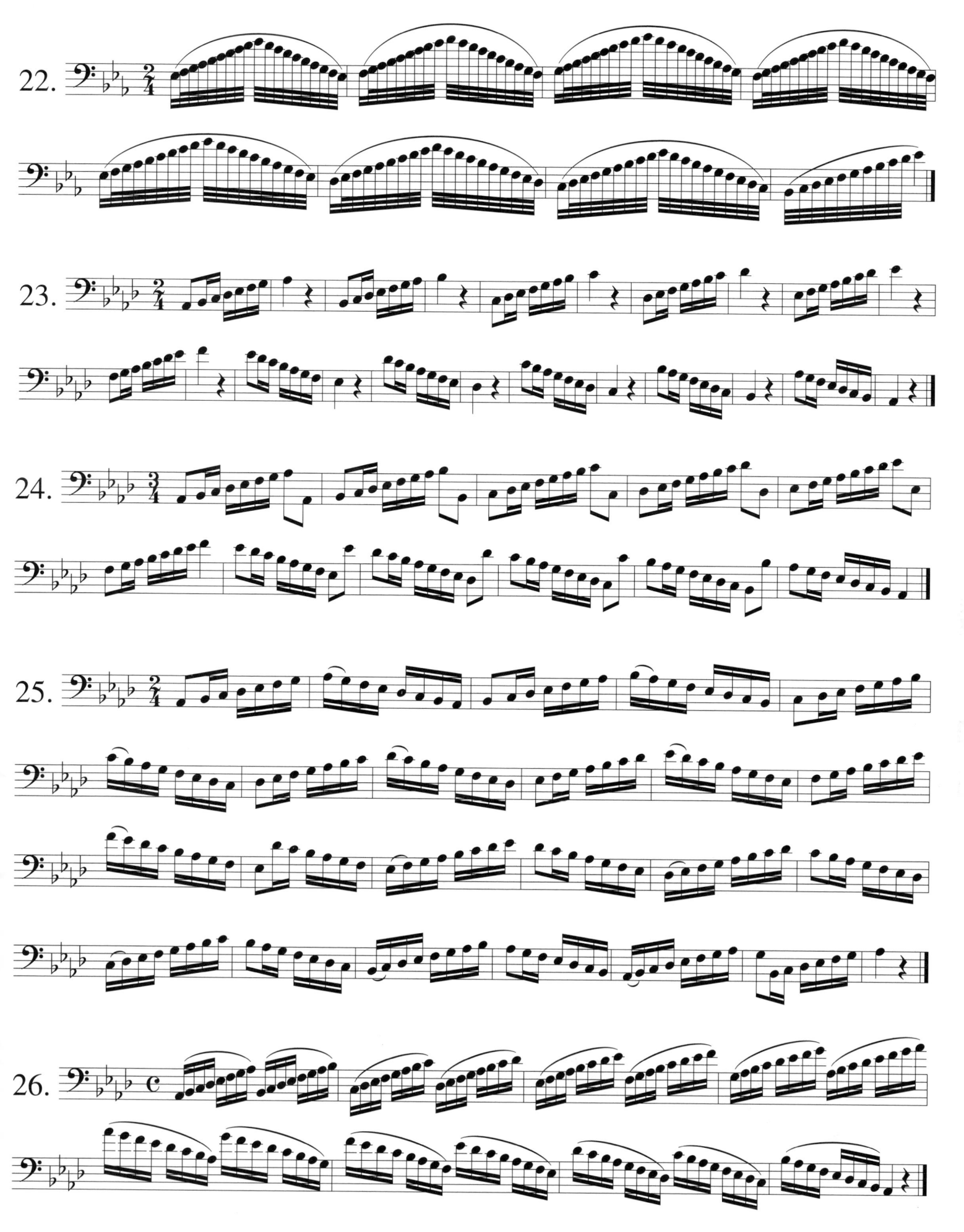

70 • Arban SCALES

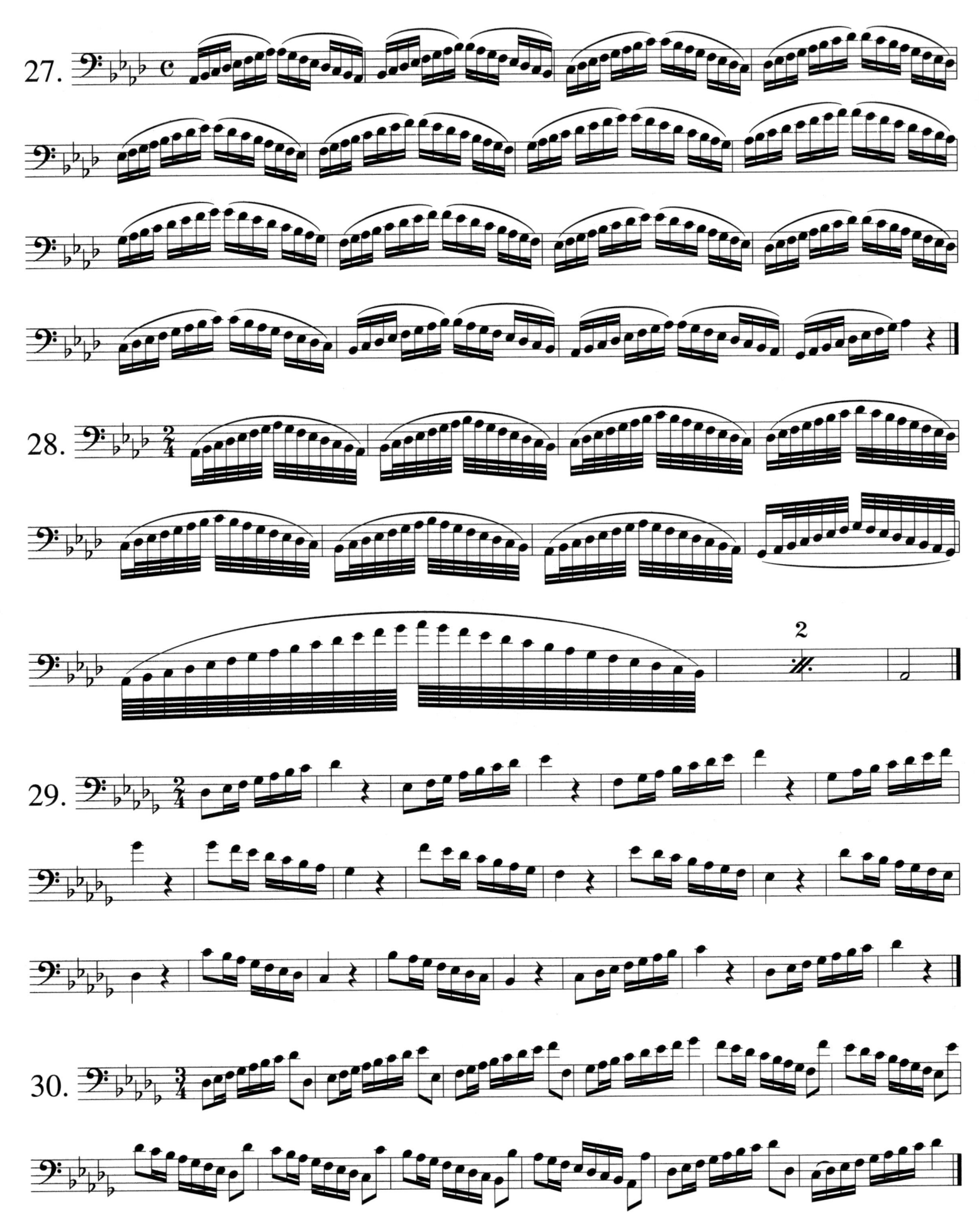

SCALES Arban • 71

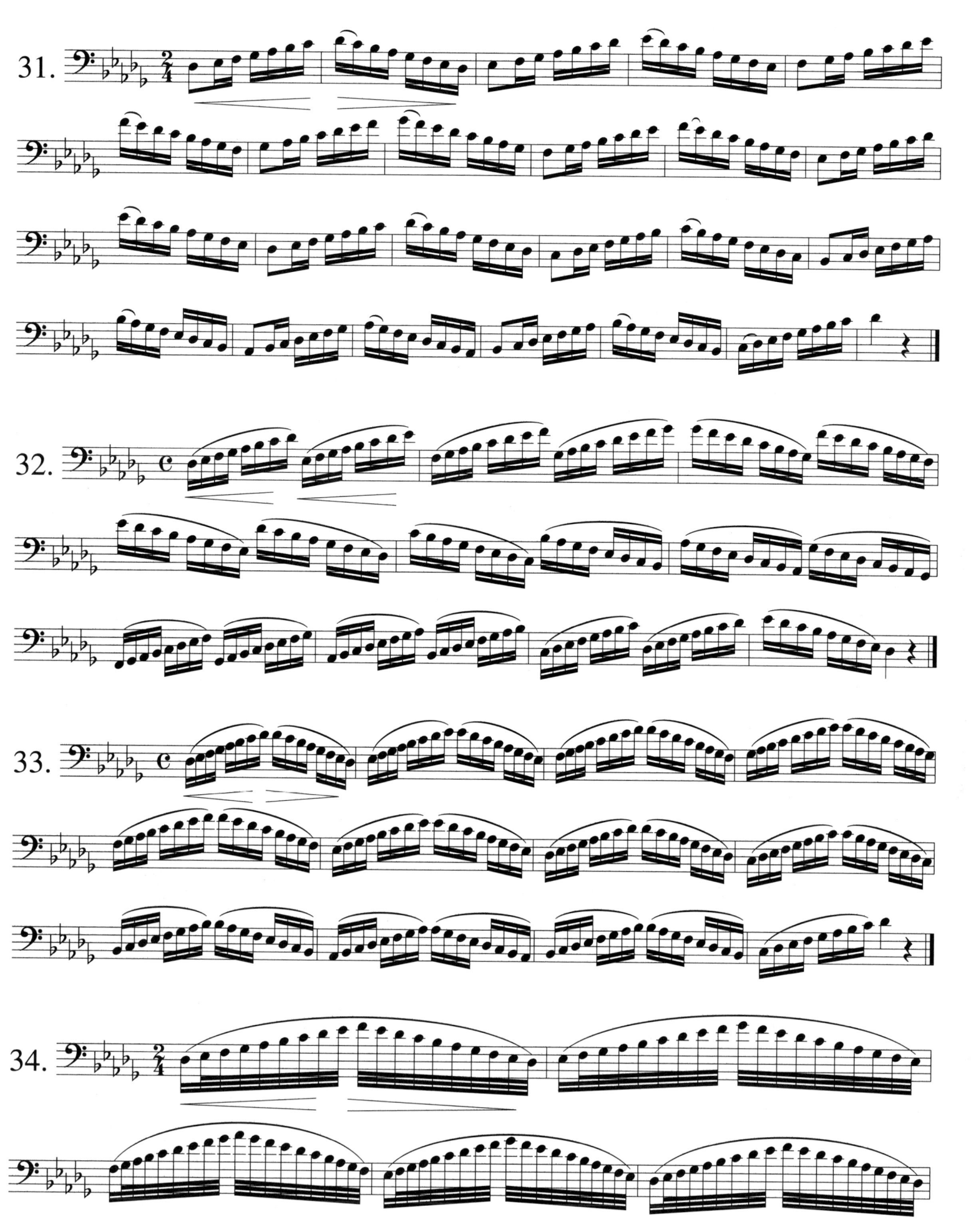

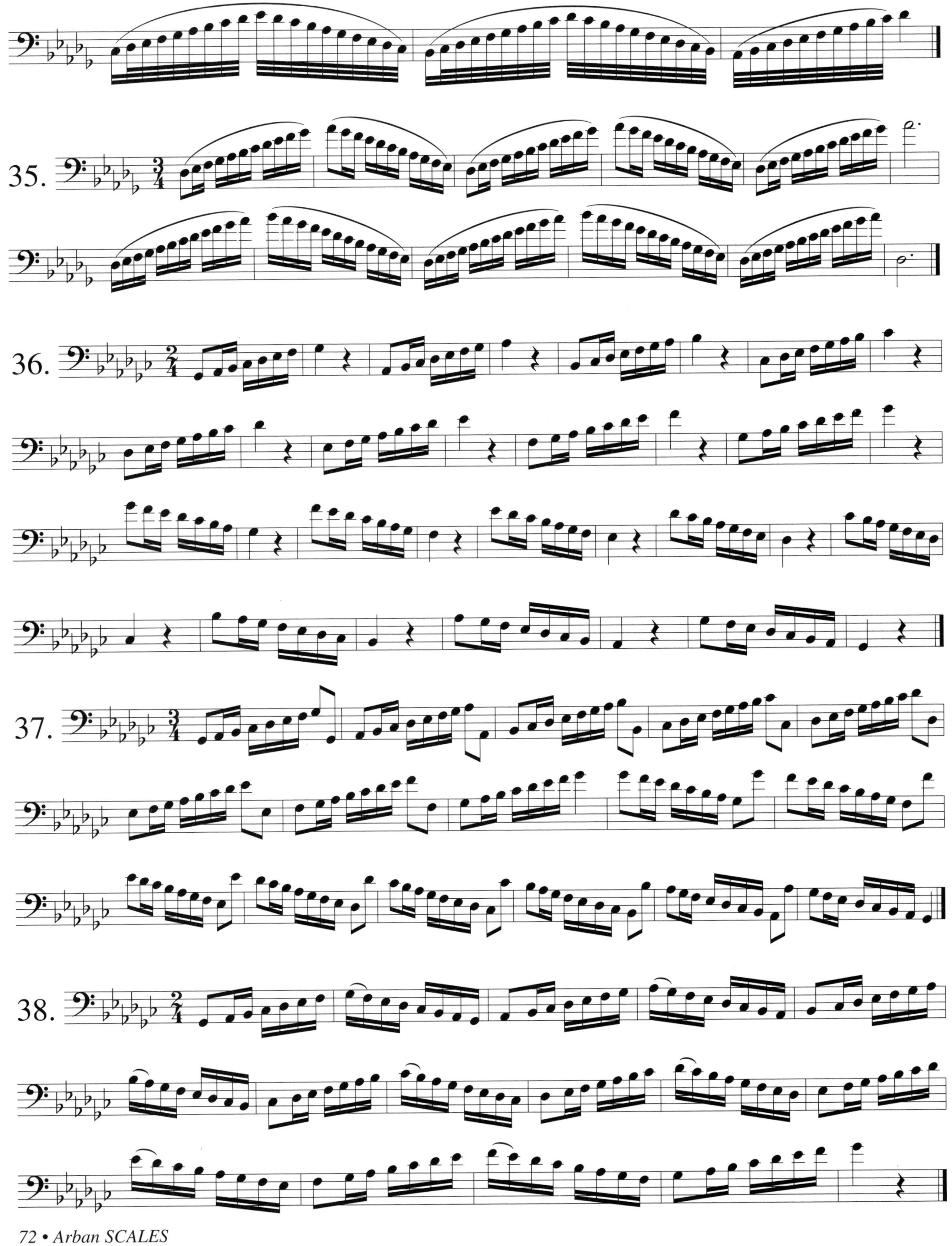
35.
36.
37.
38.

SCALES Arban • 73

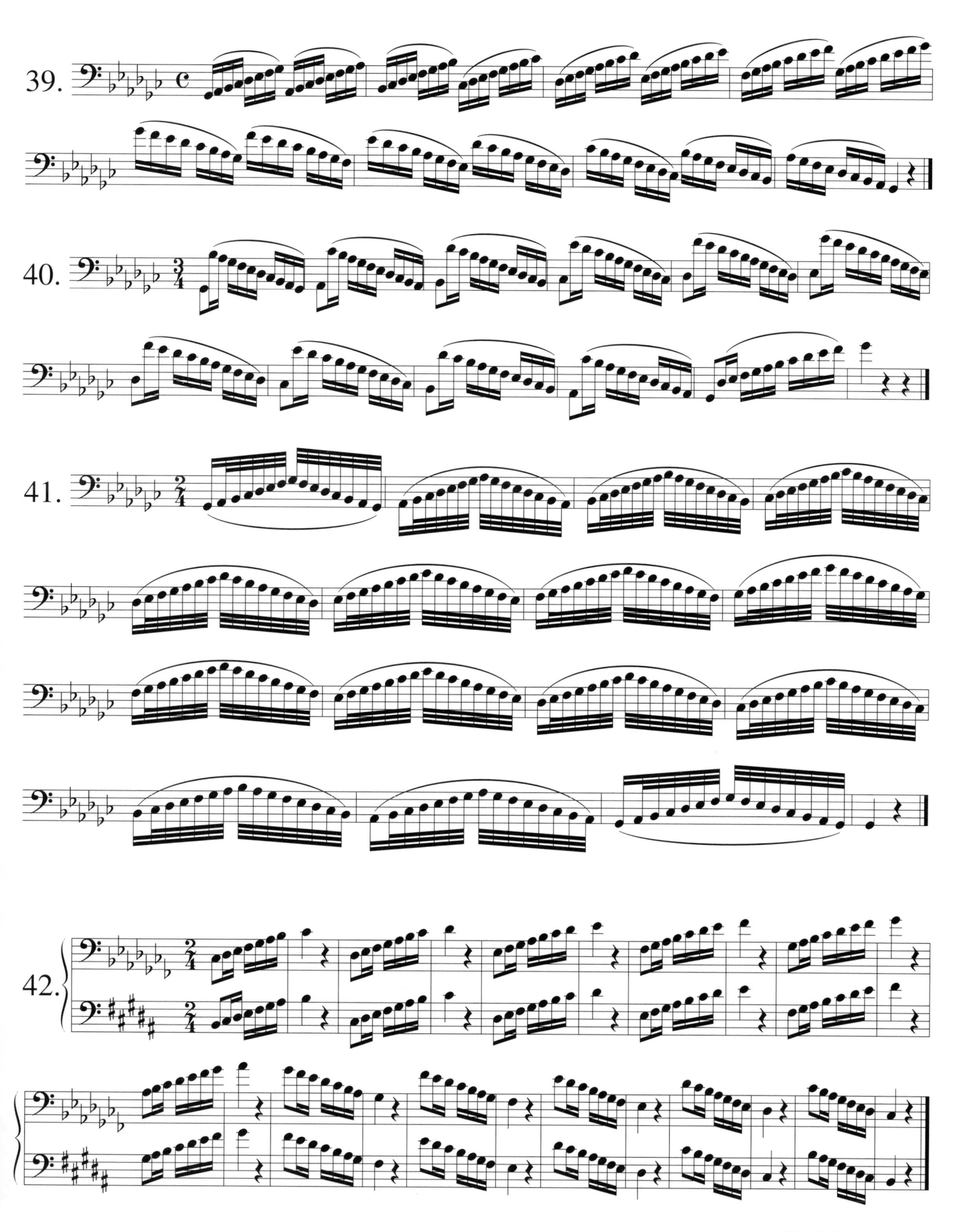

74 • Arban SCALES

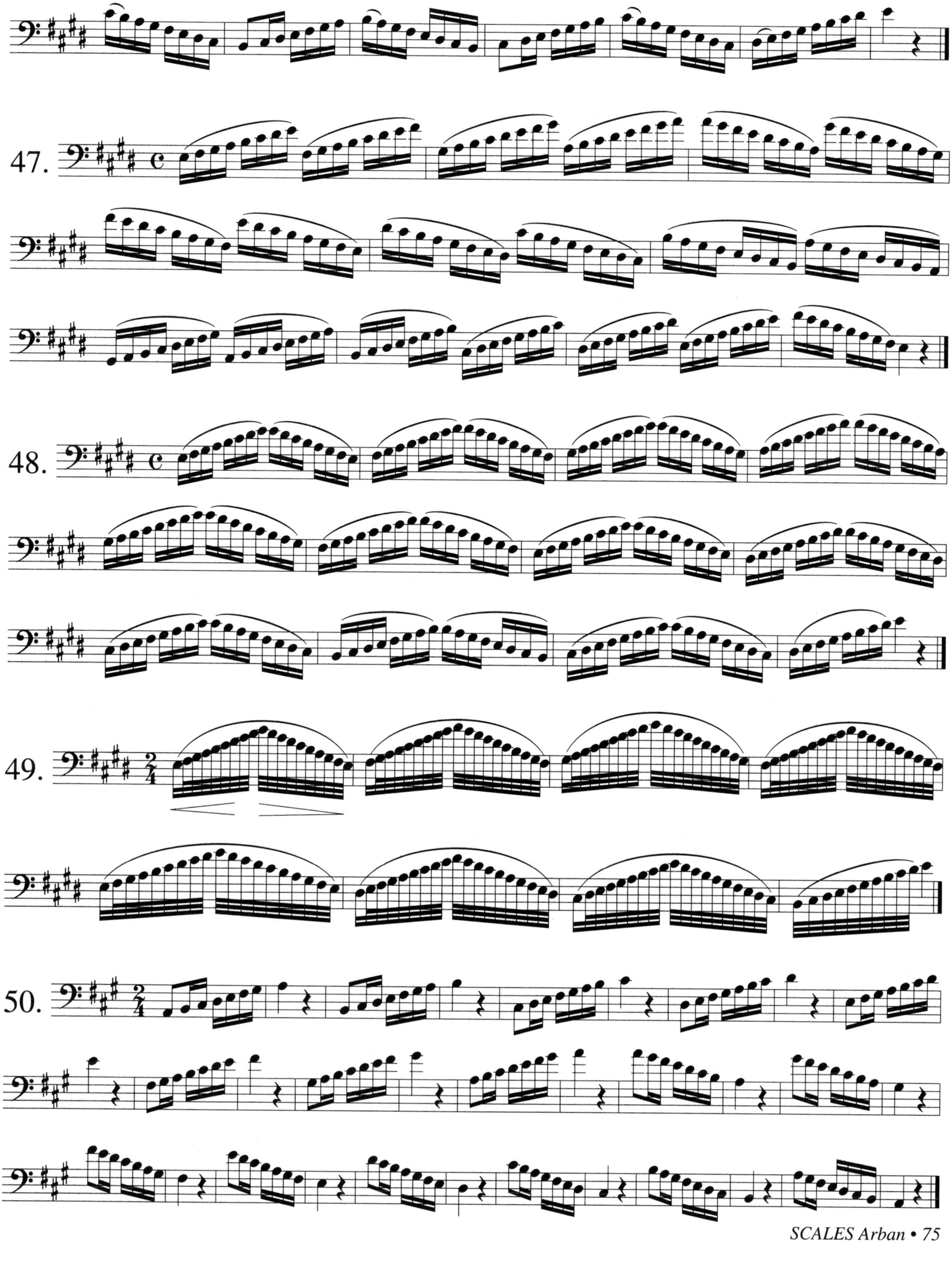
47.
48.
49.
50.

76 • Arban SCALES

SCALES Arban • 77

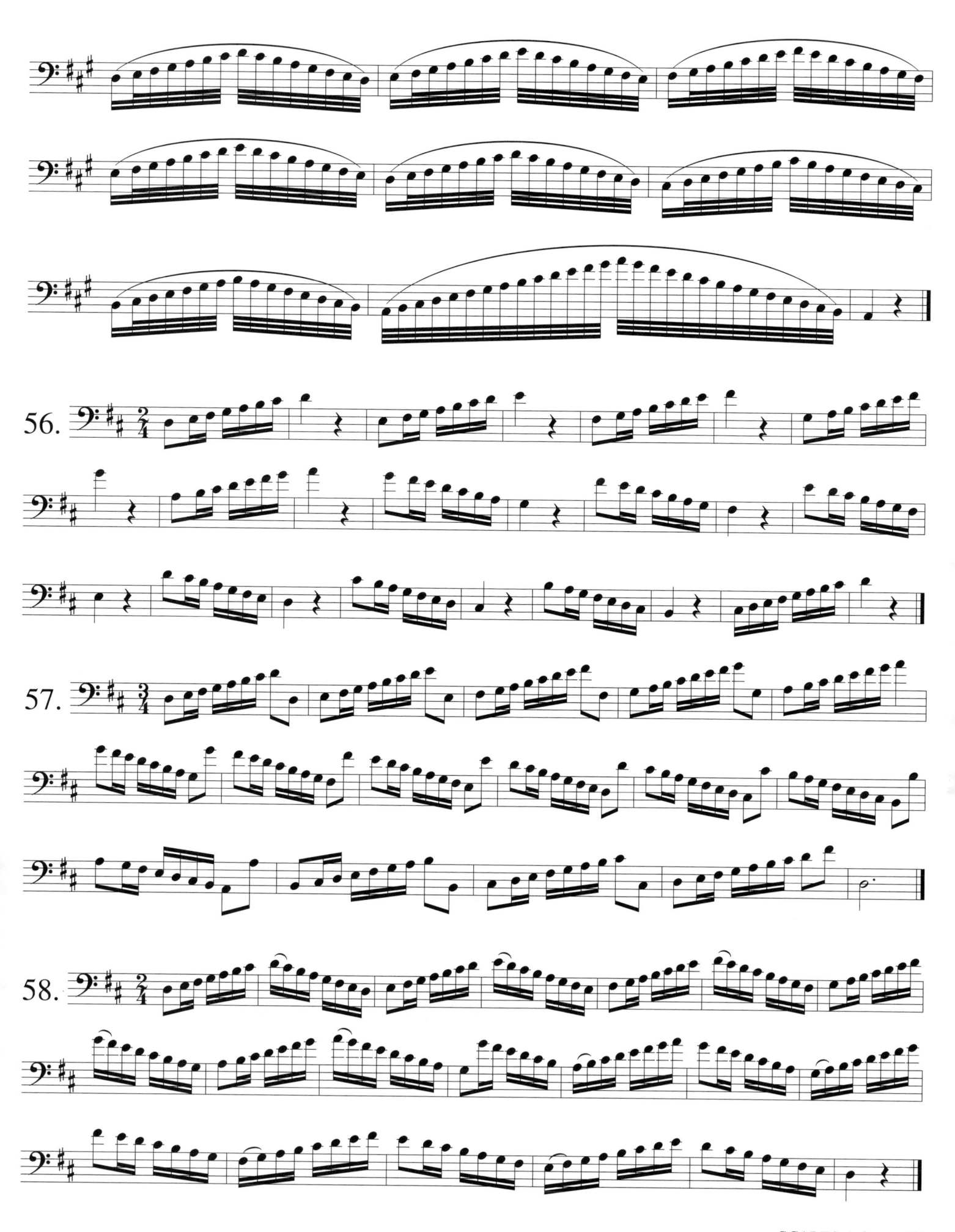

59.

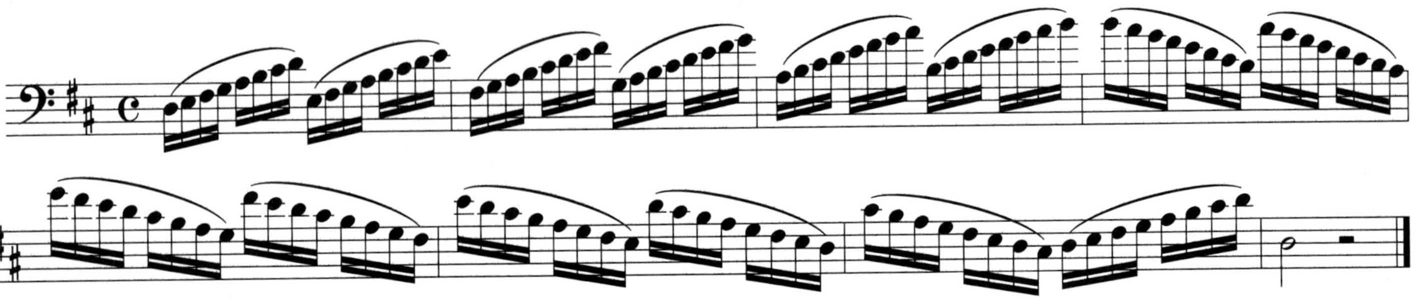

60.

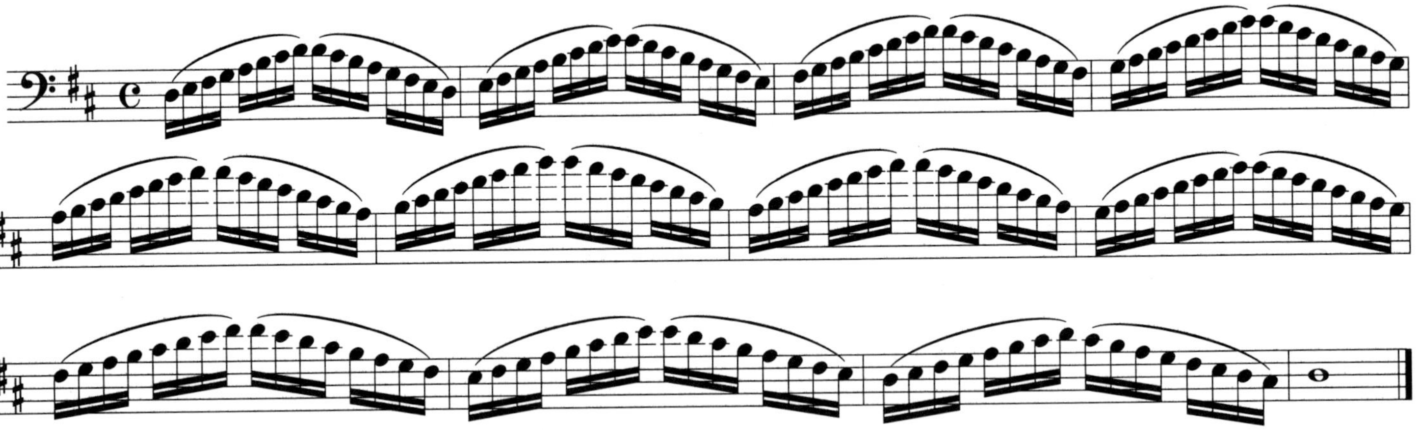

61.

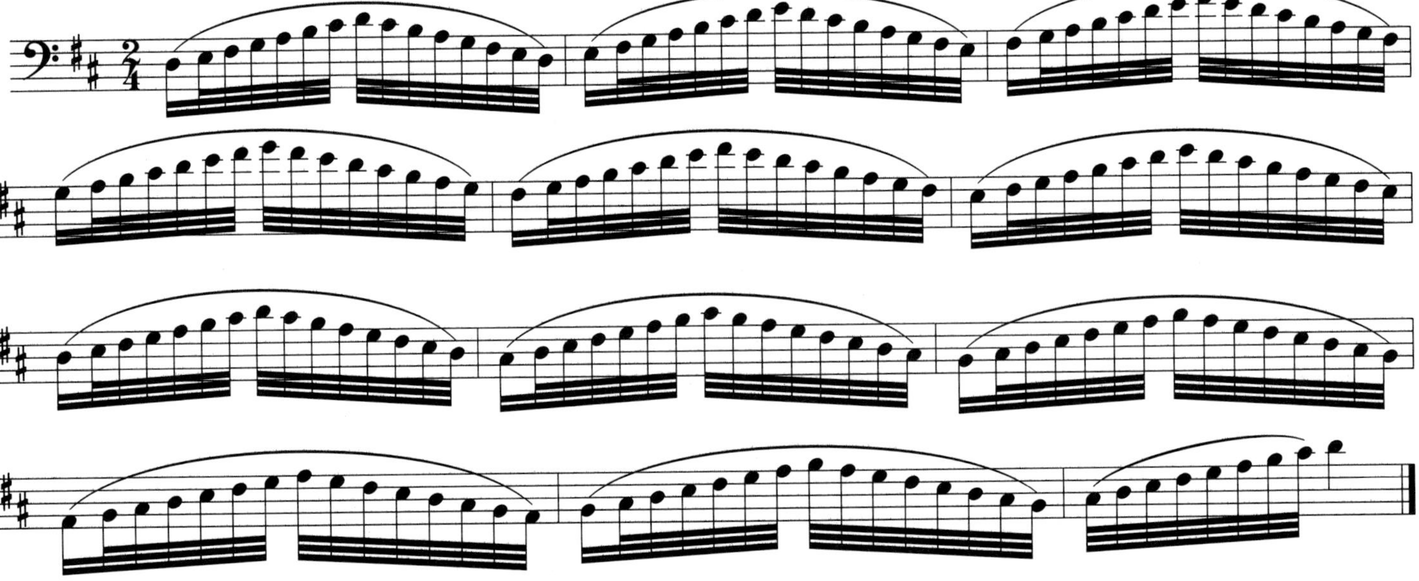

62.

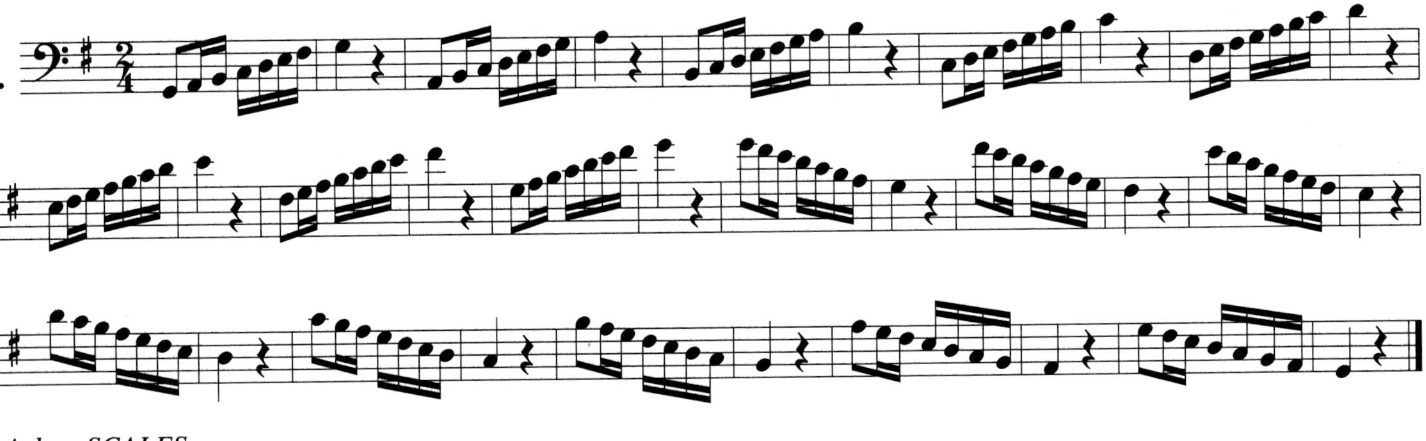

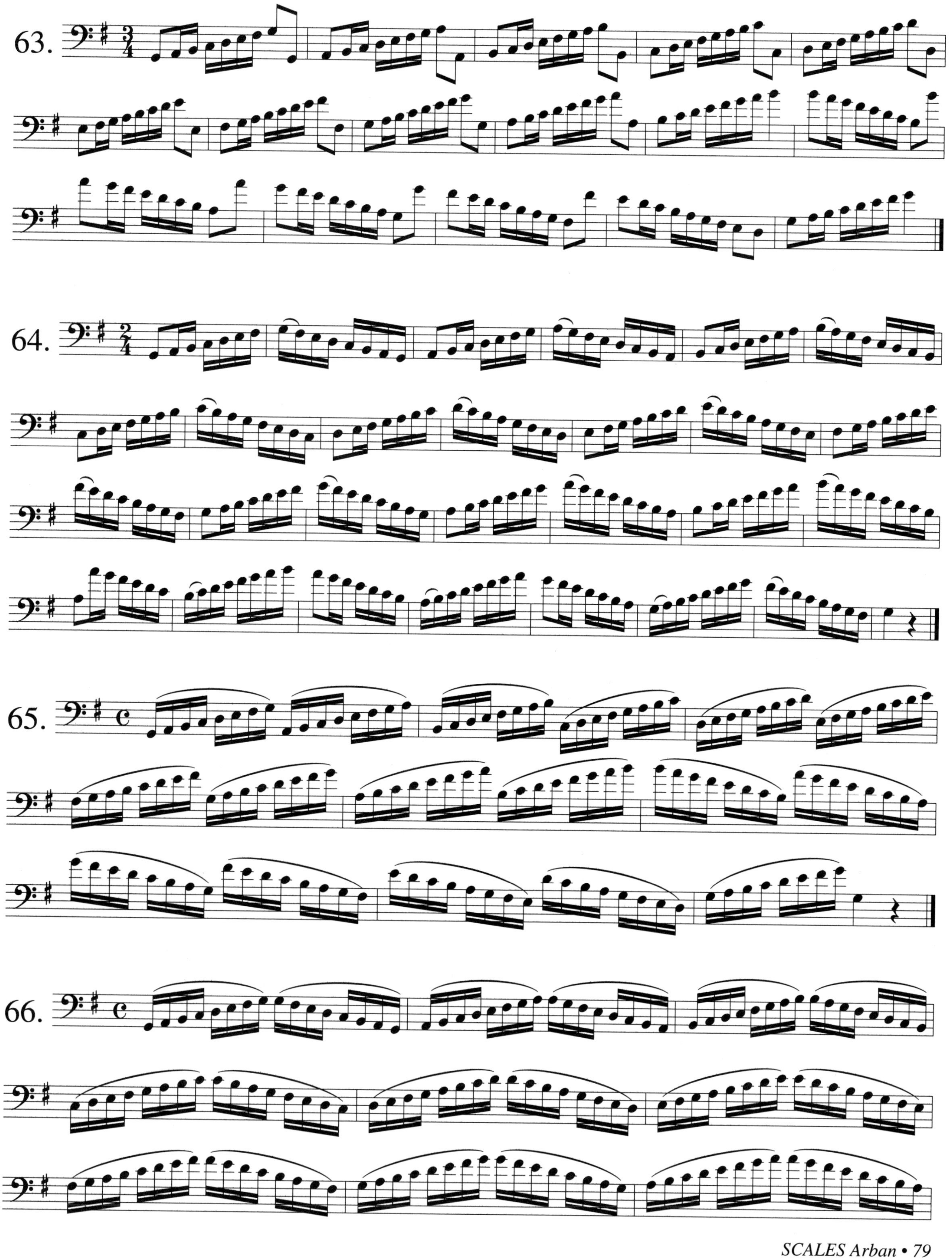
63.
64.
65.
66.

80 • Arban SCALES

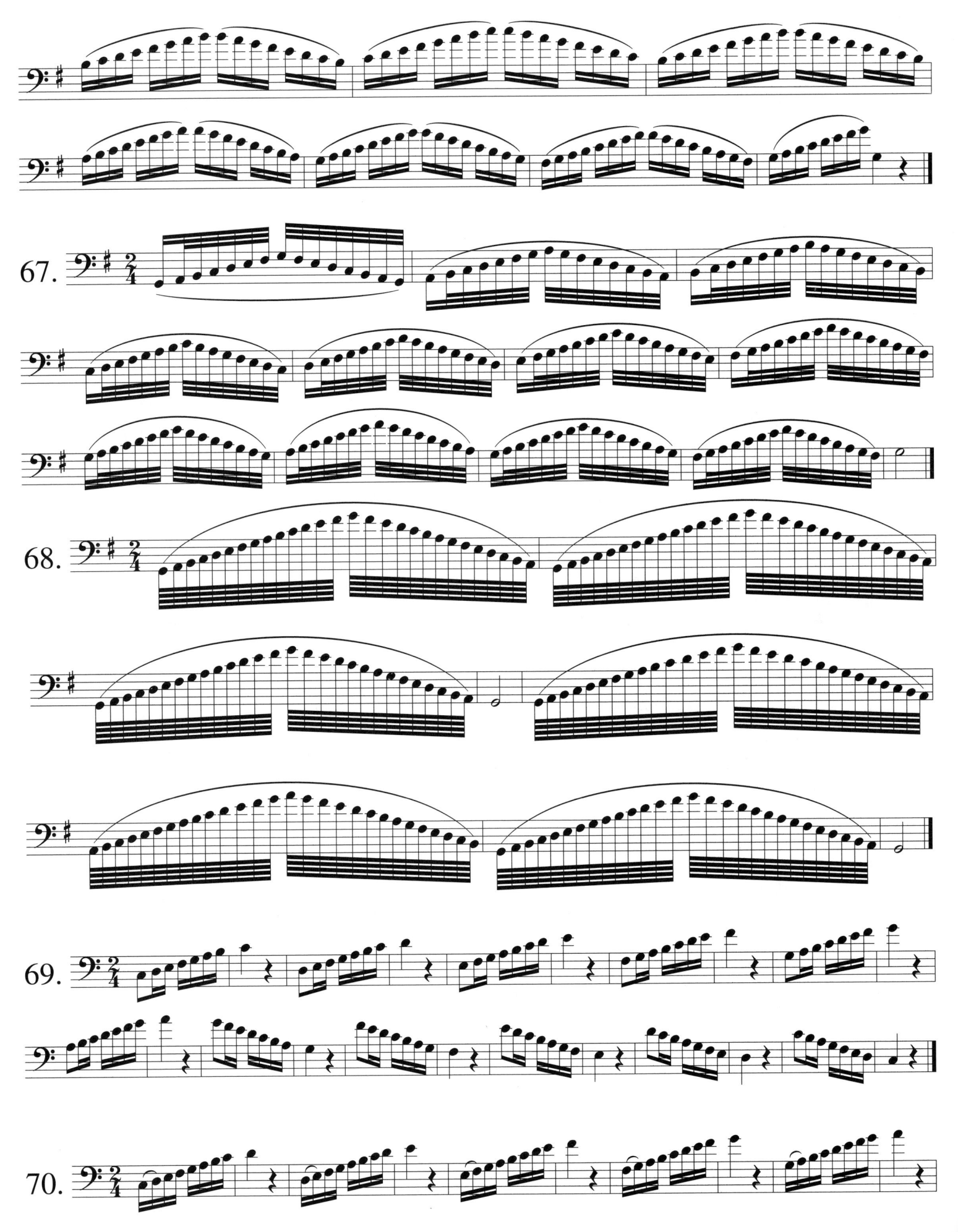

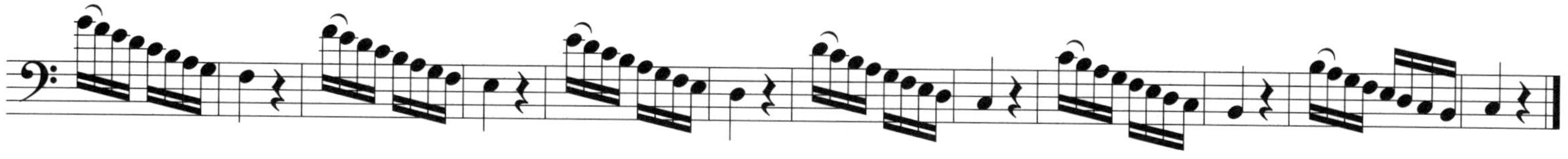

71.

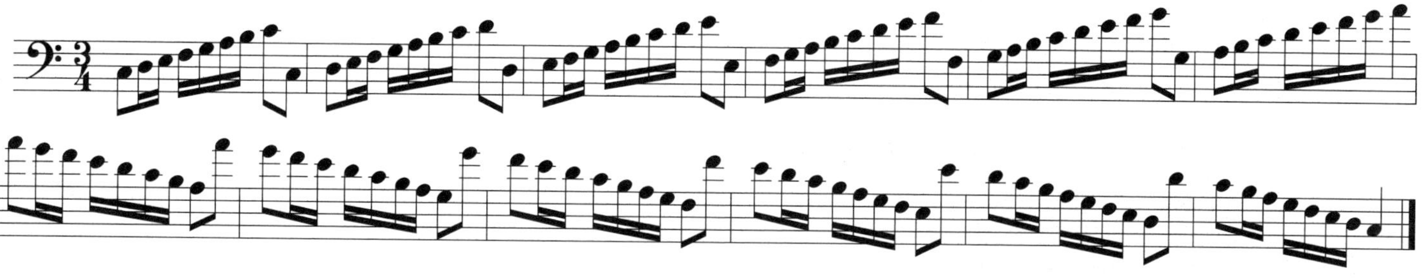

72.

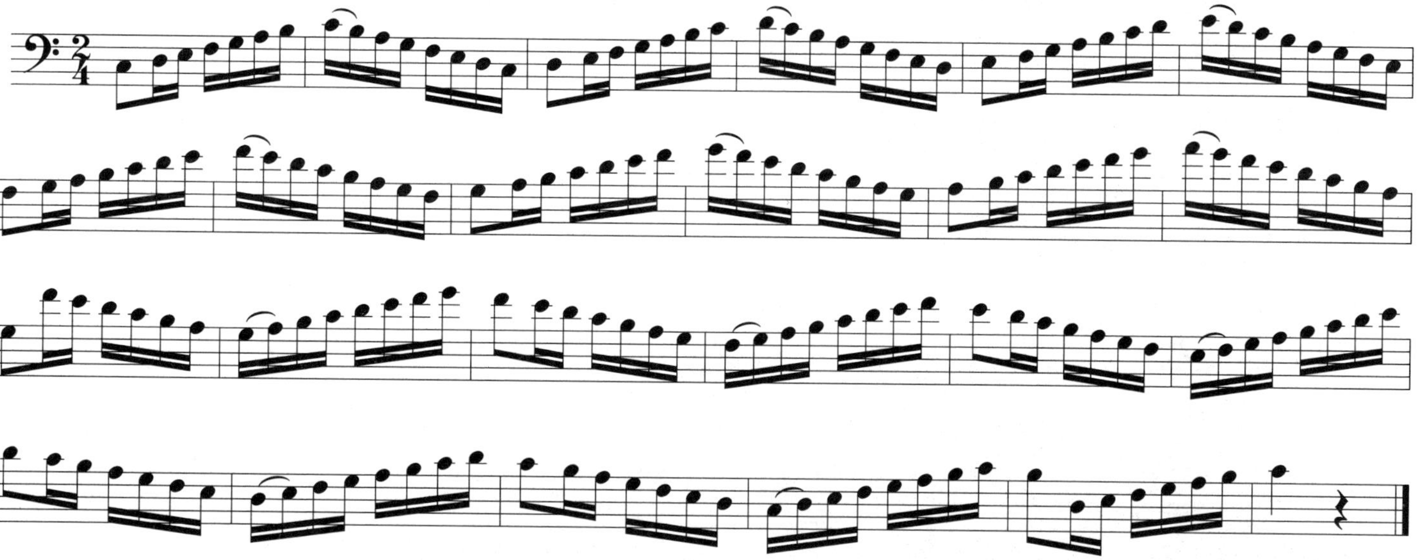

73.

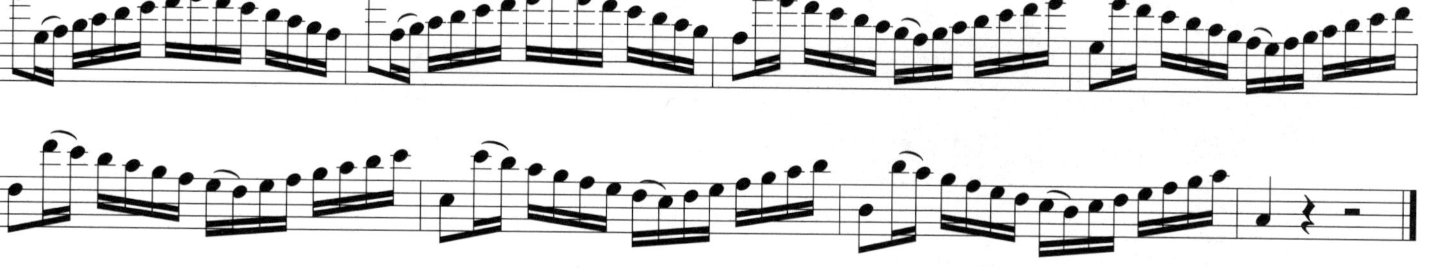

74.

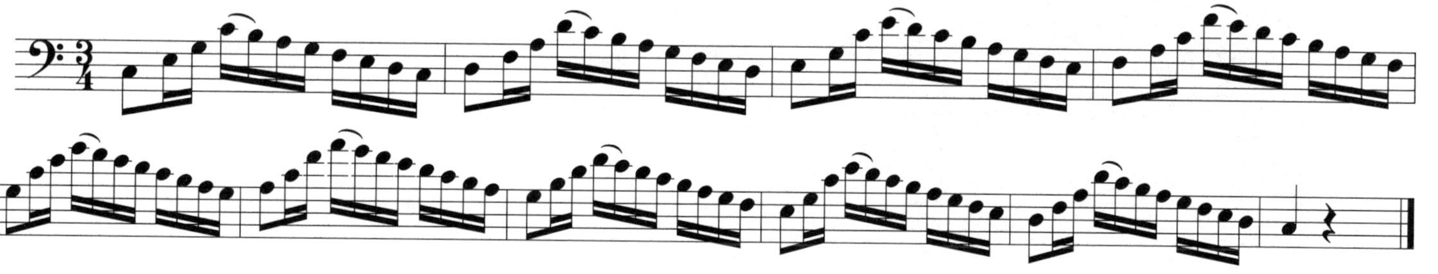

82 • Arban SCALES

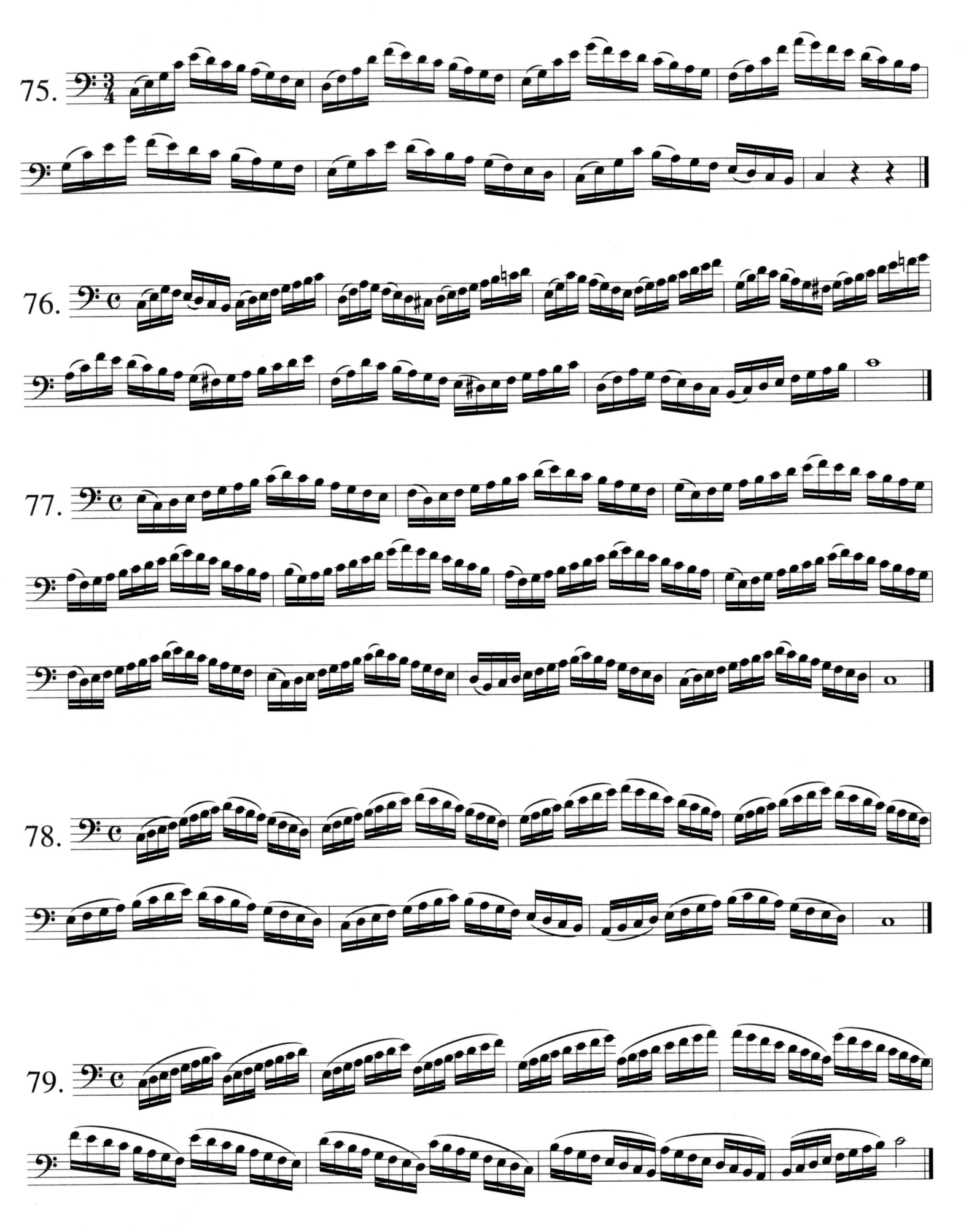

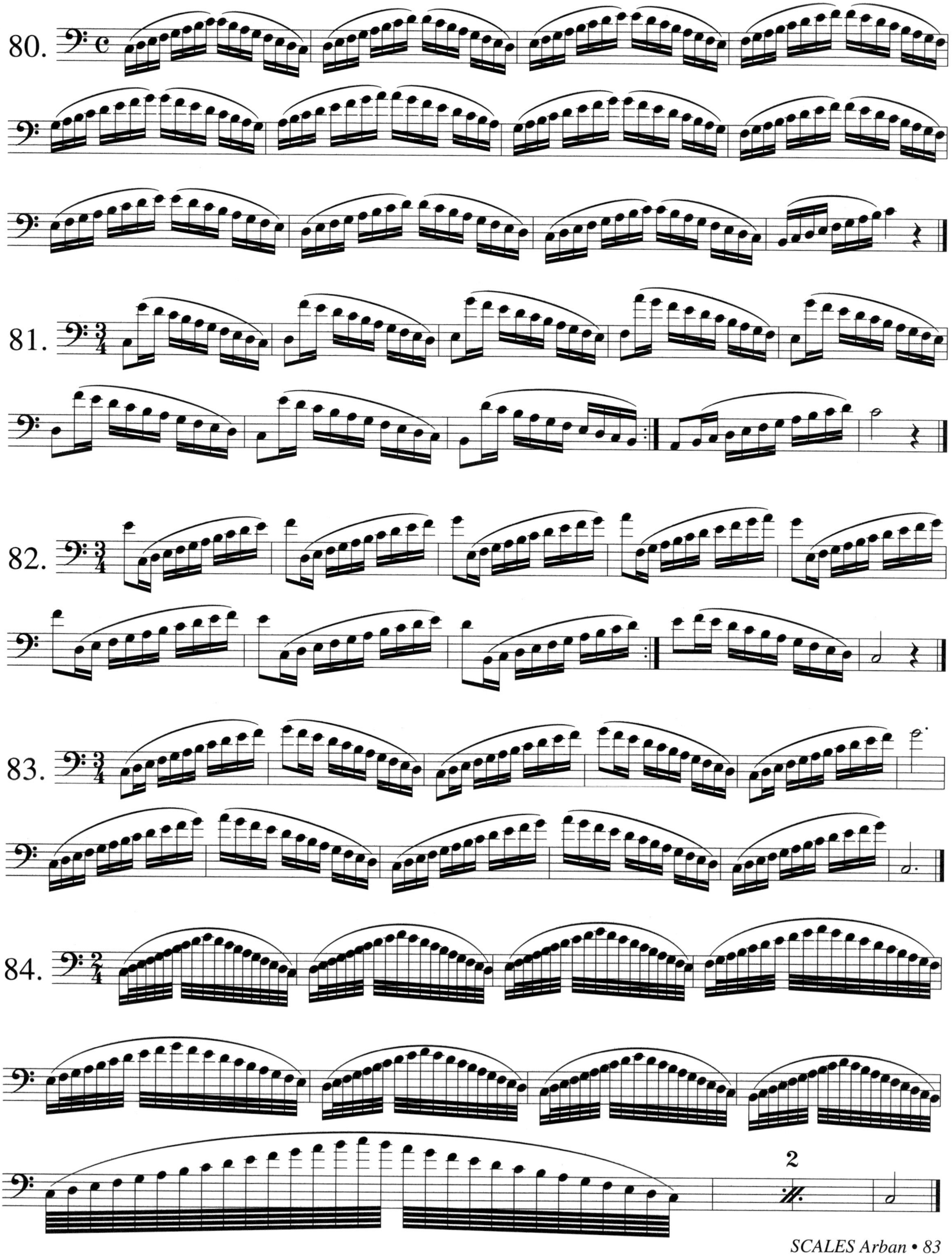
80.
81.
82.
83.
84.
2

84 • Arban SCALES

SCALES Arban • 85

86 • Arban SCALES

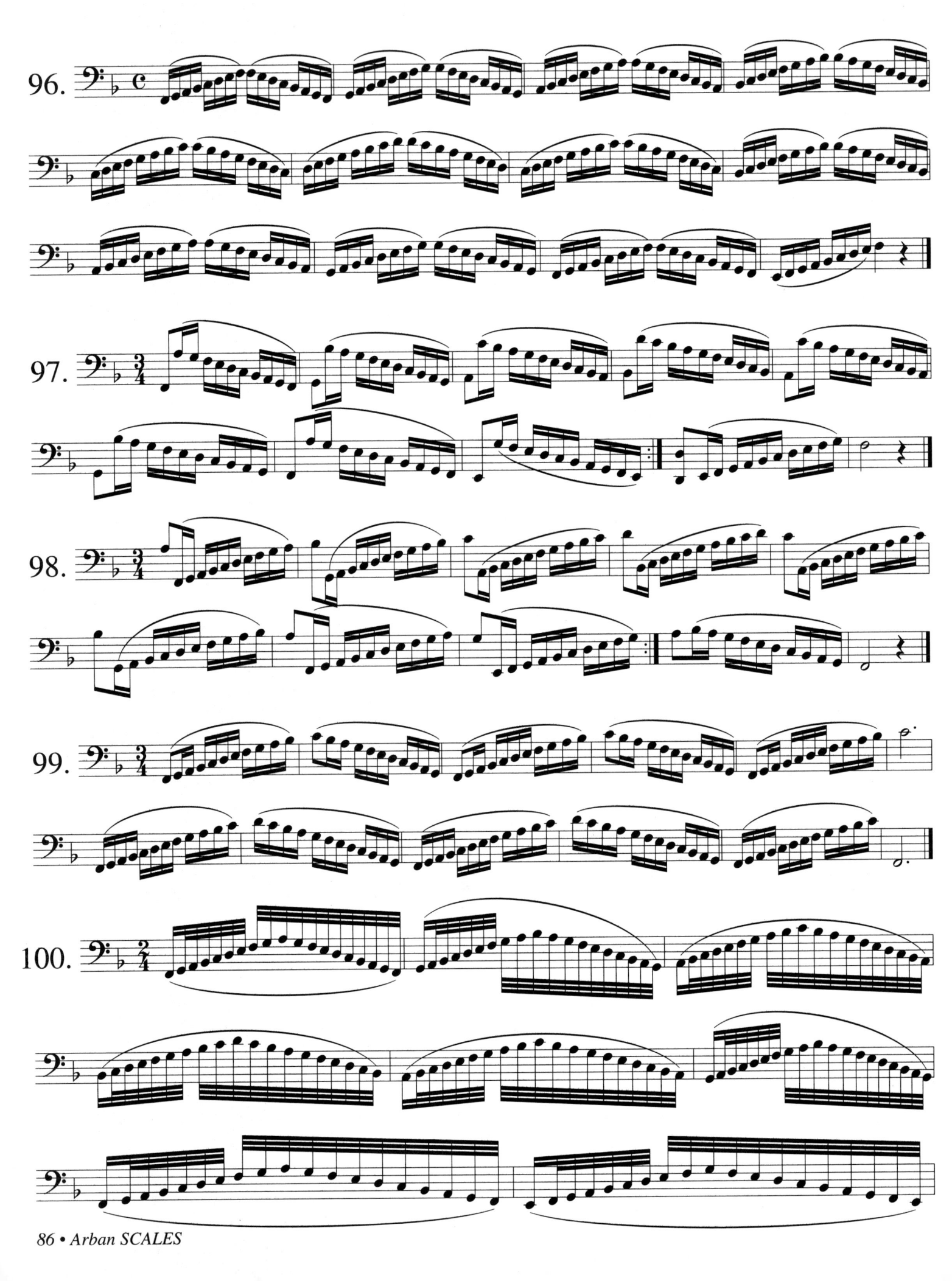

## Minor Scale Studies 101-109—Dr. Bowman

While not given much attention in the *Arban Method*, the study of minor scales can help with another complete set of fingering patterns that will aid technical development. I suggest that the student learn all the forms of the minor scale in all keys, even though they are not presented here. (A more complete presentation of Arban's scale patterns can be found in the book *Arban's Scales for Euphonium*, published by Encore Music Publishers.)

# Chromatic Scales

### Chromatic Scale Studies 1-30—Dr. Bowman

Use a metronome for this section and remember to press the fingers down all the way with security. The key to playing accurate chromatic scales in rhythm is the even and steady spacing of each note. Practice tongued as well as slurred. Start slowly and accurately and gradually increase the speed until great velocity is achieved. Listen carefully for good sound quality at all times.

For those with a 4 valve instrument, practice these exercises using the 4$^{th}$ valve and also with just the standard 3 valves.

### Chromatic Scale Studies 1-30—Mr. Alessi

Chromatics are an important part of the trombonists *daily diet*. Practicing them regularly tends to join the different registers together. Chromatics are also great for slide and tongue coordination.
- Practice these studies with a metronome at least ten minutes a day.
- Play them tongued and slurred.
- Practice them using different tempi.

When using a slower tempo, notice how the slide pauses for each position. Master this technique first before increasing speed.

At faster tempi, let the slide go in one motion so as not to stop on each position. In other words, *let the slide glide.*

One danger when playing faster is that the slide may get ahead—or fall behind—the tongue and the mind. If you are having trouble with this, slightly accent each downbeat.

At the end of each fragment, be certain to sustain longer note values, i.e. quarter and whole notes.

Make a slight crescendo when ascending.

*SCALES Arban • 89*

5.

*SCALES Arban • 91*

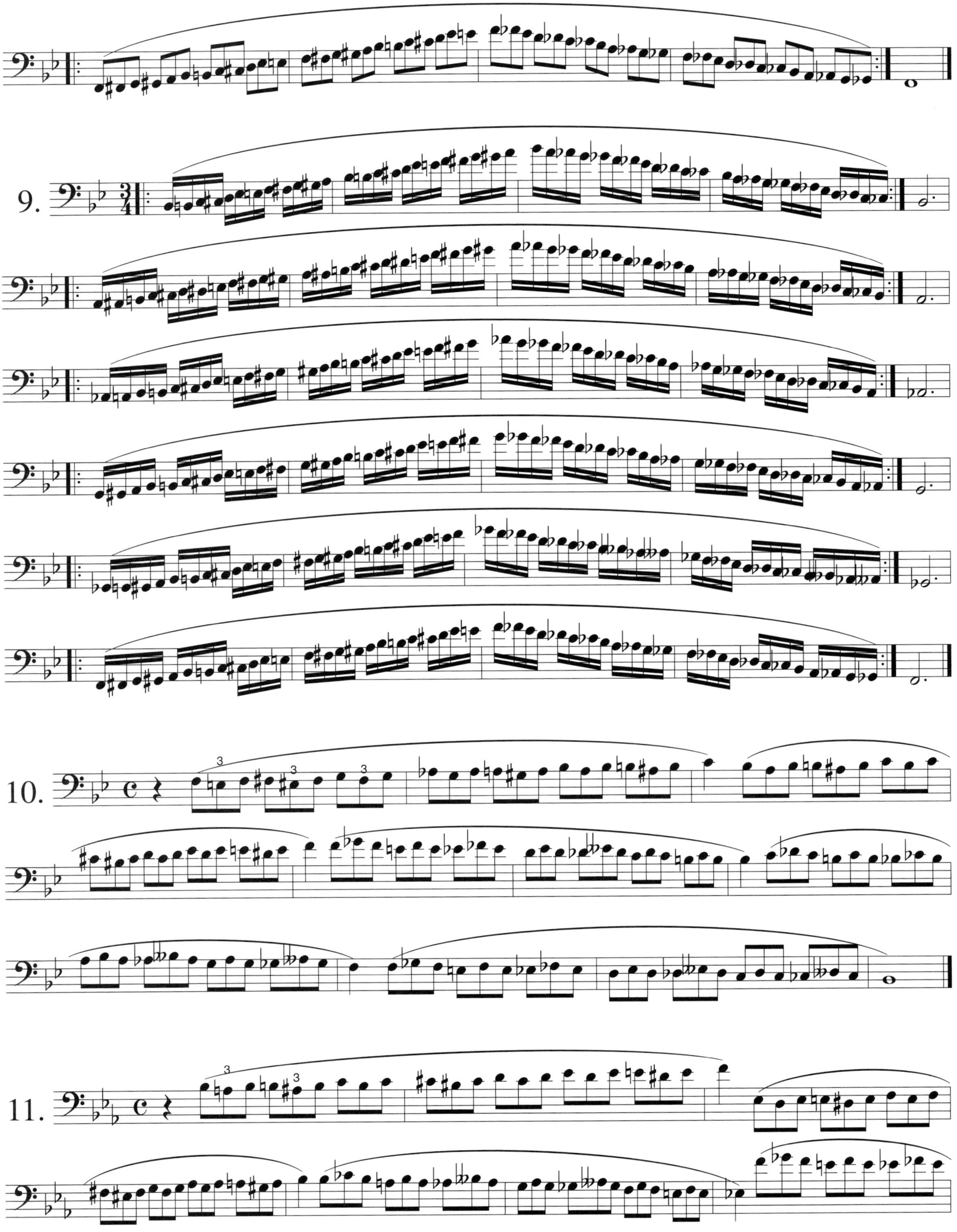
9.
10.
3
11.
3

*SCALES Arban • 93*

94 • Arban SCALES

SCALES Arban • 95

96 • Arban SCALES

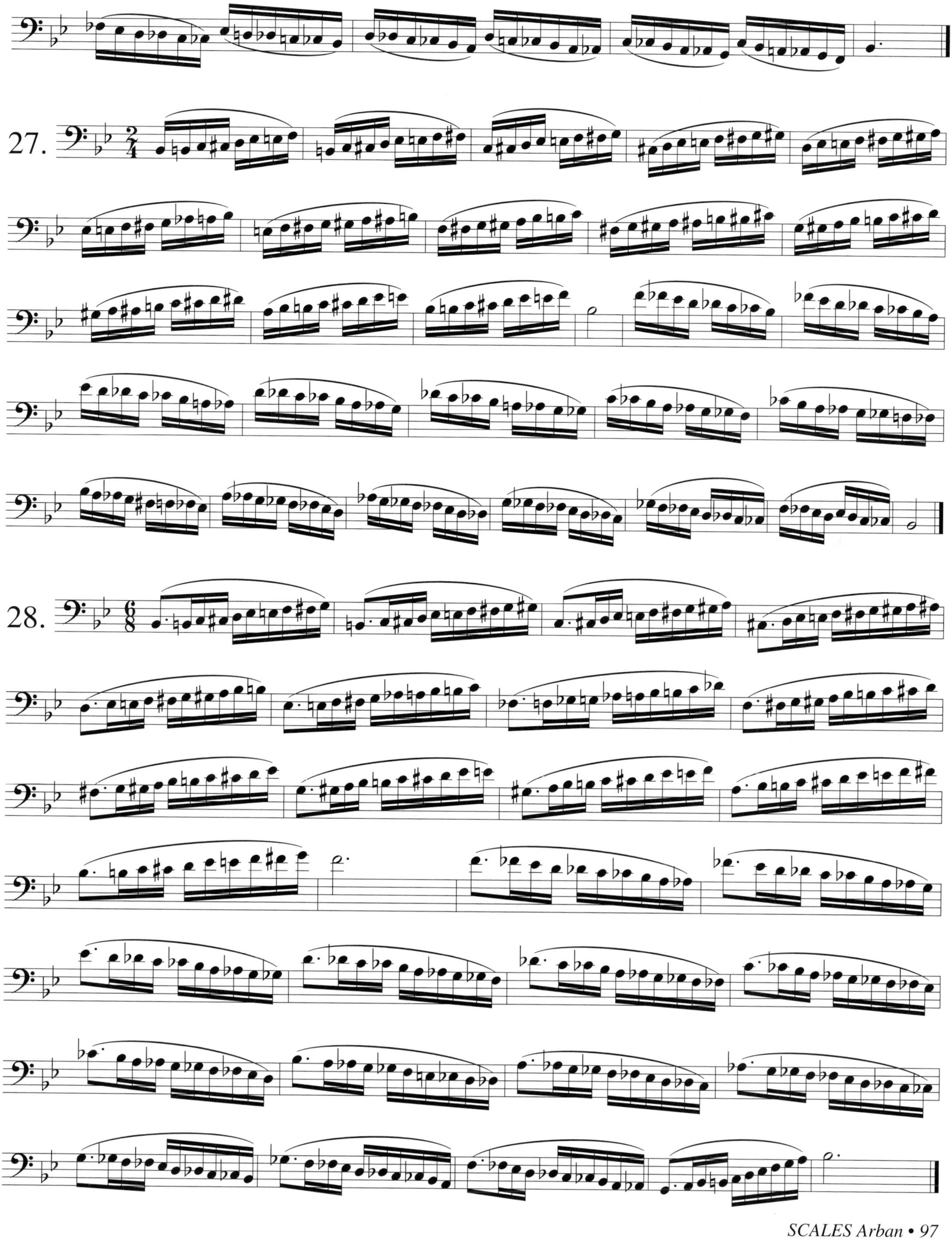
27.
28.

## —Mr. Alessi

As the exercises increase in difficulty—and when the speed increases—keep in mind to mentally subdivide using eighth notes. Also, remember to hold the slide firmly with the two fingers and the thumb. Avoid playing these studies too quickly causing you to lose control. Keep a clear and clean slur followed by staccato. When changing the slide direction quickly, be careful not to accent this connection.

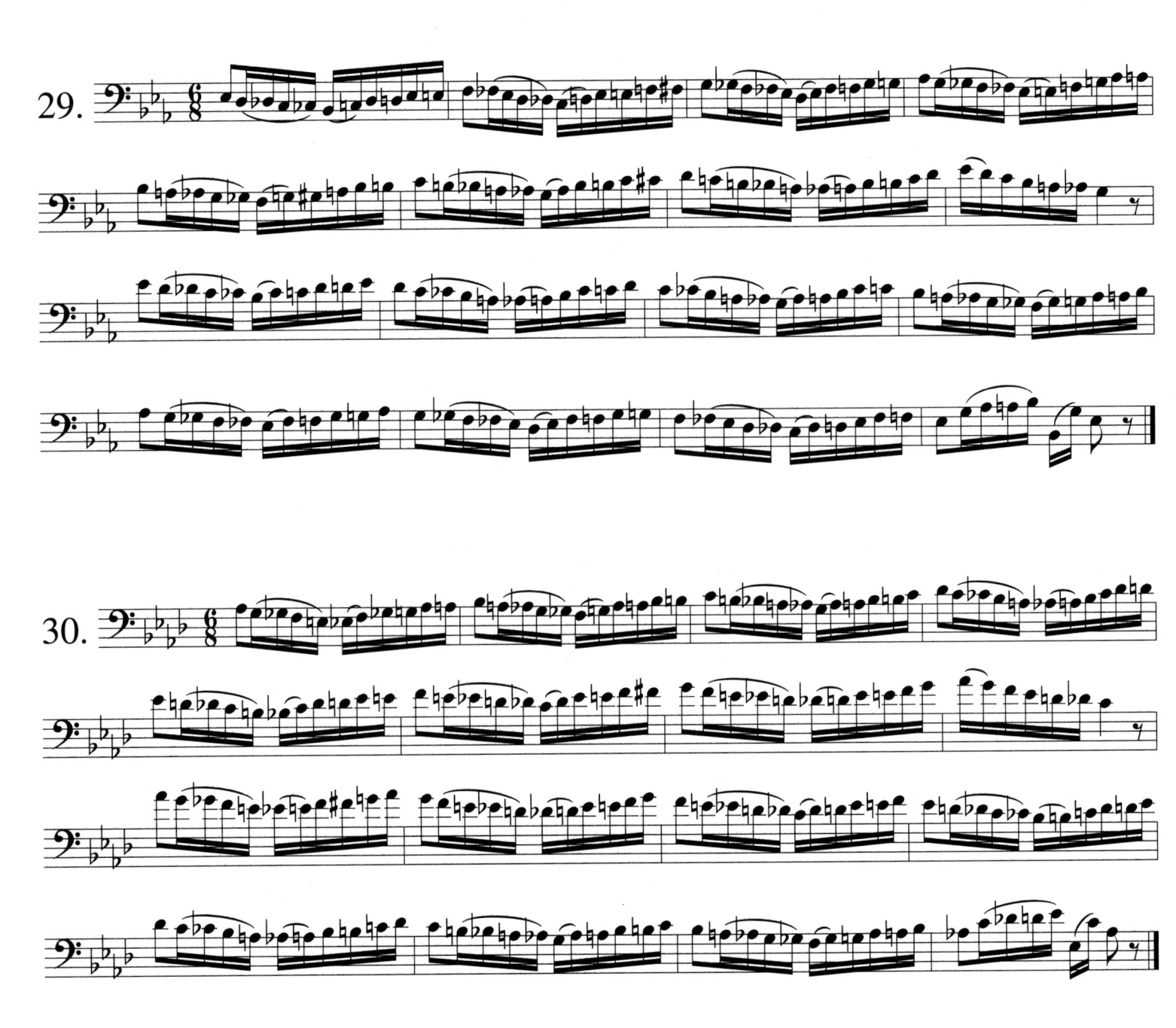

98 • Arban SCALES

31.

# ORNAMENTATION

### GENERAL COMMENTS—DR. BOWMAN

The development of skill in using ornamentation is essential to the euphonium player to prepare the ability to play all periods and styles of music. Ornamentation is frequently an important factor in the performance of borrowed literature from the baroque and classical periods and is also useful in all performance areas. The mastery of all the ornamental techniques presented in the *Arban Method* gives a good basis for the interpretation and performance of this borrowed literature.

The first 23 exercises are excellent studies in accuracy and melodic interpretation. Stress the melody note in each figure while keeping the tone quality and sound as consistent as possible.

### GENERAL COMMENTS—MR. ALESSI

While most of this section is applicable to the euphonium player, there are benefits to practicing some of these exercises for the trombonist. Usually, the trombonist is not confronted with traditional ornamentation, but occasionally it is written: i.e. Bordogni Etudes, Pryor solos, and some concerti. The modern trombonist must acquire good lip-trilling technique. Unfortunately, Arban's original exercises for the trill in this register do not apply to the trombonist. For more pertinent exercises for trilling on the trombone, return to studies 16-22 beginning on page 47.

Certainly the gruppetto is the most common ornament encountered by the trombonist. I suggest combining the natural slur with the legato tongue to make a smooth gruppetto turn. It is also important to mentally subdivide when executing this ornament.

Exercises 1-23 are excellent for developing slide technique, accuracy, and intonation as well as combining natural slurs with the legato tongue. Be careful not to *splat* short low notes, which is a most unpleasing sound on the trombone. When studying these exercises, take the opportunity to make a natural slur by using the alternate position to create a no tongue event. Number 26 is a good example for this concept. In the first measure, use the $4^{th}$ position *D* and *F*. In the second measure, use the $5^{th}$ position $B^b$. Take advantage of these opportunities when it makes sense to do so.

*ORNAMENTATION Arban • 101*

102 • Arban ORNAMENTATION

3.

ORNAMENTATION Arban • 103

104 • Arban ORNAMENTATION

ORNAMENTATION Arban

106 • Arban ORNAMENTATION

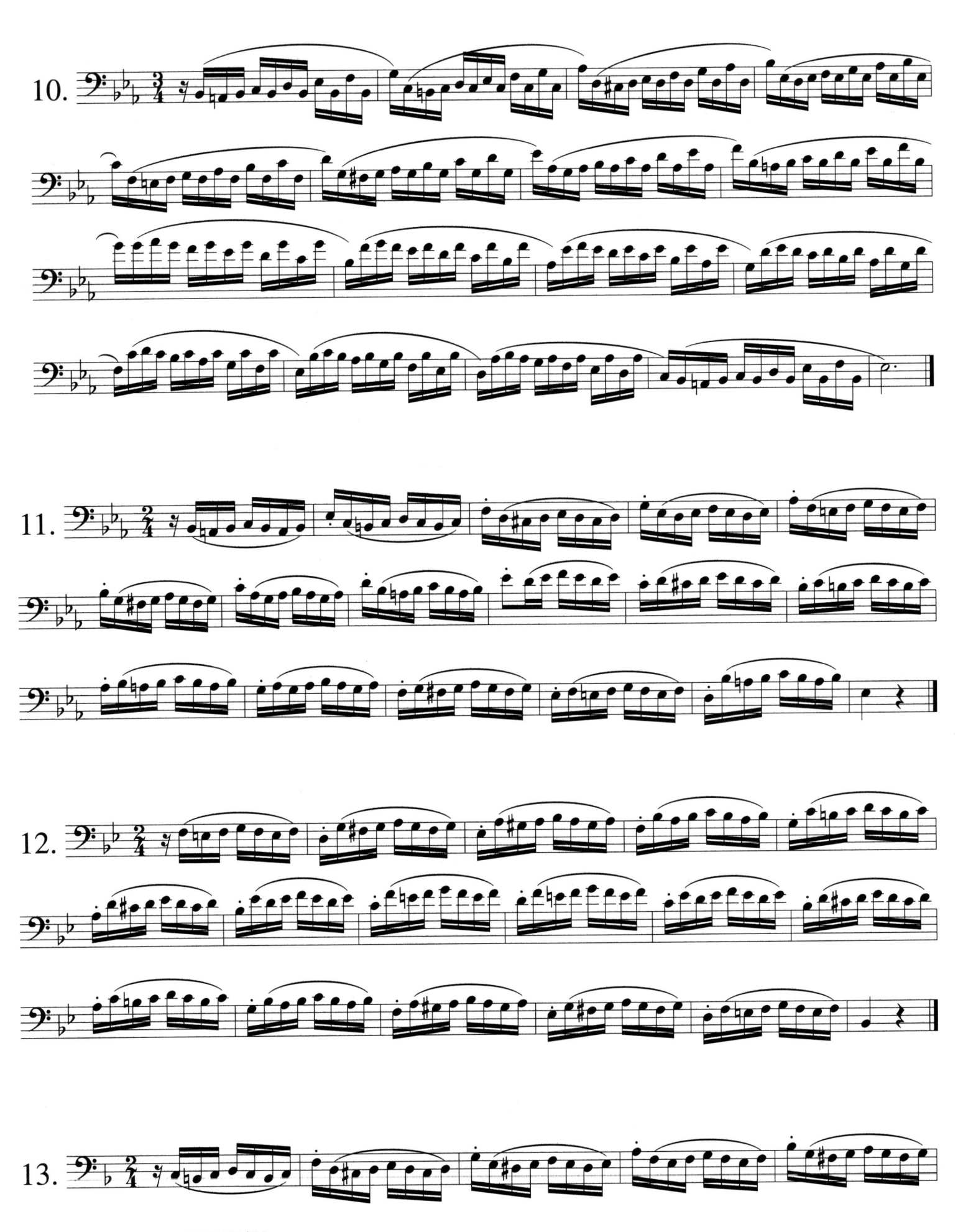

ORNAMENTATION Arban

108 • Arban ORNAMENTATION

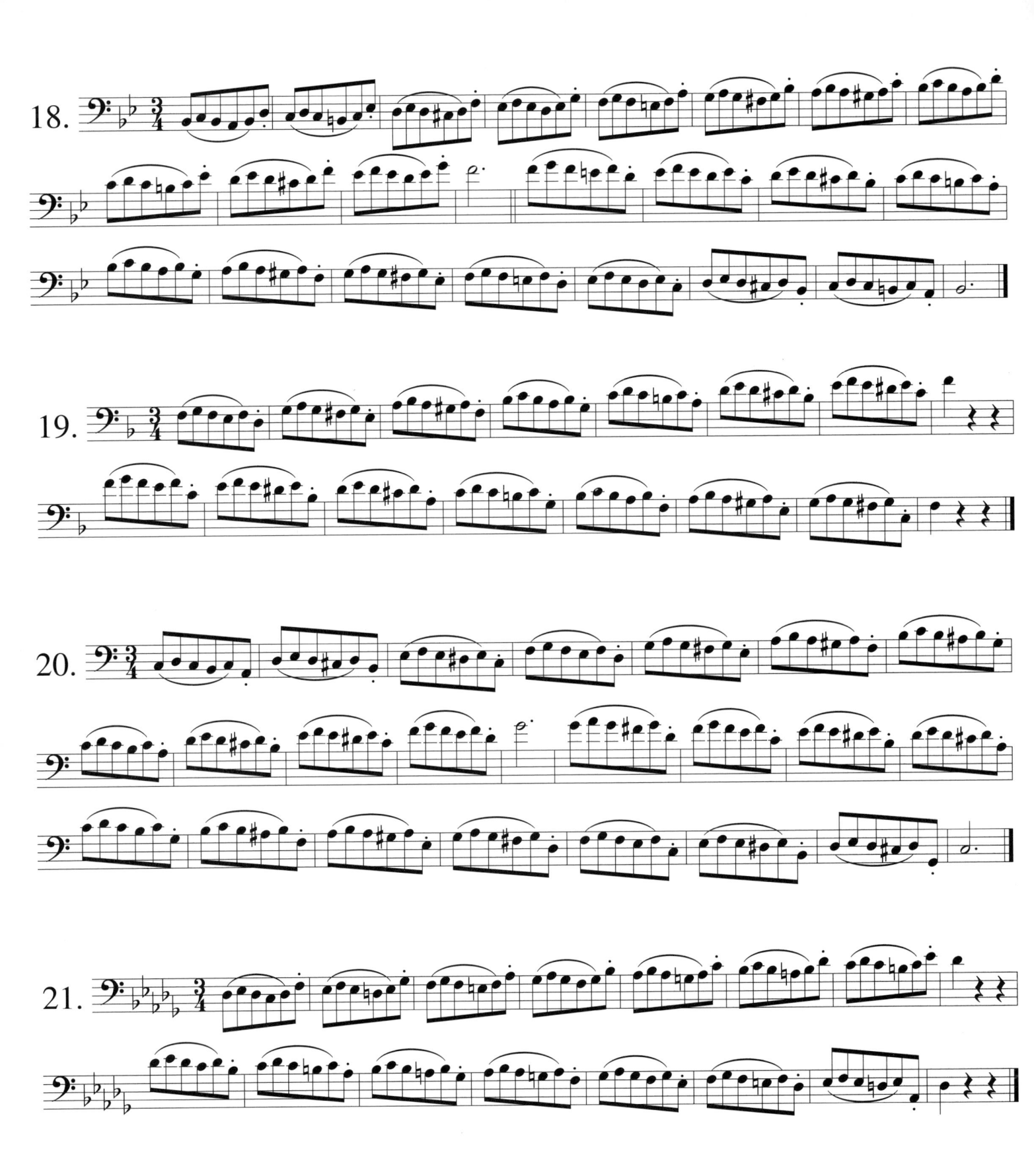

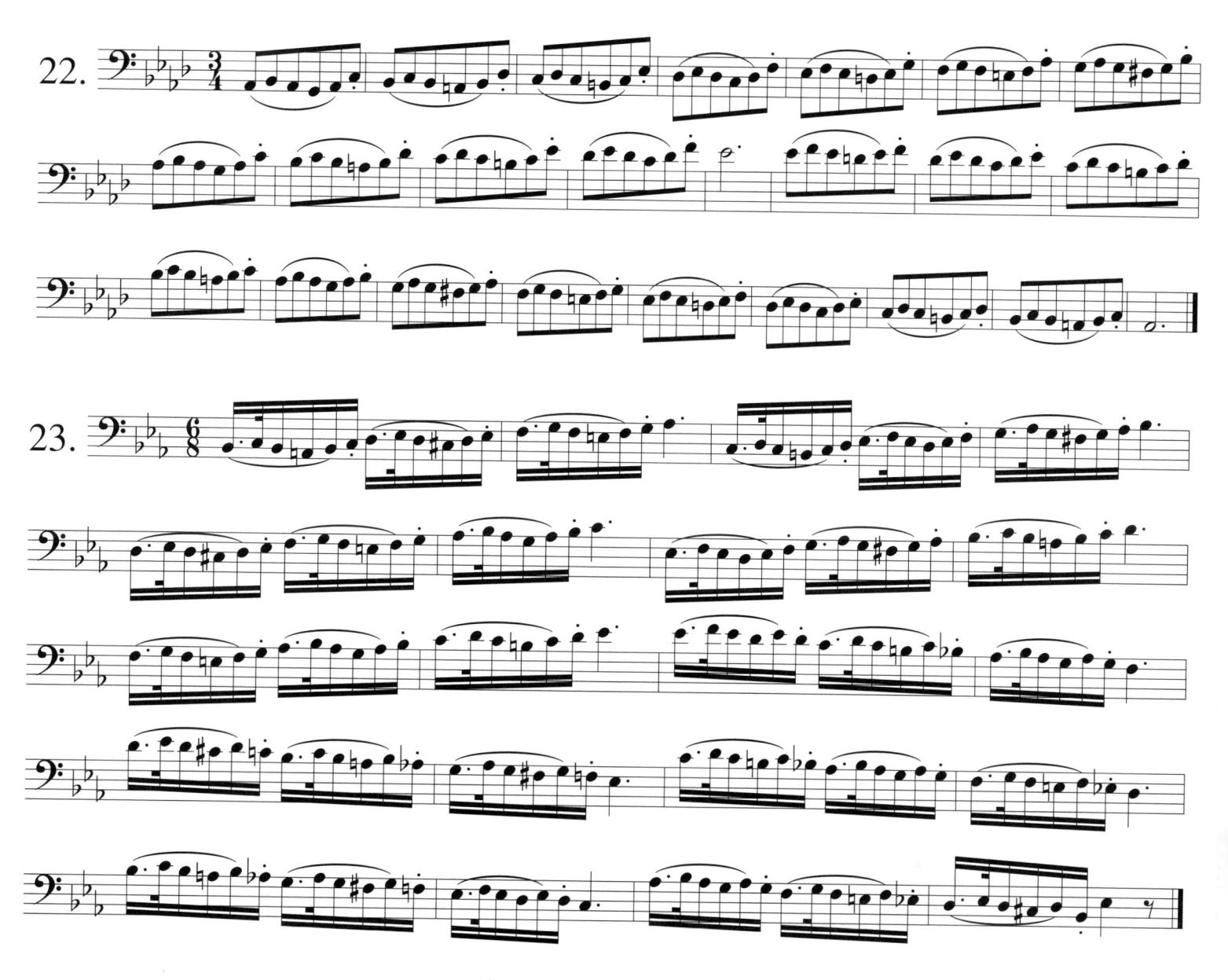

## GRUPPETTO—DR. BOWMAN

More commonly called a *turn*, the gruppetto has two basic interpretations: ascending and descending. The most common is the ascending form playing the four notes involved as: the note itself, the note above the note itself, the note below, and the note itself. This is notated by the symbol ∽.

The gruppetto may be inverted to the descending form of the note itself, the note below, the note itself, and the note above. This inverted form is usually notated rather than indicated by a symbol. In either case the choice of notes to be played should be in the key signature of the piece unless chromatically altered by a sharp or flat placed above or below the sign (or notated in the case of the inverted gruppetto), indicating that the corresponding upper or lower note should be altered appropriately. Often editors or publishers do not carefully follow this notation practice. As with all ornamentation, the rhythm of these four notes should be compatible with the main melodic content of the piece and be in good musical taste.

110 • Arban ORNAMENTATION

ORNAMENTATION Arban • 111

112 • Arban ORNAMENTATION

ORNAMENTATION Arban • 113

### Three Note Gruppetto or Anticipation—Dr. Bowman

The two types of three note gruppetti, or anticipations, are ascending and descending. Either one can be a minor or diminished third but not a major third. Rhythmically, this figure should be treated as a grace note coming before the beat.

114 • Arban ORNAMENTATION

ORNAMENTATION Arban • 115

## DOUBLE APPOGGIATURA—DR. BOWMAN

Actually this figure is a grace note figure of two notes before the main note of the melody. There are two types. The first type can be two notes played diatonically either below or above the main note. The second type has one note below and one note above the main note as demonstrated.

ORNAMENTATION Arban

118 • Arban ORNAMENTATION

**43.**

## Simple Appoggiatura—Dr. Bowman

Played as half of the value of the note it precedes, often this type of appoggiatura is notated by a small note with no slash on the stem. It is often used in baroque literature but, as with other ornamentation, some editors and publishers have added their own style of notating these figures.

**44.** Andante con spirito

*p*

*cresc. poco a poco*  *f*

*p < sf   sf   f*

*p*

rall.

ORNAMENTATION Arban • 119

Allegro moderato
45.
rall.

Andante con espressione
46.

Allegro con spirito
47.

### SHORT APPOGGIATURA-GRACE NOTE—DR. BOWMAN

The notated grace note (with a slash through the note stem) should usually be played before the regular sized note that follows. It should be played softly and quickly. Avoid playing the grace note with an accent and making it sound more prominent than the note to which it is leading.

ORNAMENTATION Arban • 121

122 • Arban ORNAMENTATION

## Portamento—Dr. Bowman

In actual musical practice the portamento is a very smooth rapid glissando type feeling between two notes. This is done very easily by vocalists and by musicians performing on stringed instruments. Although euphoniumists cannot play the portamento in this exact manner, it can be duplicated by the flexibility of the embouchure. The same concept can be practiced by playing the exercise on the mouthpiece alone, sliding or glissing between the two tones. Then work for the same smooth legato sound while playing on the instrument.

124 • Arban ORNAMENTATION

## Trills—Dr. Bowman

Basic trilling technique involves accurate rhythmic control of the fingers and, at times, the use of alternate fingerings. Trills should never sound frantic nor become so rapid that the pitches are not distinguishable. Learn to use alternate fingerings that work well. The smoothest trills are those that stay in the same harmonic series, and alternate fingerings make that possible in most cases.

126 • Arban ORNAMENTATION

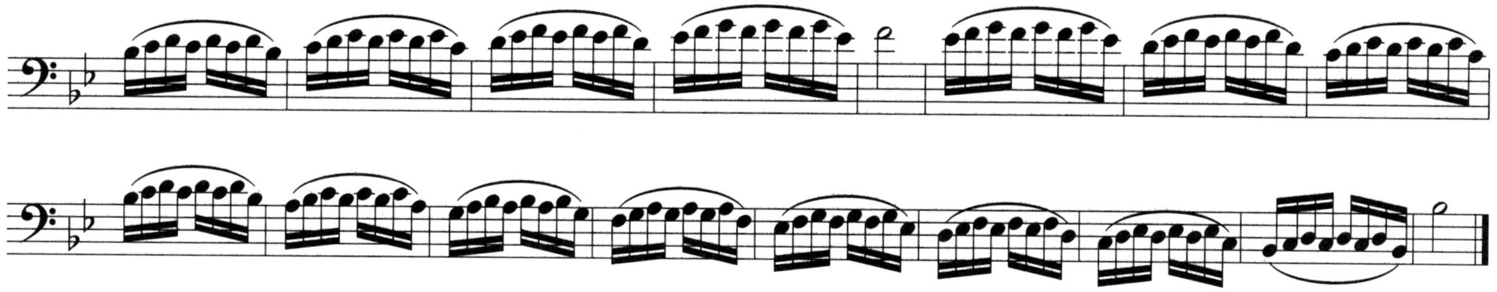

65.

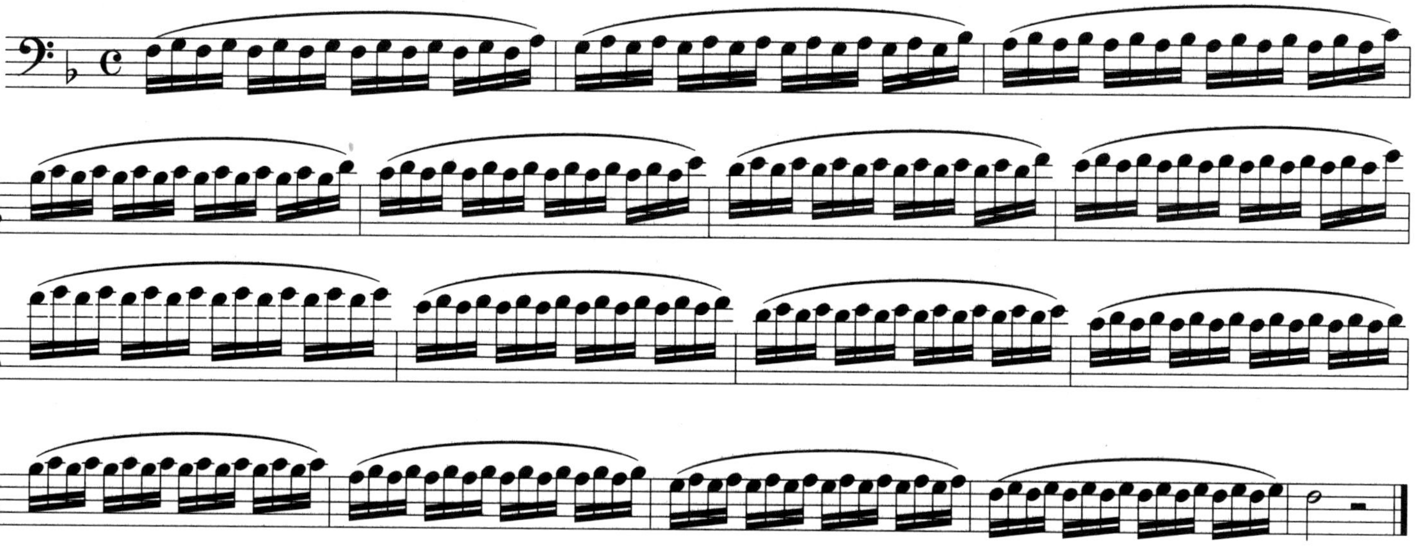

66.

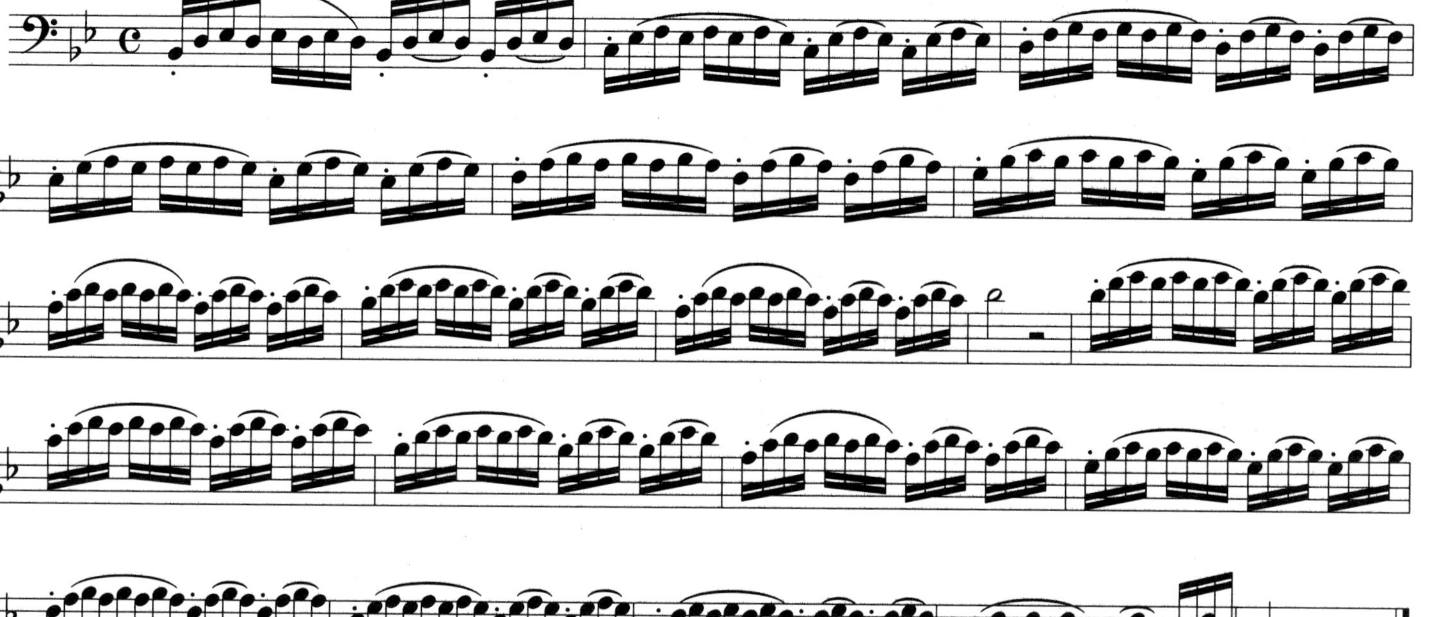

128 • Arban ORNAMENTATION

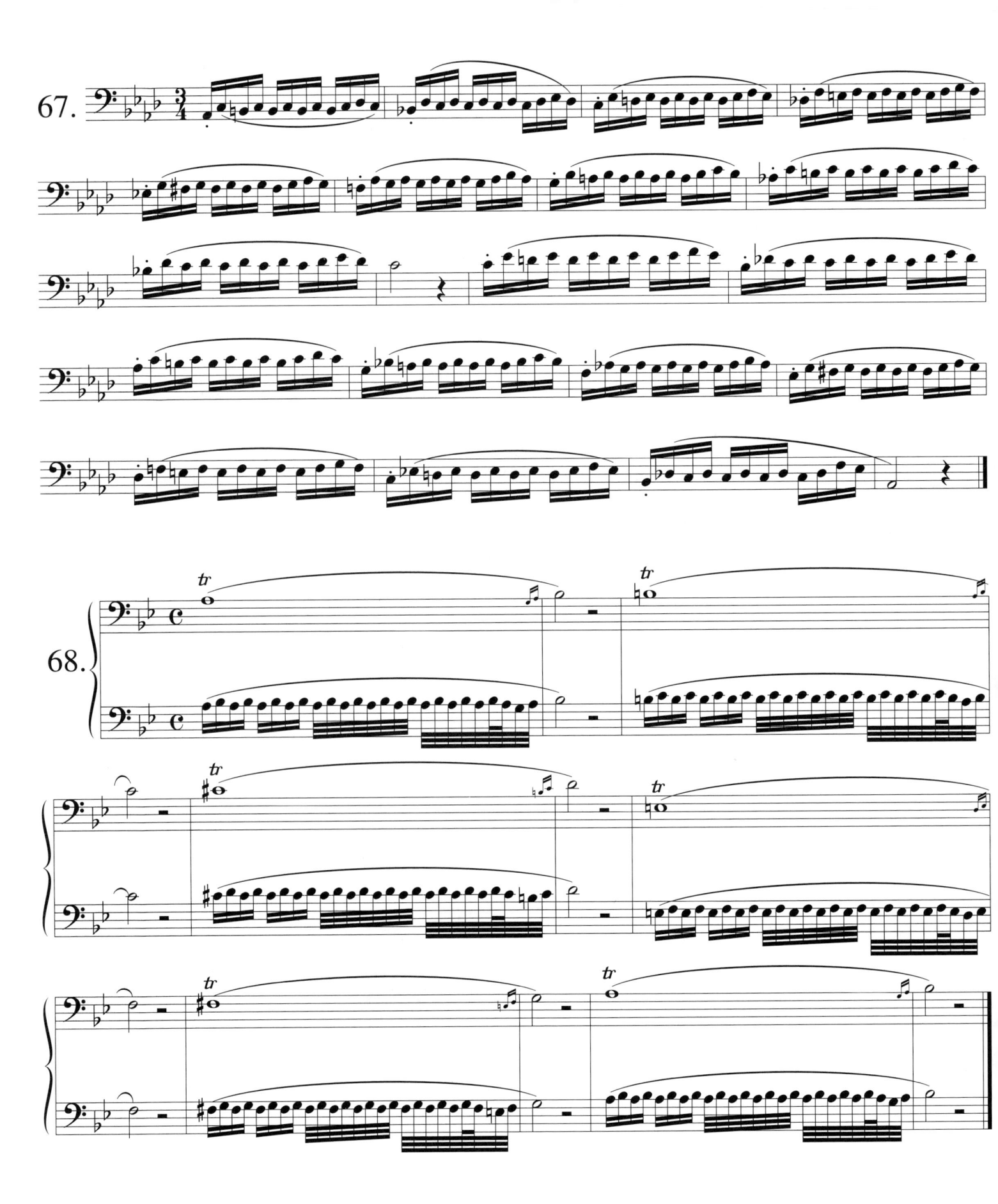

ORNAMENTATION Arban • 129

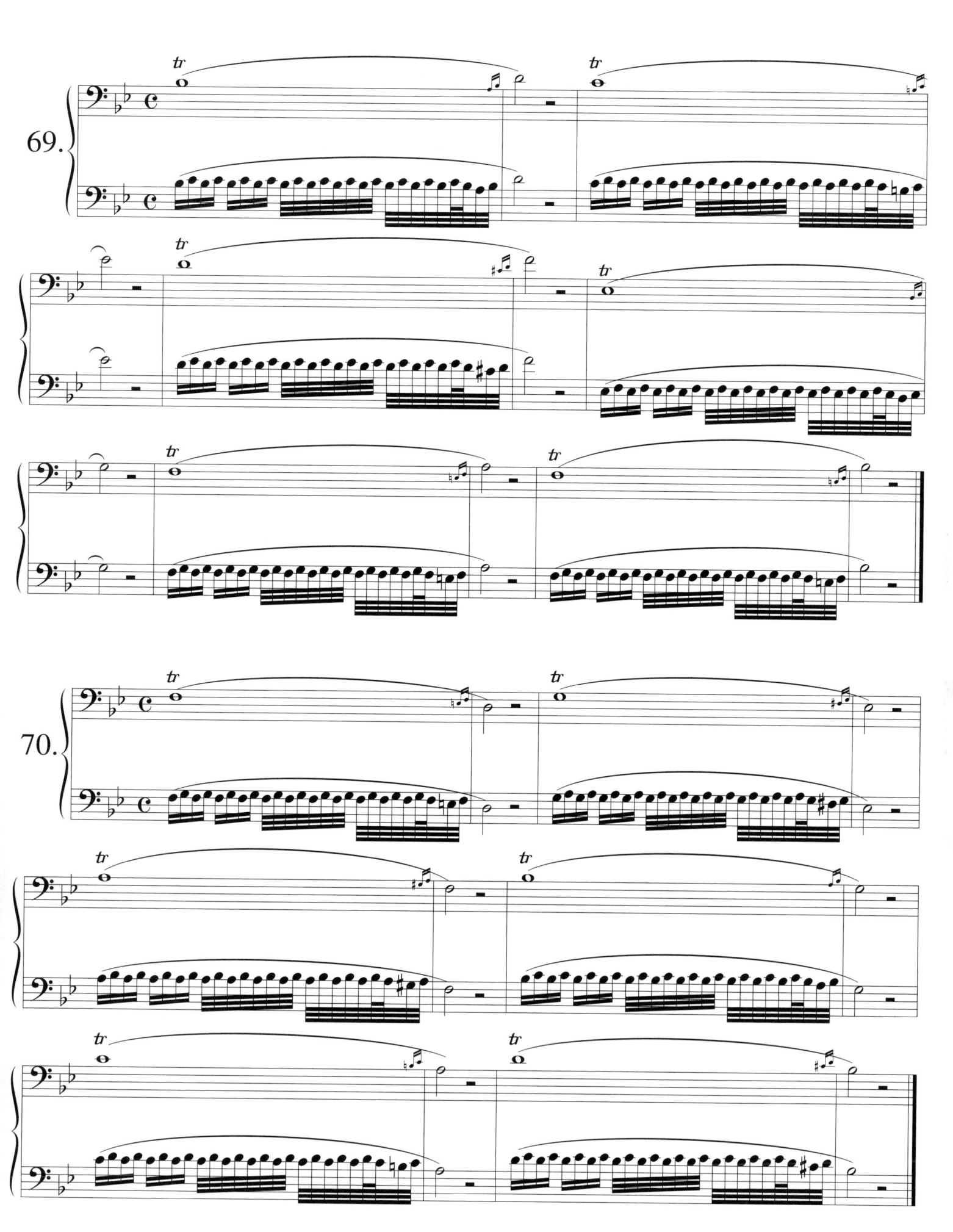

130 • Arban ORNAMENTATION

ORNAMENTATION Arban

132 • Arban ORNAMENTATION

ORNAMENTATION Arban • 133

## Mordant—Dr. Bowman

The mordant is a fast trill placed directly on the beat. It may be several repetitions or just one depending upon the speed of the figure. Avoid making too many repetitions that are unclear or too fast.

134 • Arban ORNAMENTATION

ORNAMENTATION Arban • 135

136 • Arban ORNAMENTATION

ORNAMENTATION Arban • 137

# INTERVALS

### GENERAL COMMENTS—DR. BOWMAN

One of the most demanding and taxing sections of this volume, the *Interval Studies* are also among the most valuable for the development of embouchure flexibility and control. Work for accuracy and tone quality before increasing speed in each exercise. Every exercise should be played with different articulations including slurring two notes and all-slurred. After all the lines in a specific exercise are mastered, a good way to review is to play all the sharp keys one day and all the flat keys the next.

### EXERCISES 1-7—MR. ALESSI

Since I began playing a brass instrument, the following exercises on intervals have been among my favorite studies. They are very good for development of consistent tone production in all registers, for flexibility, and for embouchure development. Keep in mind:

- Strive for the same tone throughout.

- Concentrate on the scale notes, making them even-sounding and in a consistent style.

- Do one set of exercises a day in a continuous manner.

- Anchor your mouthpiece in one position. (For myself, this anchor point is the bottom of the lower lip.)

- Don't let the mouthpiece travel up and down on the lips as you switch registers. To prevent this, make use of the lower jaw by thrusting it out and down in a 45° angle when traveling down in pitch while maintaining the anchor point.

- Don't *splat* the lower note. Play with a *tenuto* style.

- suggested tempo: ♩ = mm75

INTERVALS Arban

140 • Arban INTERVALS

3.

4.

INTERVALS Arban • 143

5.

INTERVALS Arban • 145

146 • Arban INTERVALS

### OCTAVES AND TENTHS—DR. BOWMAN

Listen carefully to the intonation in these studies. Practice the octaves two ways:

- Use the specific fingerings for each note.

- Play the octaves using the same fingering for the top note as the bottom note.

This is excellent practice for lip flexibility.

### OCTAVES AND TENTHS—MR. ALESSI

- Blow through the bottom note.

- Start the bottom note with a great sound, like a pyramid with a huge base.

- When descending, thrust the lower jaw forward and slightly downward and never use the tongue for this type of slur.

- Think of the diaphragm as an elevator. When ascending, raise it and when descending, let it drop or relax.

- Make use of vowels; *ee* for the upper notes and *ah* or *oh* for the lower.

10.

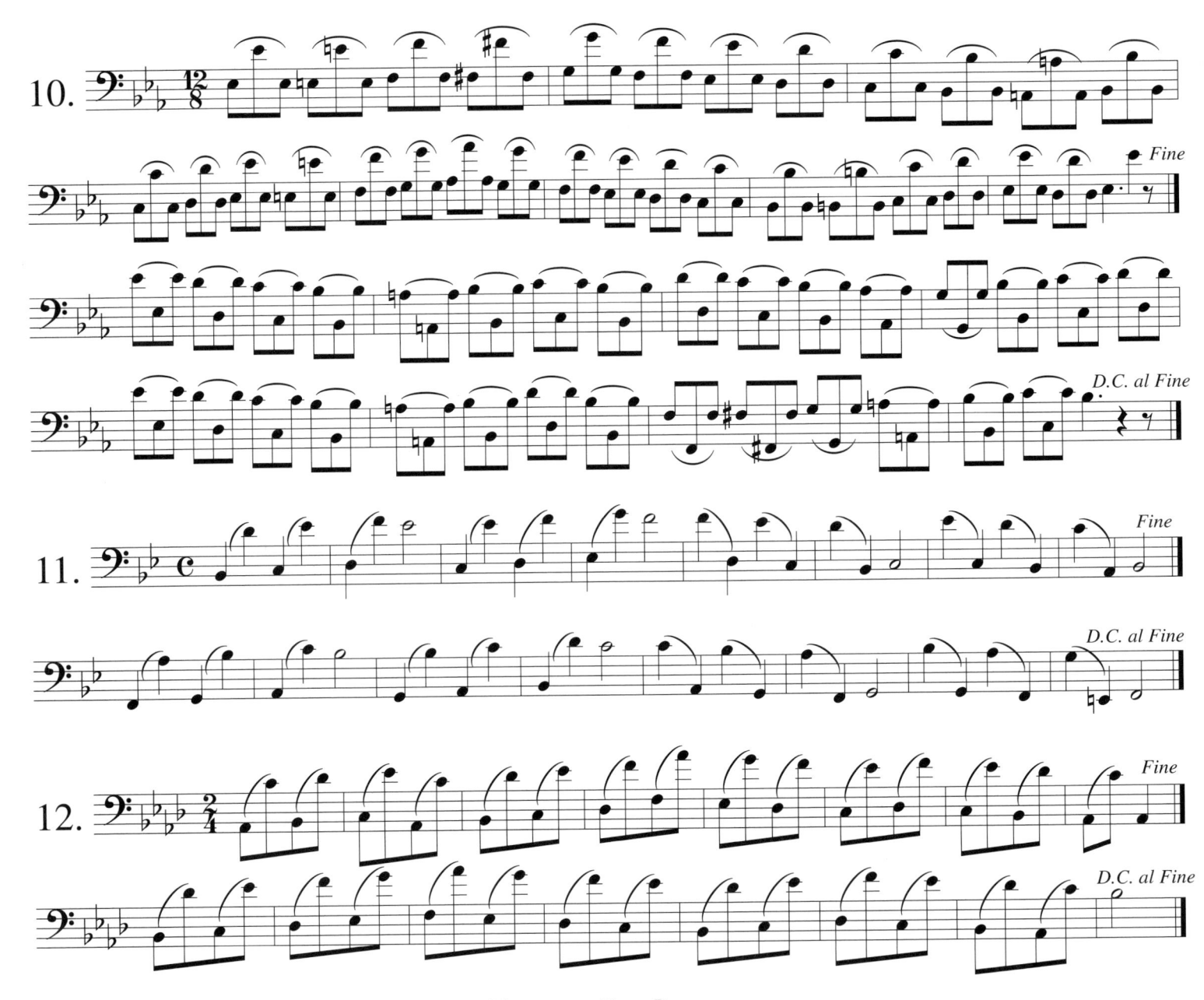

11.

12.

### TRIPLETS—DR. BOWMAN

In these exercises, the fingers must be completely under control rhythmically. Practice slowly at first but increase speed as much as possible without losing rhythmic integrity.

### TRIPLETS—MR. ALESSI

- Combine natural slurring with light legato tonguing for agility.
- Play full quarters.
- Use a metronome.
- Slightly pulsate downbeats if needed.
- Keep the air moving.

13.

148 • Arban TRIPLETS

*TRIPLETS* Arban • 149

150 • Arban TRIPLETS

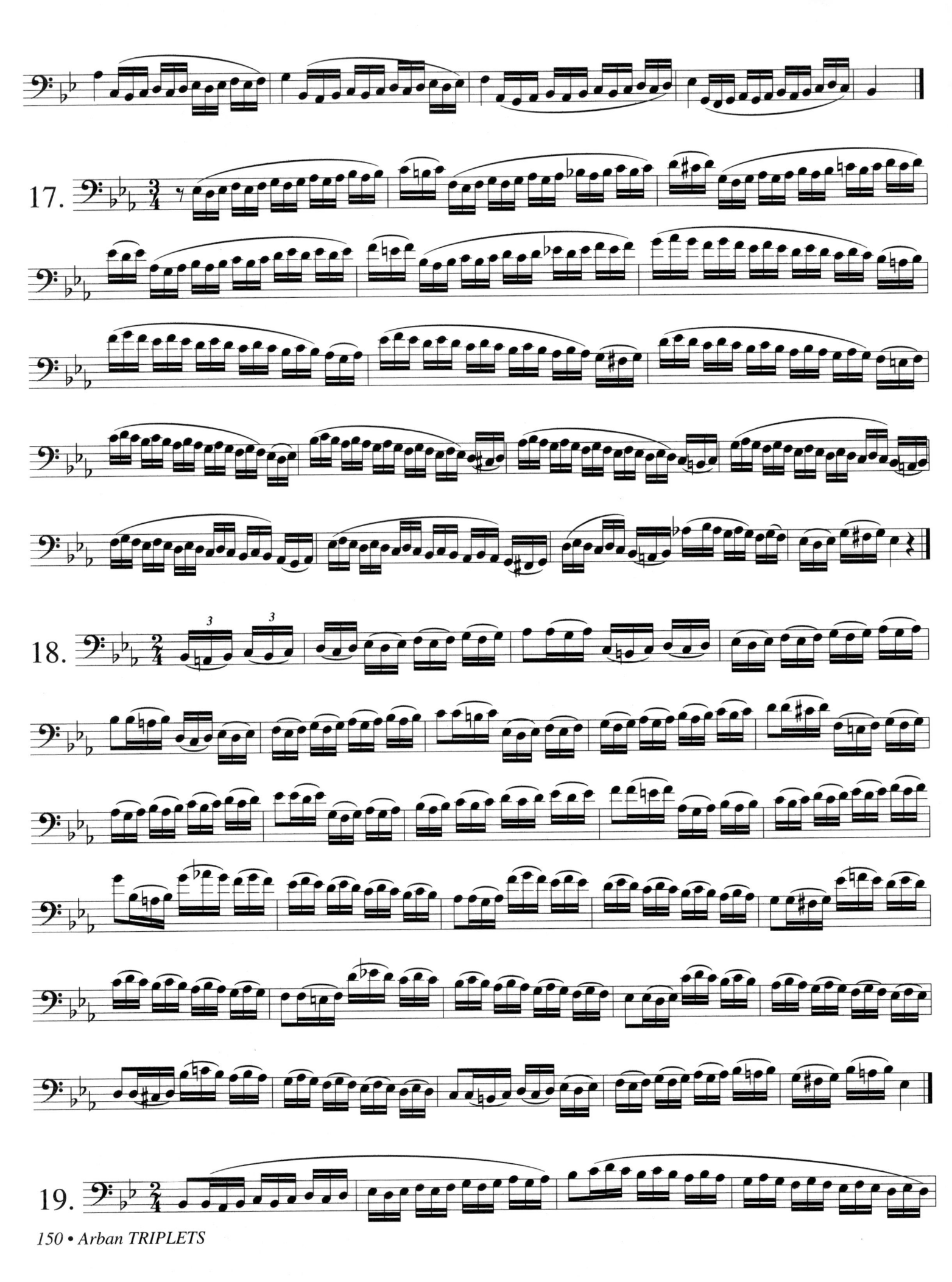

TRIPLETS Arban • 151

152 • Arban TRIPLETS

TRIPLETS Arban • 153

## 27.

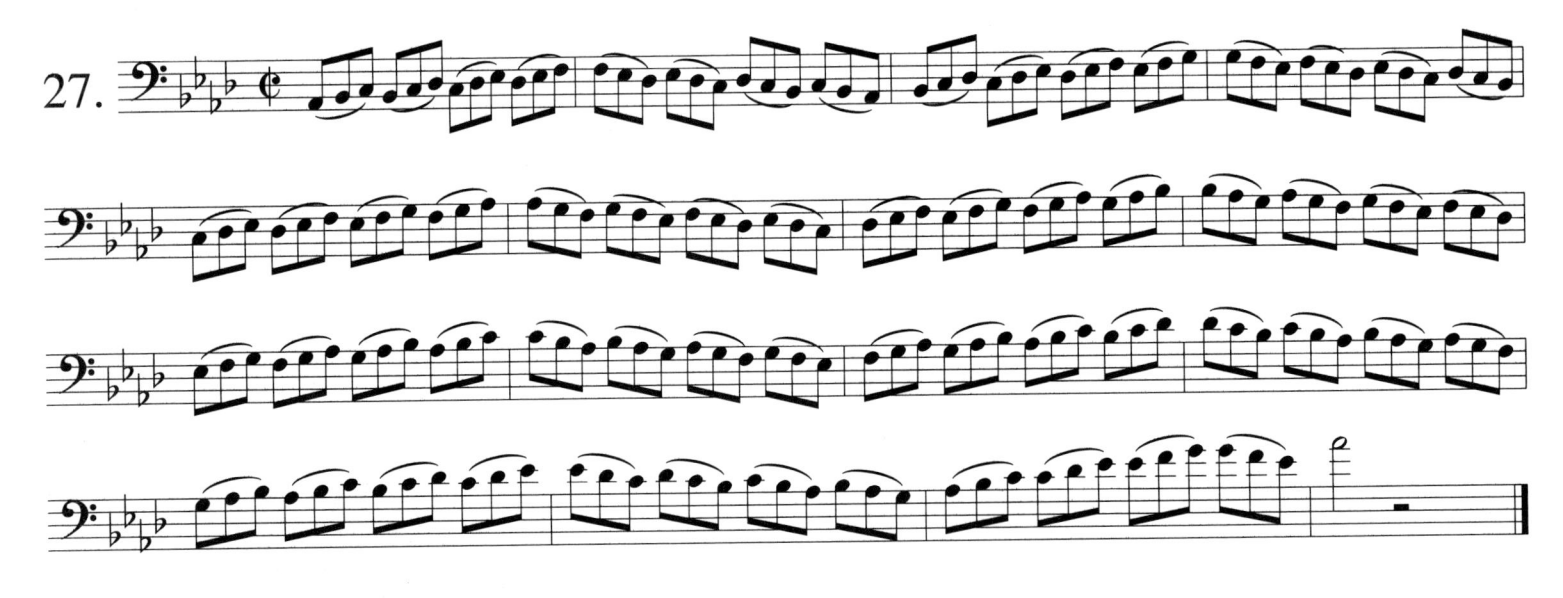

### Studies in Sixteenth Notes—Dr. Bowman

I have used these exercises (#28-47) to improve the technical ability of my students. Play these exercises as rapidly as possible—even though not perfectly in rhythm at first. Then slow them down and perfect the rhythm with precision to a lightening speed.

### Studies in Sixteenth Notes—Mr. Alessi

- Always think in eighth notes.
- Concentrate on blowing through notes.
- When making a natural slur, think *tah-hah*.
- Think lyrically by giving contour to each exercise using crescendi when ascending and decrescendi when descending.
- Play each exercise with no flaws. If you make a mistake, go back to the beginning and repeat the exercise slowly.

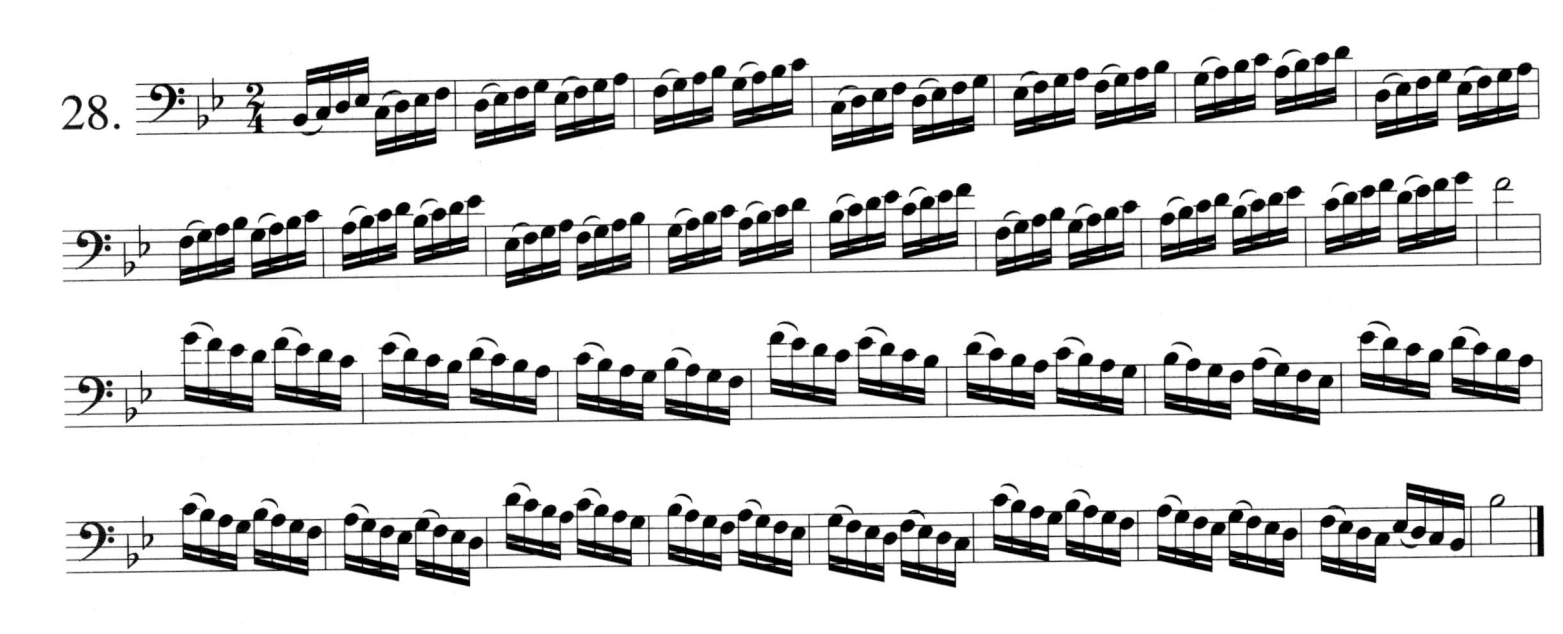

## 28.

29.

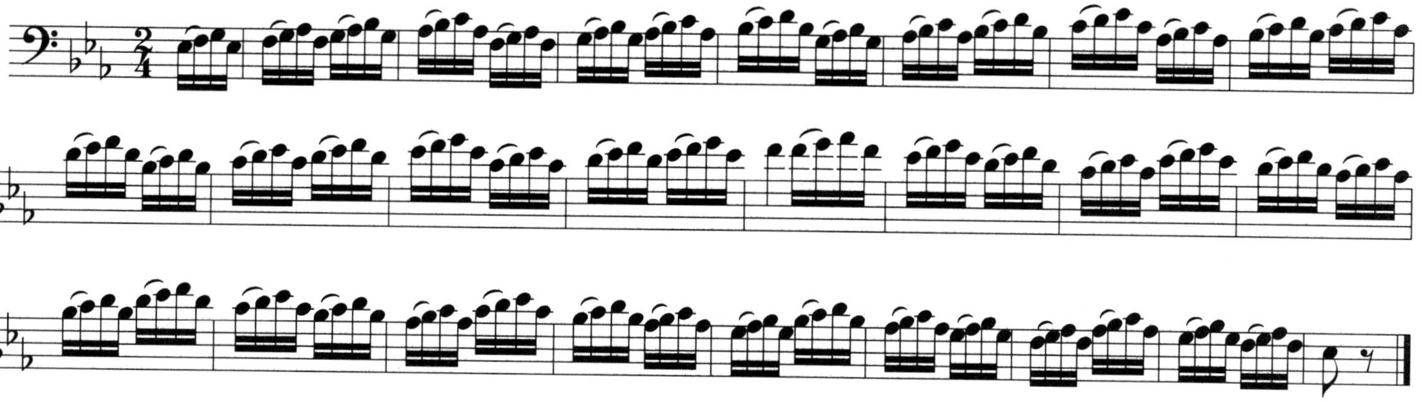

30.

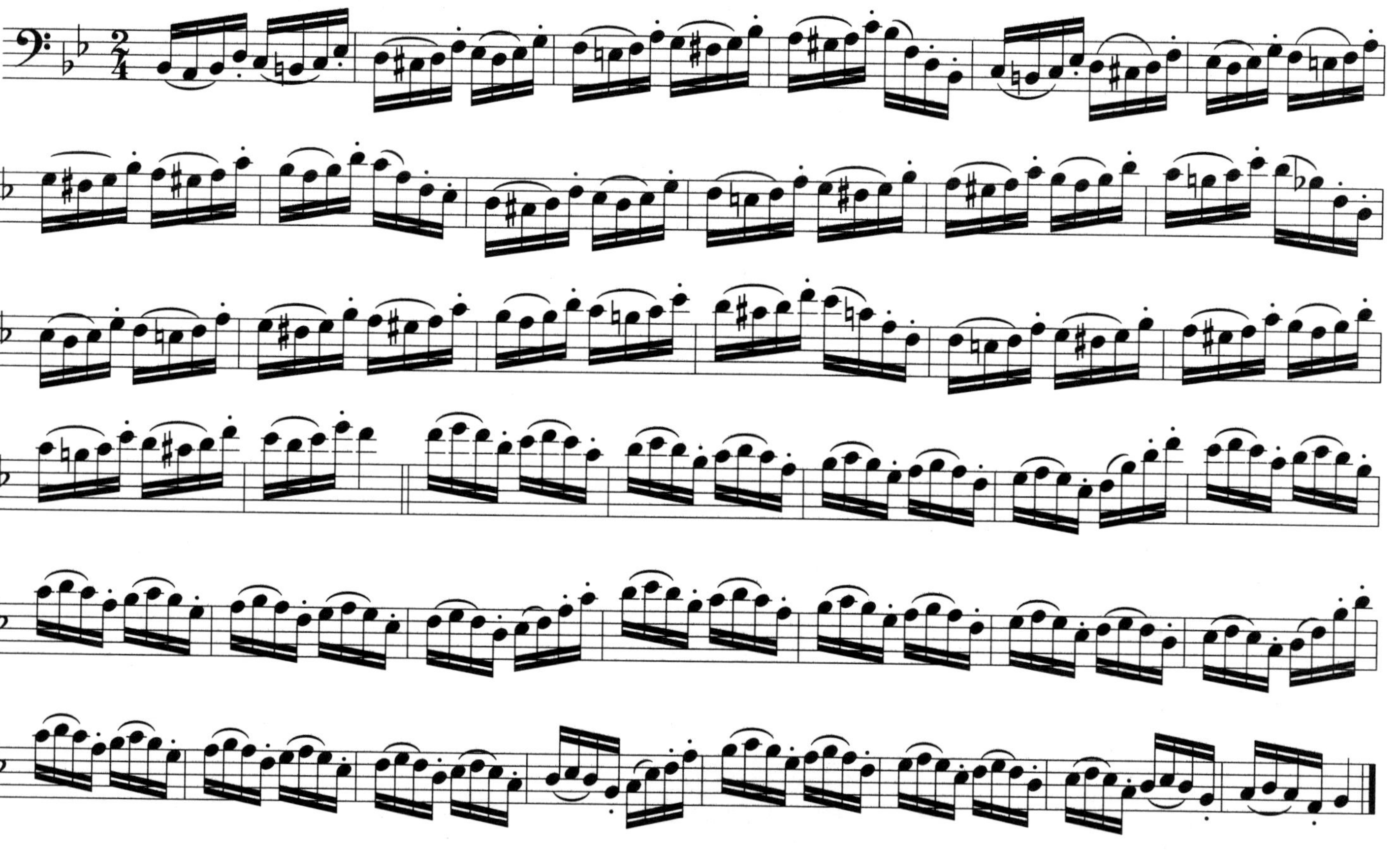

31.

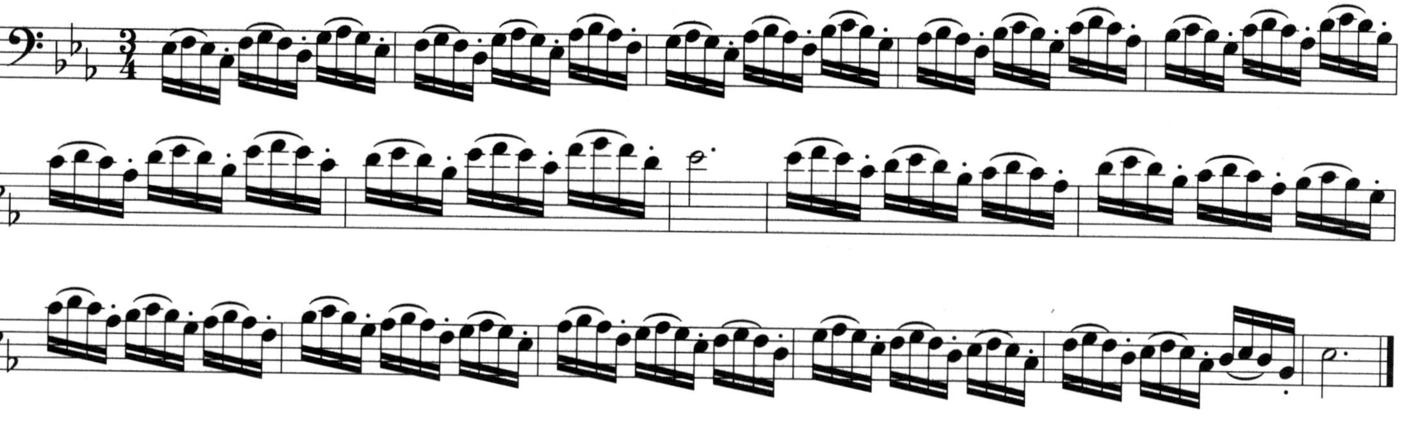

156 • Arban SIXTEENTH NOTES

SIXTEENTH NOTES Arban

158 • Arban SIXTEENTH NOTES

SIXTEENTH NOTES Arban • 159

## THE PERFECT MAJOR AND MINOR CHORDS

### CHORDAL PATTERNS—DR. BOWMAN

The study of chords in all the keys will help develop fingering patterns and listening skills that will be useful not only in reading music but in improvisational playing. Keep track of the tonality both mentally and aurally.

### CHORDAL PATTERNS—MR. ALESSI

This section is one of my favorites. Use these patterns to help develop your knowledge of music theory by memorizing all of these exercises. Notice that most of these patterns proceed through the circle of fourths. Learning these patterns thoroughly at a young age will help you when it becomes time to study music theory in college. Make the same sound and tone for every note throughout each exercise! Trombonists can omit number 52, if desired, as it is designed mainly for the euphonium player.

48.

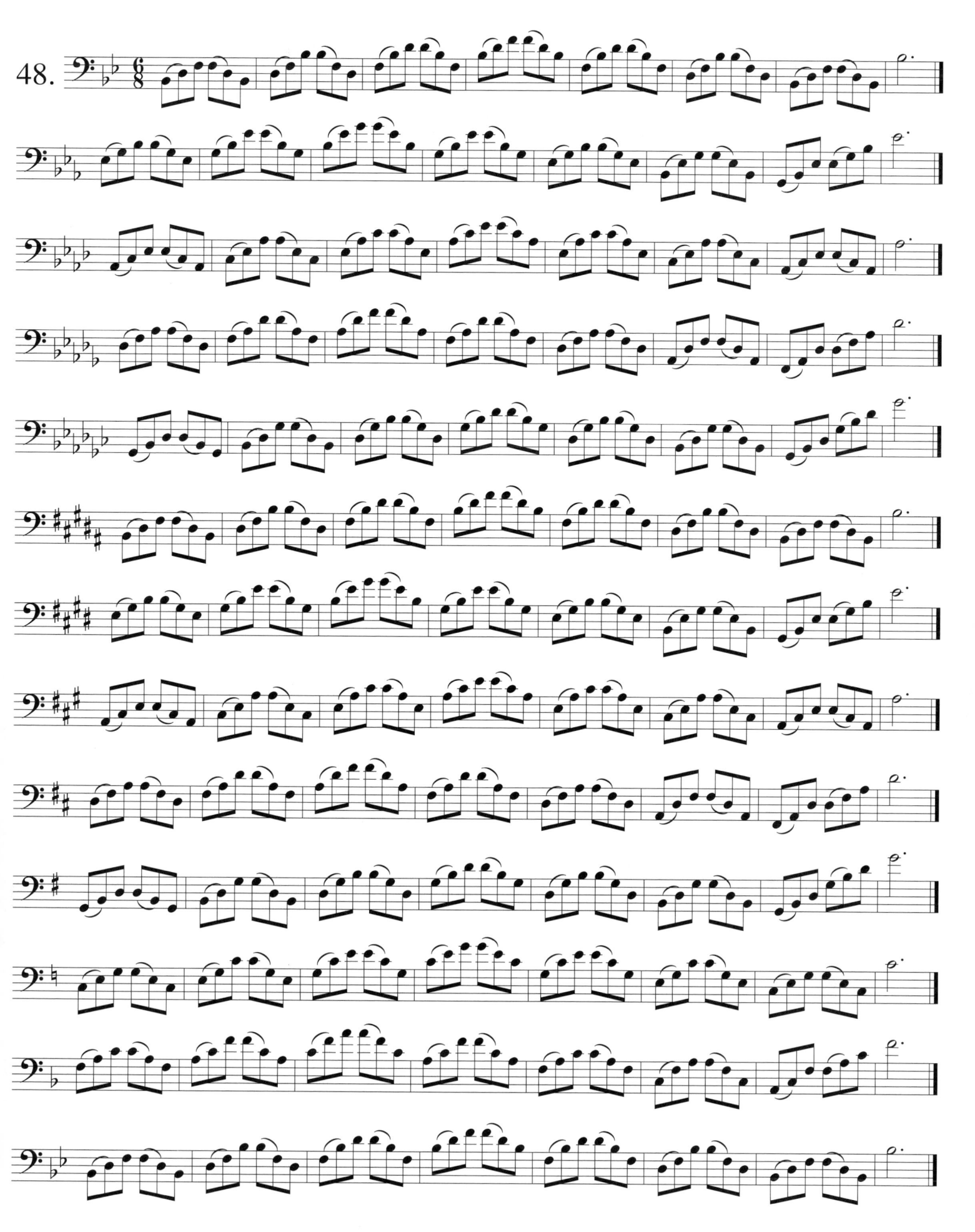

**49.**

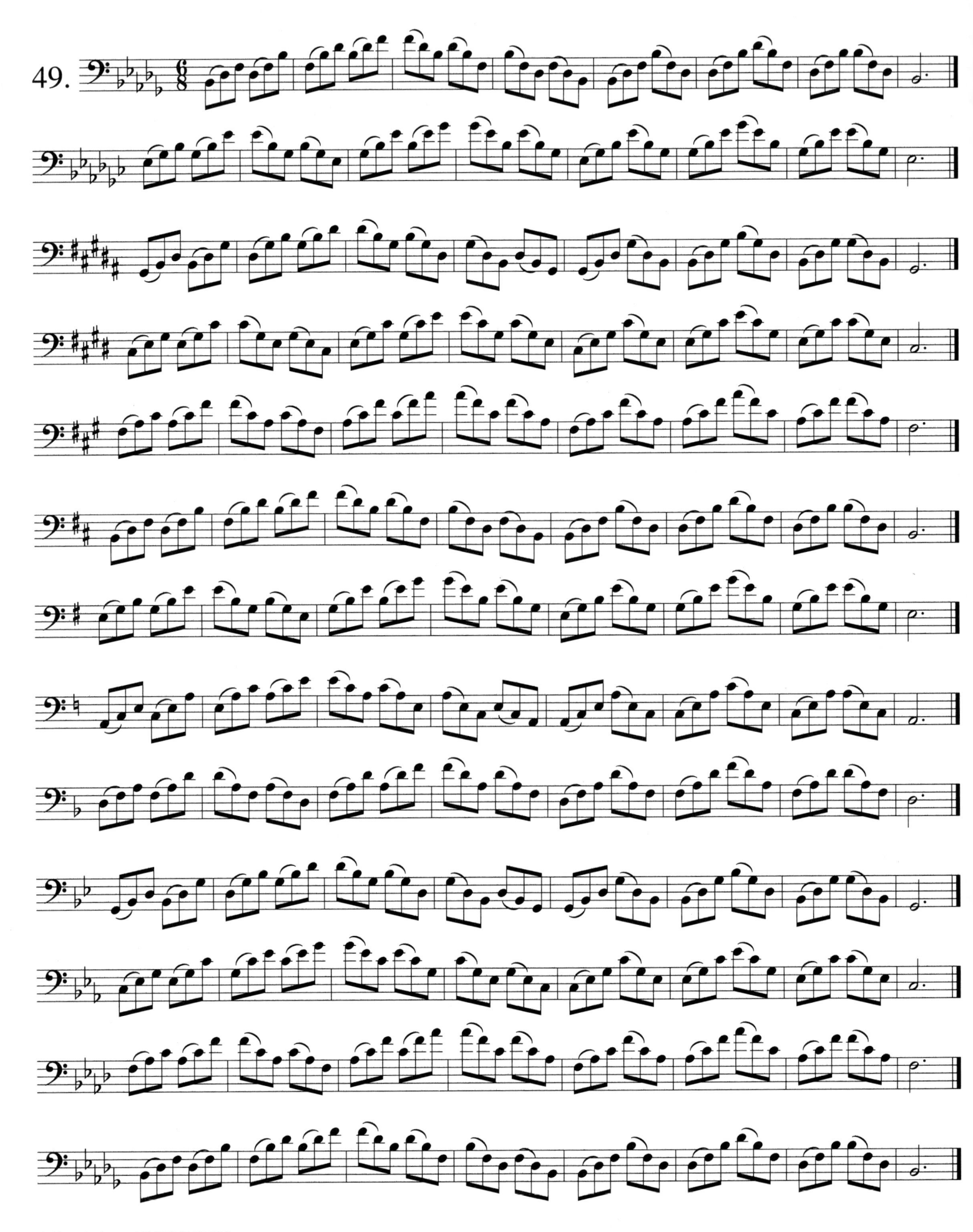

50.

51.

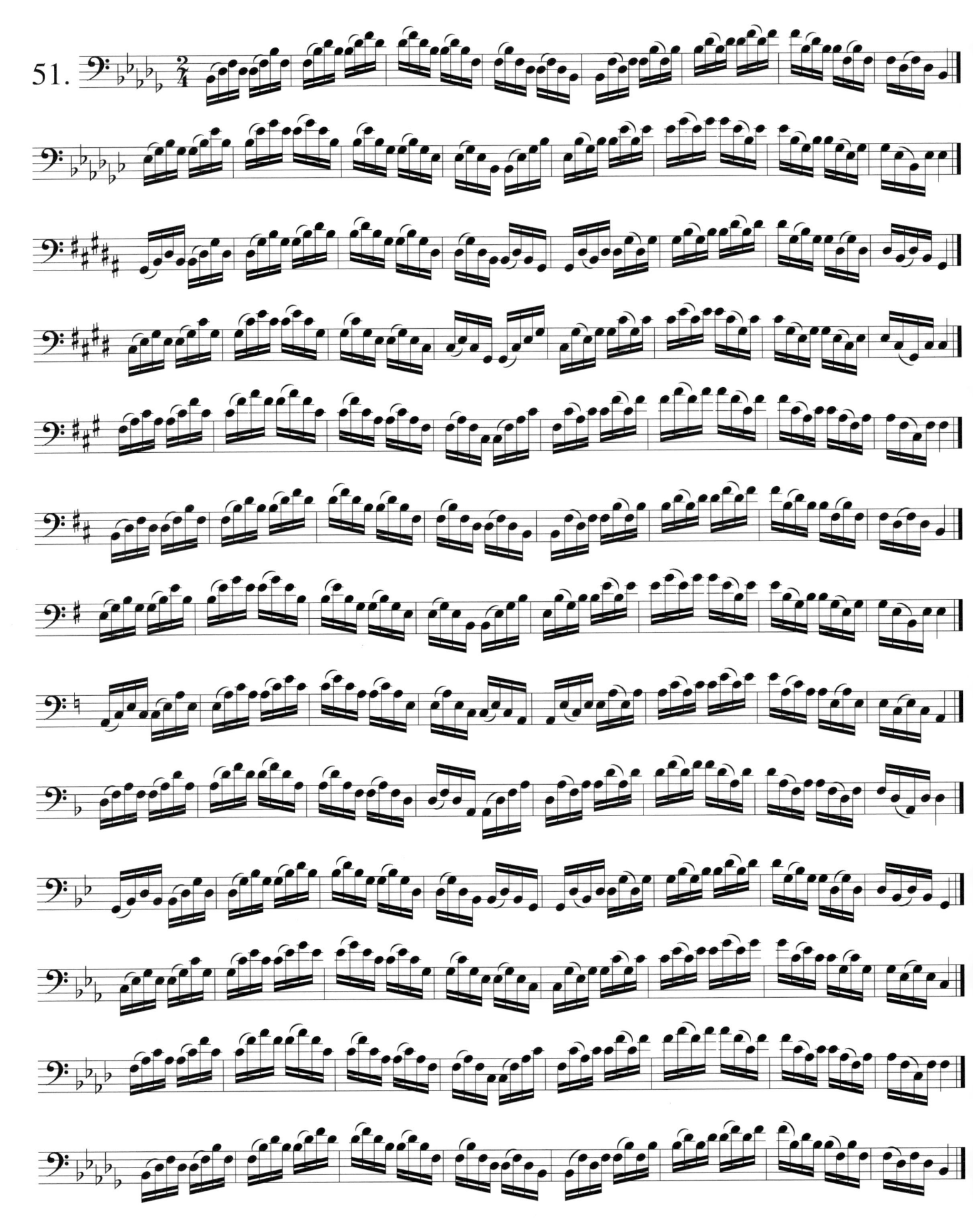

164 • Arban ARPEGGIOS

**52.**

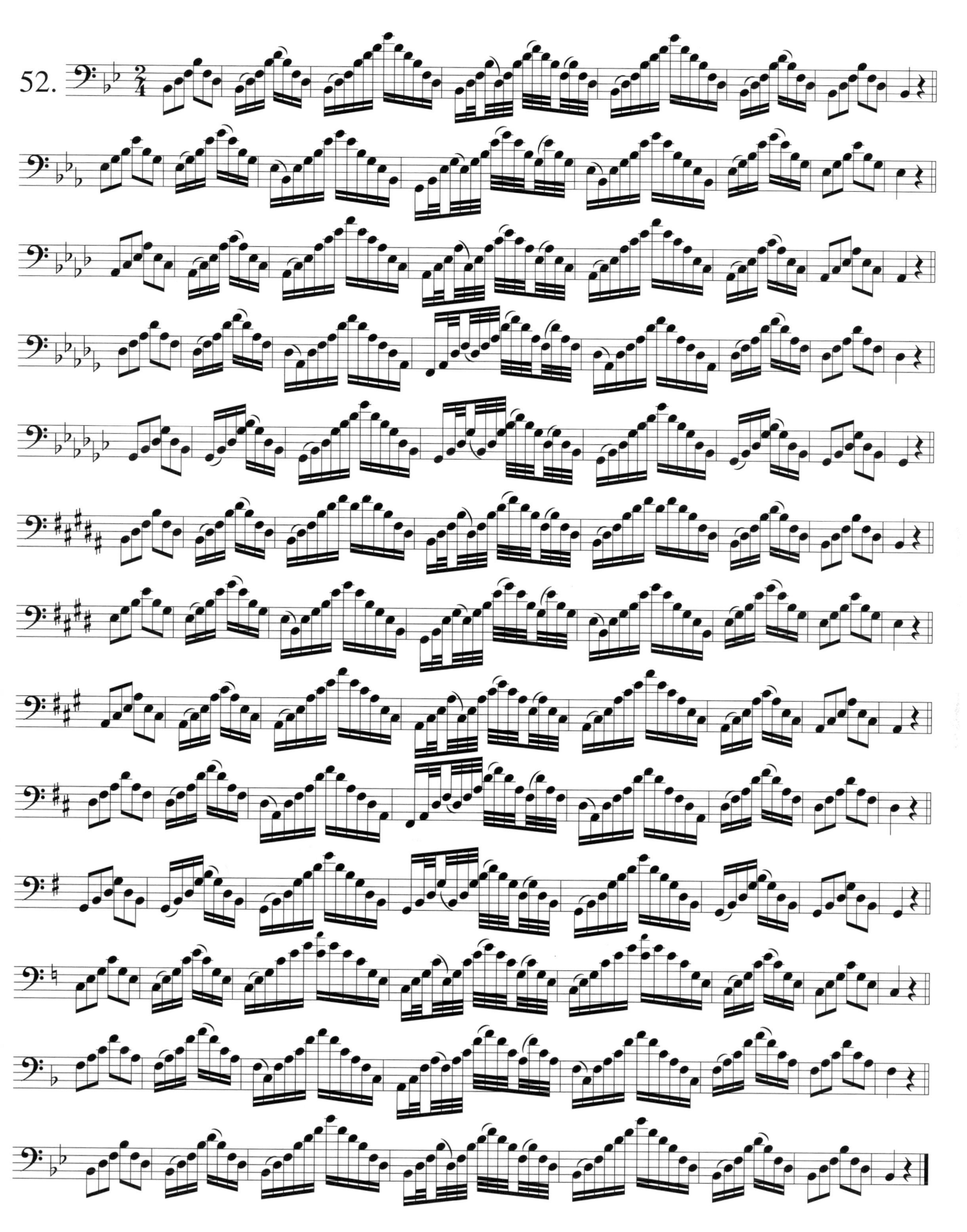

**53.**

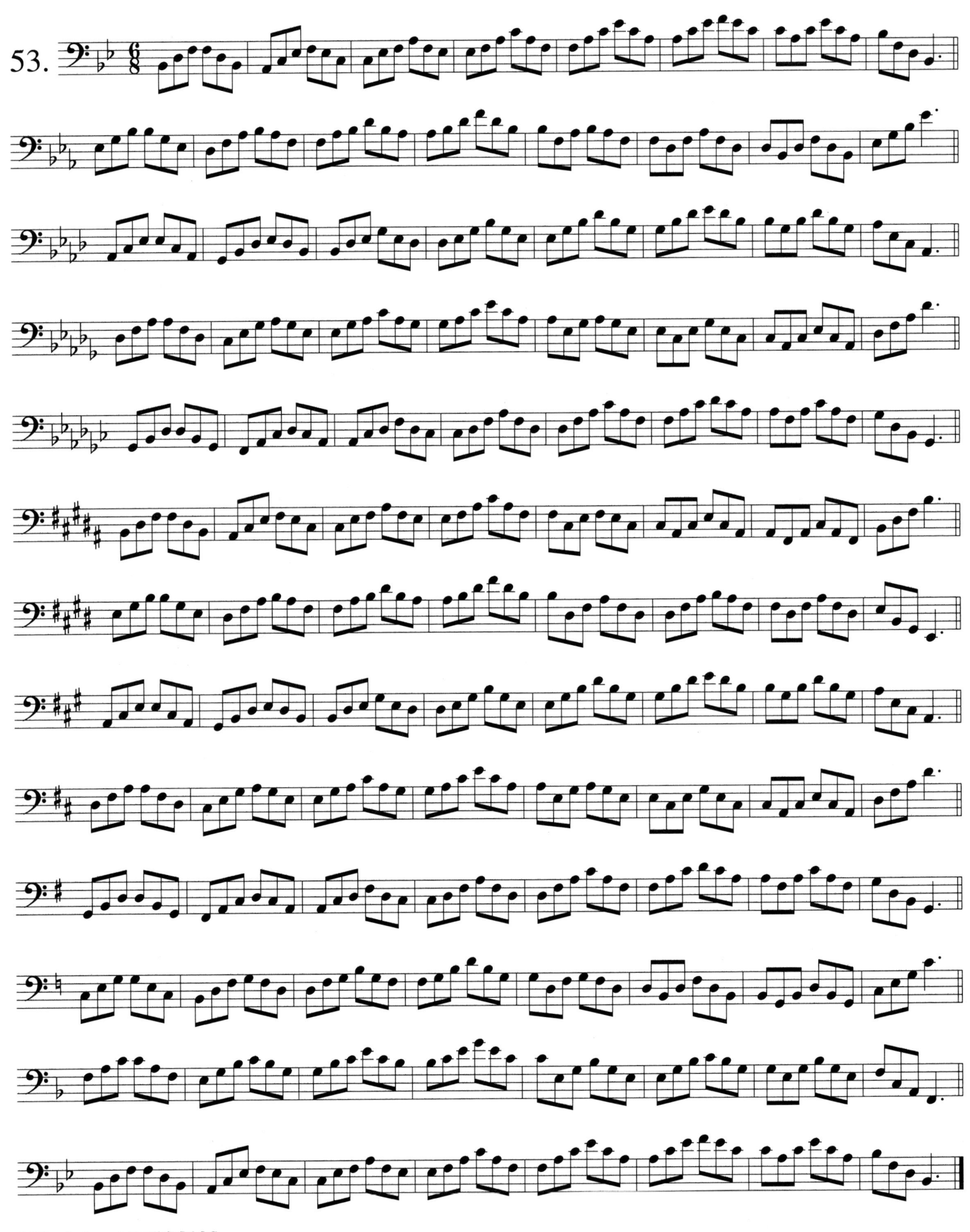

166 • Arban ARPEGGIOS

## Dominant Seventh Chords

**54.**

## Diminished Seventh Chords

**55.**

*ARPEGGIOS Arban • 169*

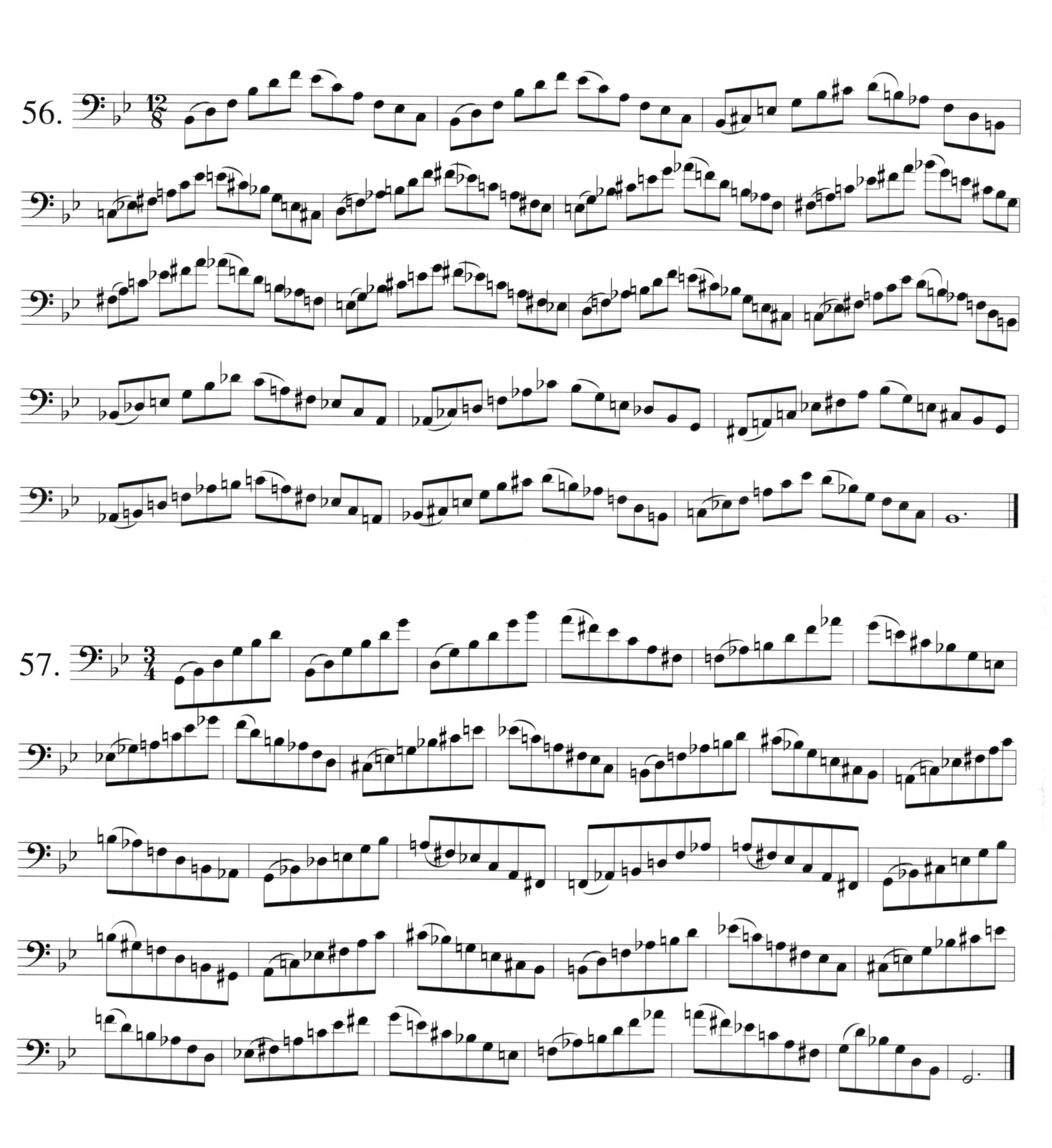

170 • Arban CADENZAS

### Cadenzas—Dr. Bowman

These cadenzas in 19th century style are useful for acquainting the student with the period music of the early virtuoso brass soloist. Try combining different examples together and also transposing them into different keys.

### Cadenzas—Mr. Alessi

While these cadenzas were designed originally for the euphonium player, there are benefits to trombonists who practice these awkward studies—awkward in the sense that they are written with many ornaments and rapid scales that would be much easier on a valved instrument. When performed in the preferred slower tempo, the phrases and scale runs become a bit long for the air supply—so plan your breaths carefully. In order to make these cadenzas sound appropriate for the trombone, do not rush the tempo. Strive for an *elegant* style by not letting the music sound frantic. While playing the fast scale passages think *poco a poco accelerando,* to aid in the development of an elegant style.

Practicing these difficult cadenzas will prepare you for the *turn of the century* repertoire that includes this style of cadenza.

**62.**

*CADENZAS Arban • 173*

# MULTIPLE TONGUING

### Multiple Tonguing—Dr. Bowman

A famous euphonium soloist once said that the secret to learning multiple tonguing was simple: "…just practice it two hours a day for two years!"

The key to this technique of articulation is the consistency of five aspects of performance:
- Articulation—Each tongued note should have the same sound and clarity.
- Weight—Each note should have the same weight, do not play some notes accented more than others.
- Length—Each note should be the same length, not some long, some short.
- Spacing—The space between the duration of each note should be identical.
- Volume—All notes should be the same volume.

### Triple Tonguing—Dr. Bowman

In current practice there are several ways of developing triple tonguing. Some use the *KAH* syllable in the middle—*TAH-KAH-TAH*—and others alternate syllables actually using a double tongue with changing accents—*TAH-KAH-TAH-KAH-TAH-KAH*. I prefer the traditional syllables of *TAH-TAH-KAH*.

Begin practice by learning to pronounce the *KAH* syllable. Practice pronouncing the syllables without the instrument working for a clear and clean *K* sound that is not aspirated. Practice at a forte or fortissimo dynamic to assure complete air support. Start with exercise #1 at a very slow tempo playing each note with a *KAH* articulation staccato. Work for a clean *K* sound that is very similar to the *T* sound in a *TAH* articulation.

Begin playing the exercises very slowly, staccato and forte, working for perfect equality of the points mentioned above. As the articulation becomes clean gradually increase the speed, keeping the notes equal in length and weight.

To further increase the challenge of these exercises, try eliminating the quarter notes and play articulated triplets on each beat beginning with exercise #3.

As speed increases many players switch to a different syllable and use *DAH-DAH-GAH*—which is much smoother at the faster tempi. It is important to maintain clarity as speed increases and not to play so rapidly that the articulation and rhythm are crushed together and become unclear.

When performing exercises that articulate changed notes, maintain the same clarity, precision and dynamic control as the repeated note articulations.

### Multiple Tonguing—Mr. Alessi

As a young lad, I was lucky enough to have a teacher who stressed the importance of multiple tonguing and who knew how to practice it. I also prefer the traditional method of multiple tonguing—*TAH-TAH-KAH* for triple and *TAH-KAH* for double. The most difficult aspect of multiple tonguing is to train the tongue to be comfortable with the *KAH* syllable. I recommend students practice speaking these patterns with repetition. Speaking these patterns for 5 minutes each day will accelerate progress in this area.

Practice very slowly using *TAH-TAH-KAH* for triple and *TAH-KAH* for double tongue, always accenting the *KAH* syllable. The amount of accent should equal the dynamic of fortissimo. Be certain not to speed up in the slightest and to continue this tonguing pattern to the very end of the exercise. Practice in this manner will strengthen the weak *KAH* syllable to match the already-trained and stronger *TAH* syllable. In time these syllables will become even in strength and control.

***In order to be proficient at multiple tonguing it is necessary to practice at least one of these exercises every day in the following manner:***

1. In order to have an even triple or double tongue, you must be able to have a clean, even, and fast single tongue. Practice the exercise at a brisk tempo using all single tonguing.
2. Practice the entire exercise slowly using all *KAH* syllables.
3. Return to step 1 and begin very slowly, accenting the *KAH*. Gradually increase the speed but still remember to accent the *KAH*. As you accelerate, decrease the amount of the *KAH* accent, eventually eliminating it near the end of the exercise.
4. Practice the exercise with no accent at a moderate tempo accelerating to a brisk tempo. When practicing the faster tempi, I suggest using *DAH-DAH-GAH* syllables for triple-tonguing and *DAH-GAH* syllables for double-tonguing.

5.

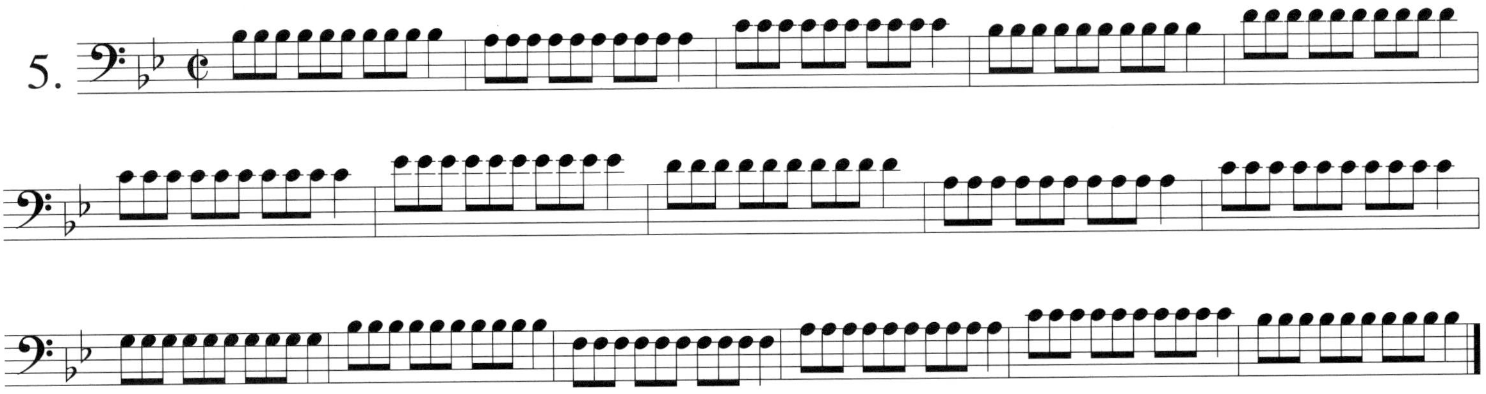

6.

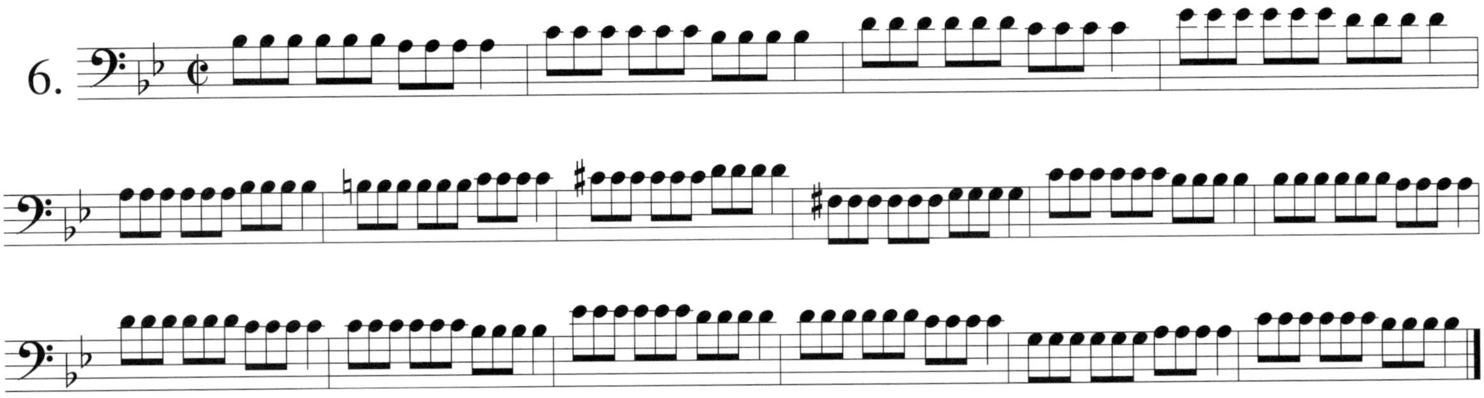

7.

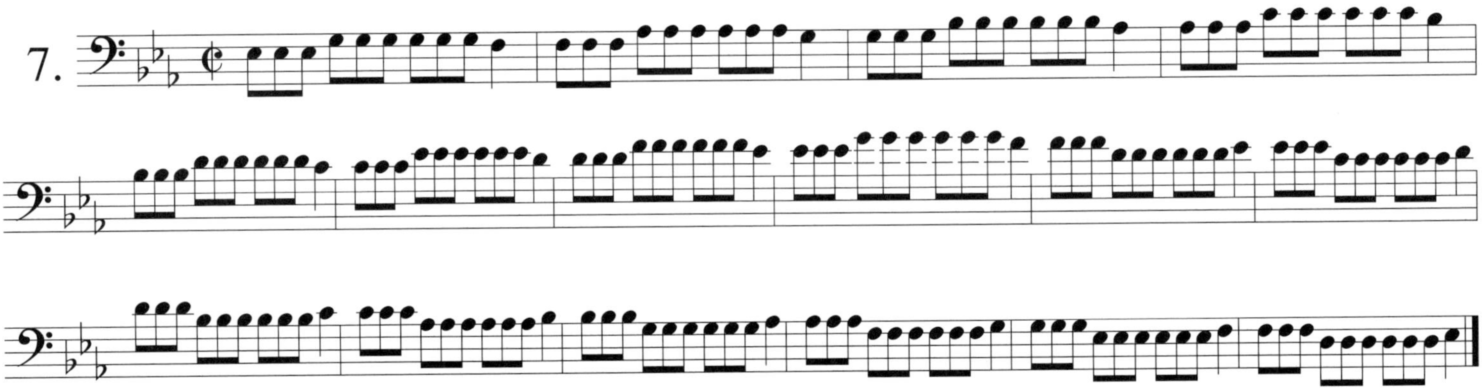

8.

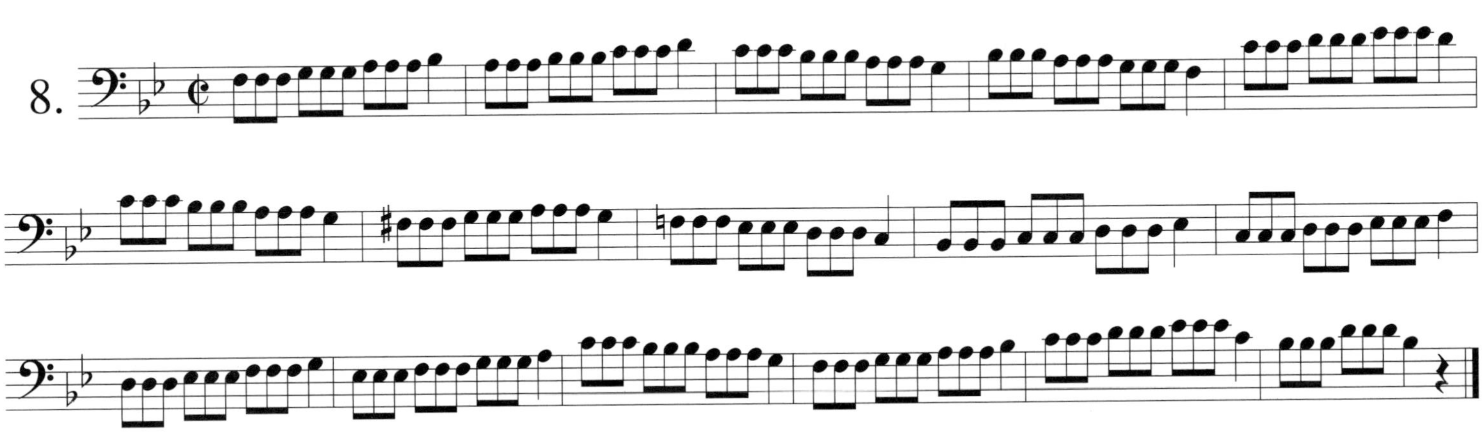

*—Mr. Alessi*

At this point, you are probably feeling a bit more comfortable with triple tonguing. This would be a good time to assess whether you have mastered the first ten exercises. From this point on, the difficulty factor will increase sharply—especially from exercise 14, where the intervals change more rapidly. In any case, it is a good idea to repeat the first ten exercises to a acquire a solid feeling about the use of triple tonguing.

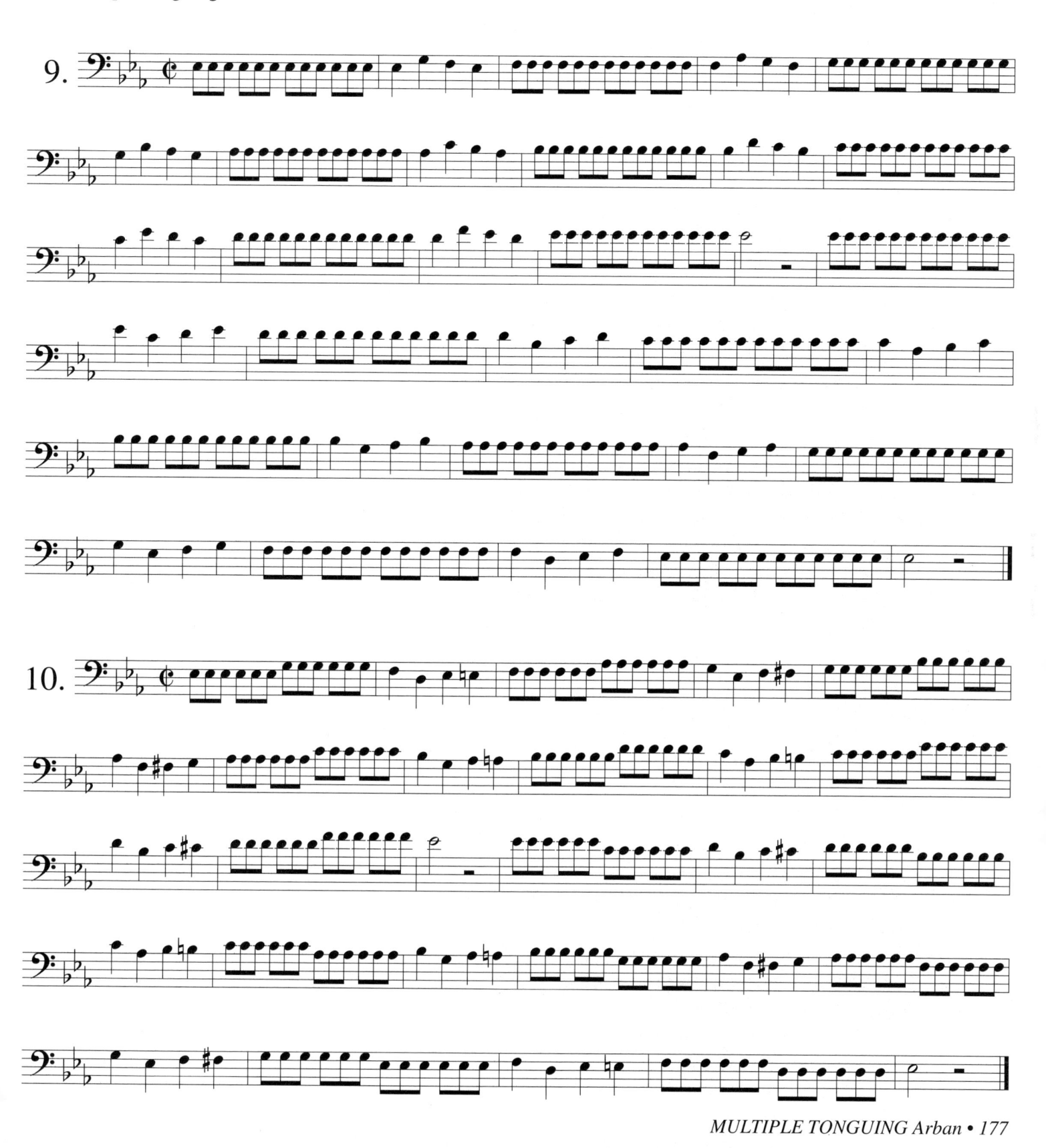

178 • Arban MULTIPLE TONGUING

MULTIPLE TONGUING Arban • 179

180 • Arban MULTIPLE TONGUING

*MULTIPLE TONGUING* Arban • 181

25.

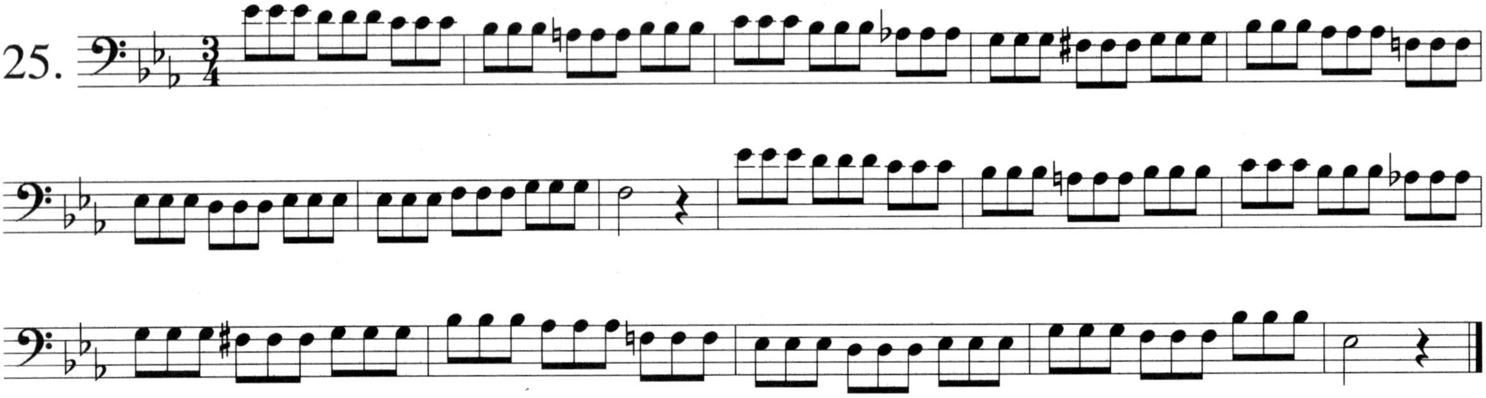

Theme

26.

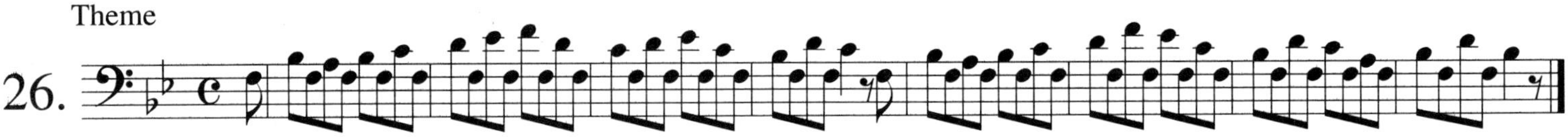

27.

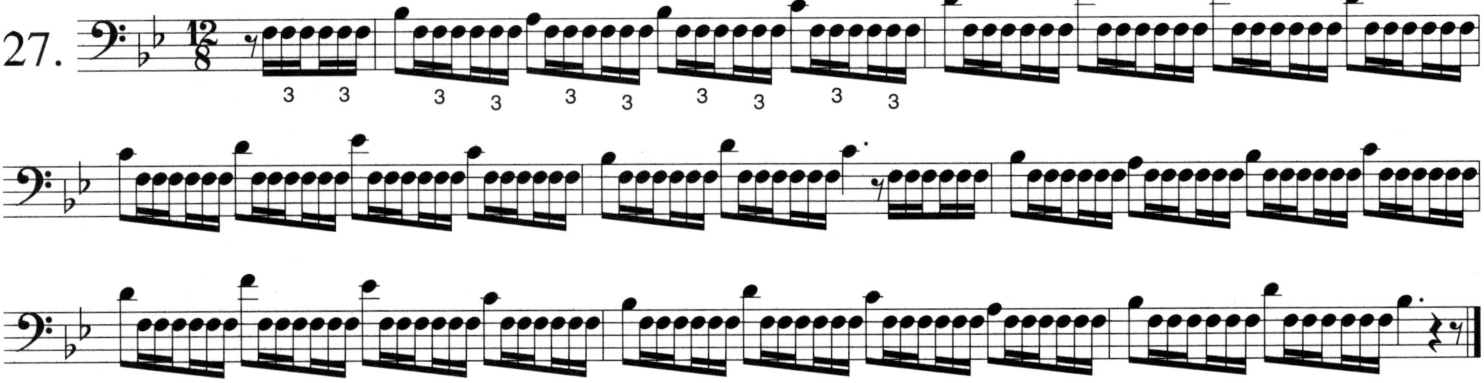

28.

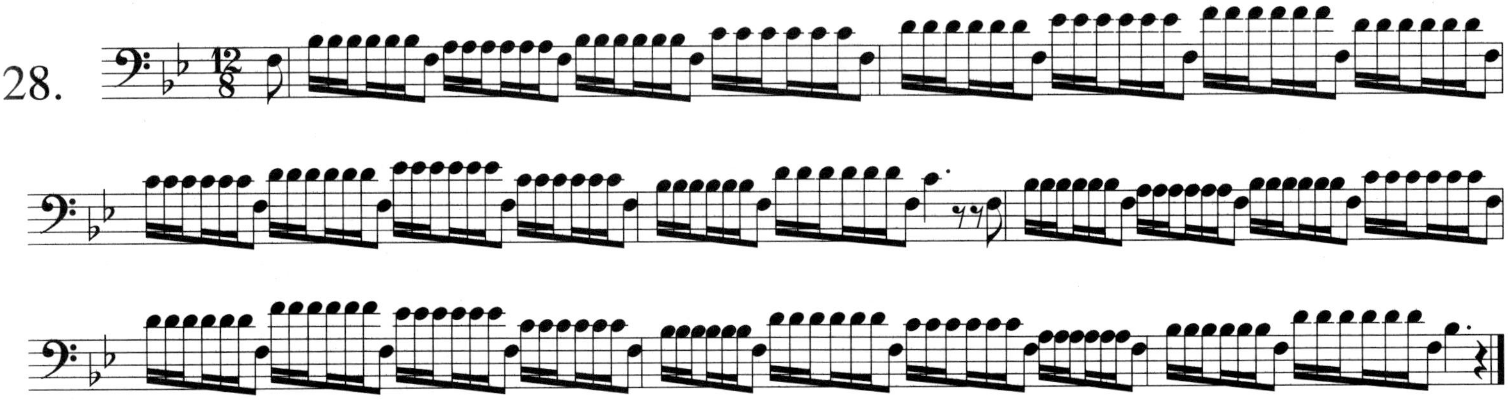

29.

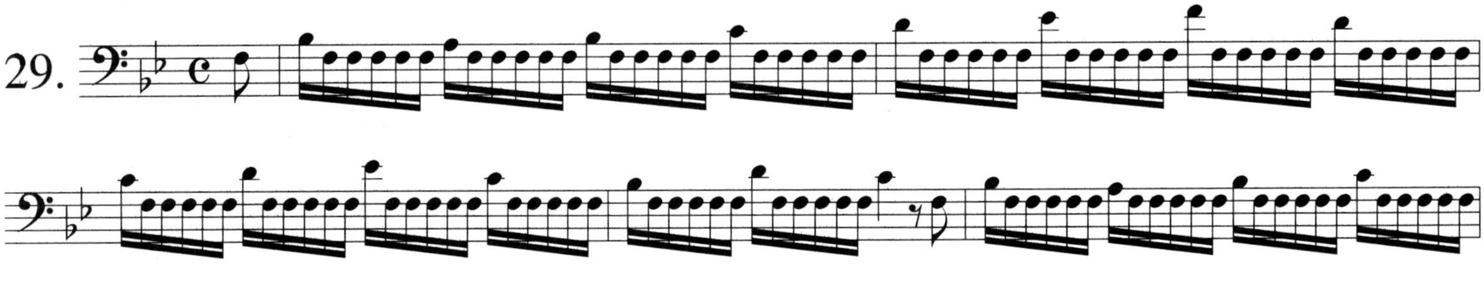

MULTIPLE TONGUING Arban

184 • Arban MULTIPLE TONGUING

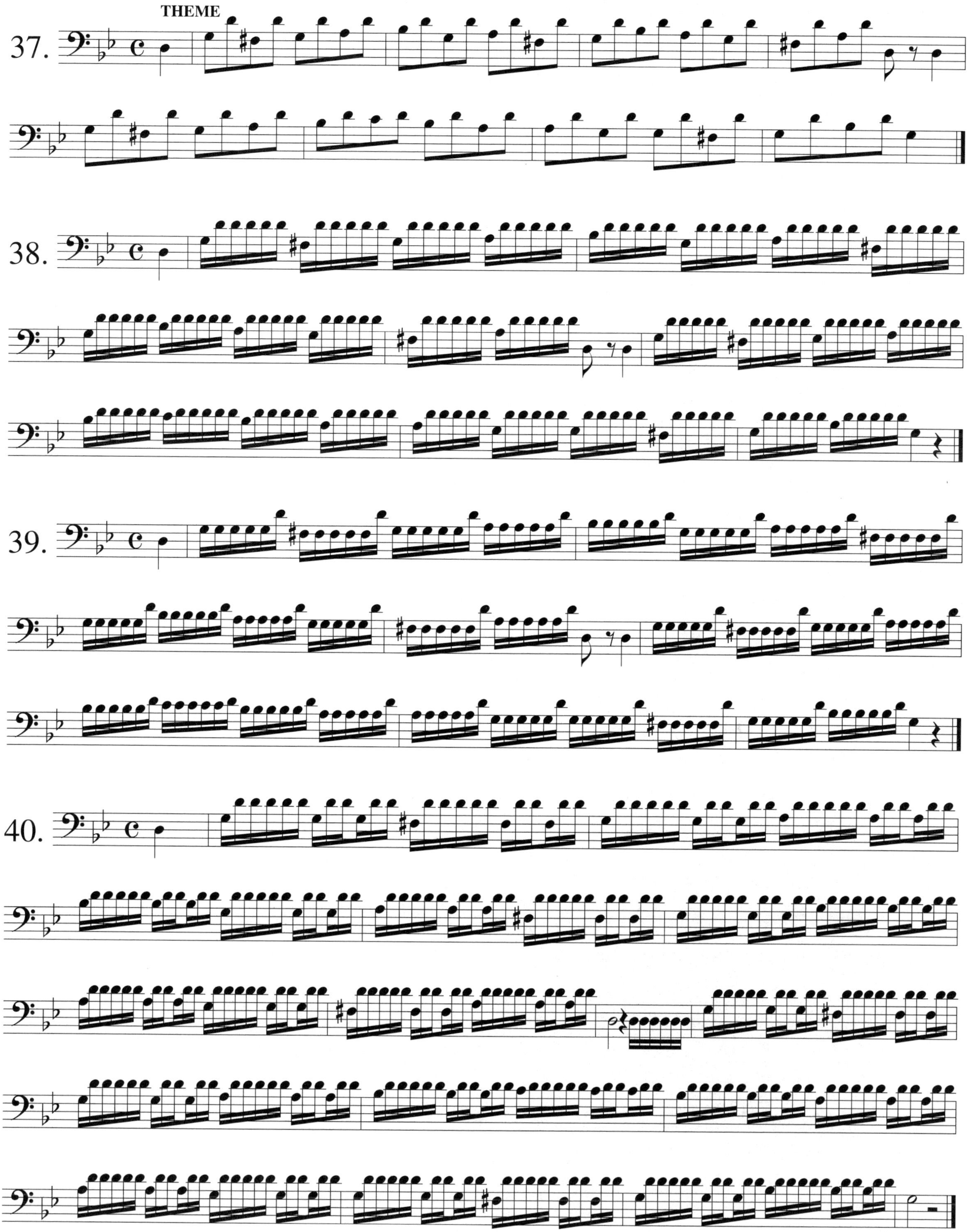
THEME
37.
38.
39.
40.

186 • Arban MULTIPLE TONGUING

MULTIPLE TONGUING Arban • 187

188 • Arban MULTIPLE TONGUING

MULTIPLE TONGUING Arban • 189

190 • Arban MULTIPLE TONGUING

MULTIPLE TONGUING Arban • 191

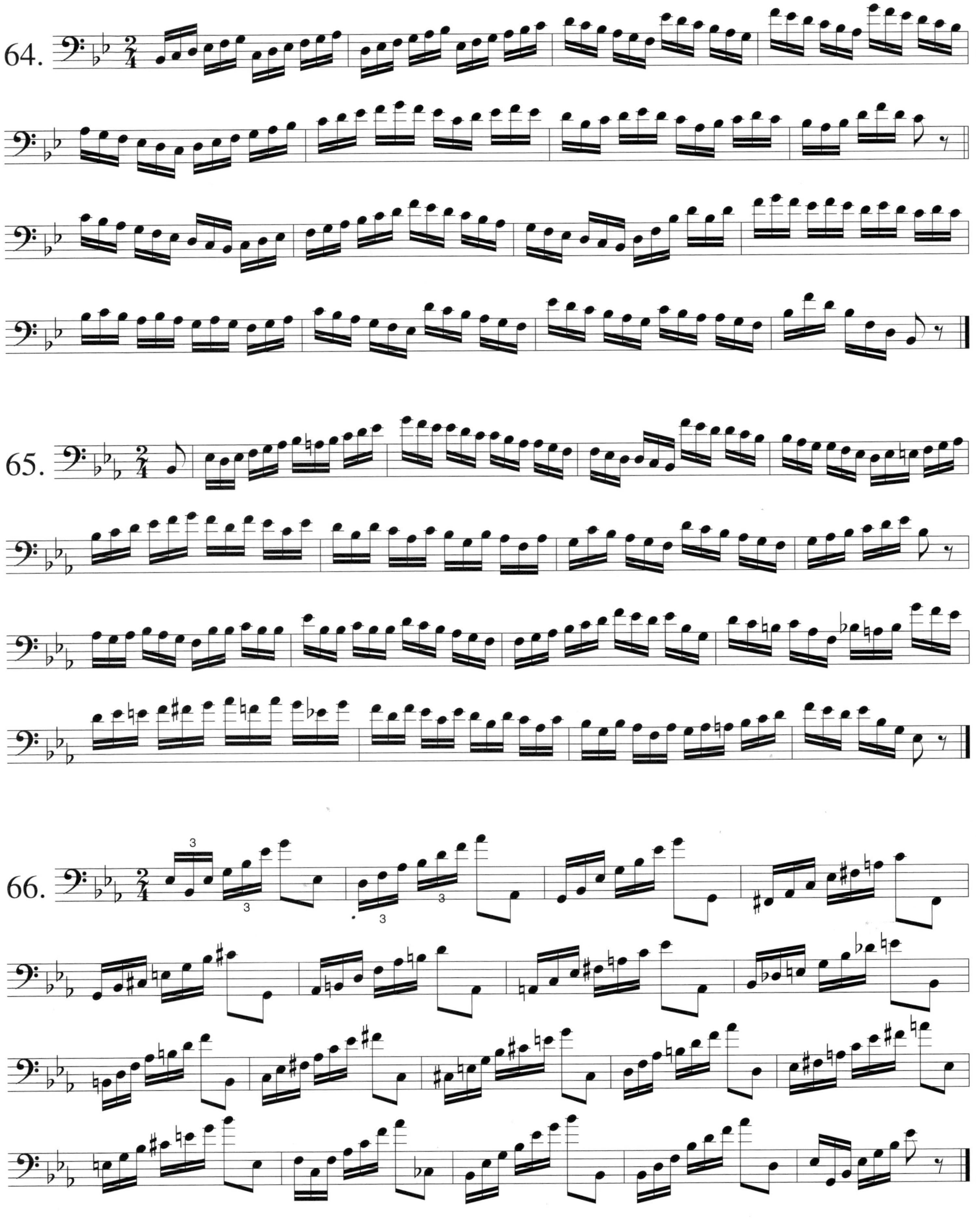
64.
65.
66.
3

MULTIPLE TONGUING Arban

194 • Arban MULTIPLE TONGUING

MULTIPLE TONGUING Arban • 195

*D.S. al Fine*

**75.** Theme — Allegro

Var.

**76.** Theme — Allegro

## Double Tonguing—Dr. Bowman

The same basic principles apply to the double tongue as the triple tongue. In addition to this section dedicated to double tonguing exercises, the scale and other sections of the book may be played double tongued with a faster tempo.

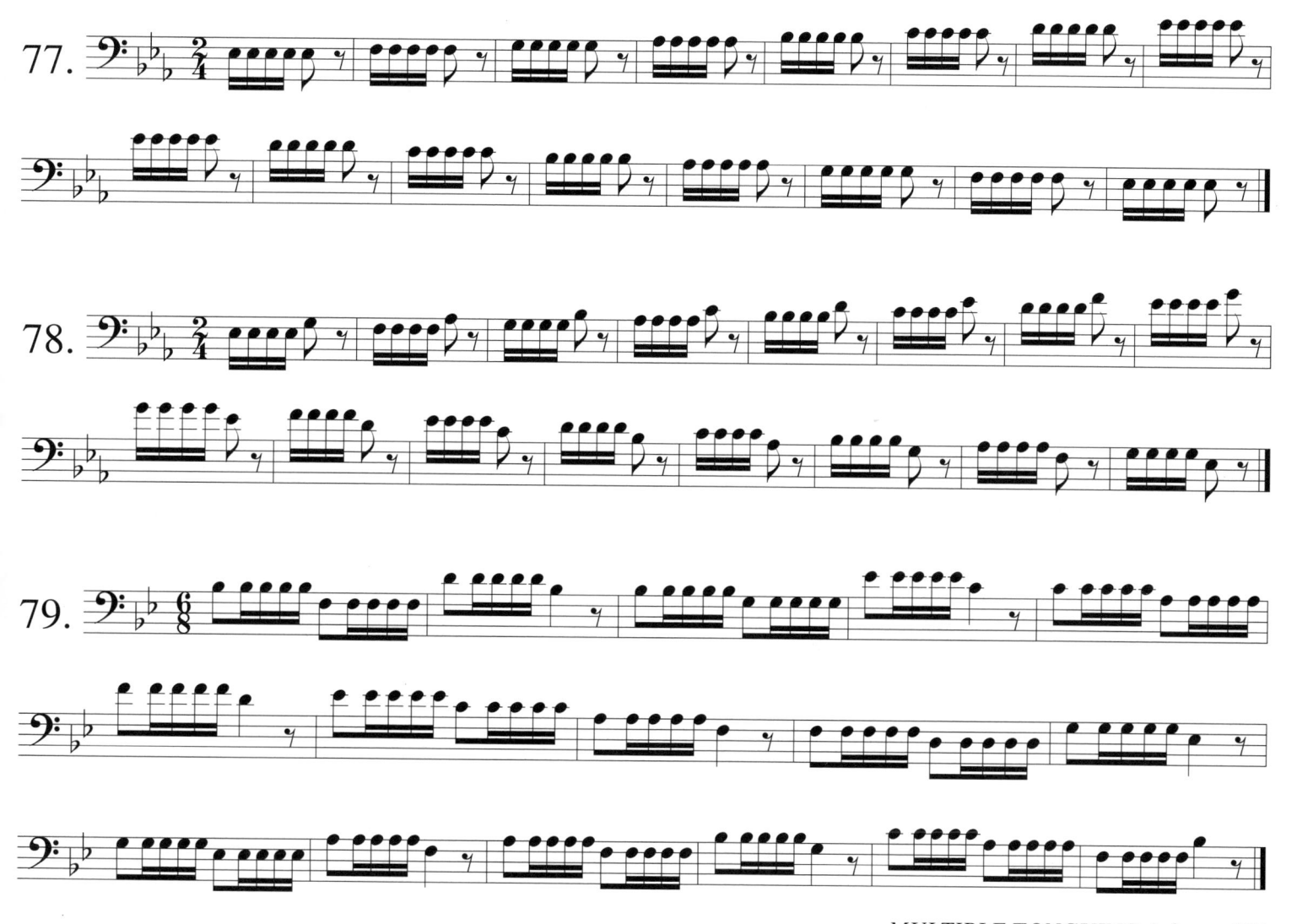

80.

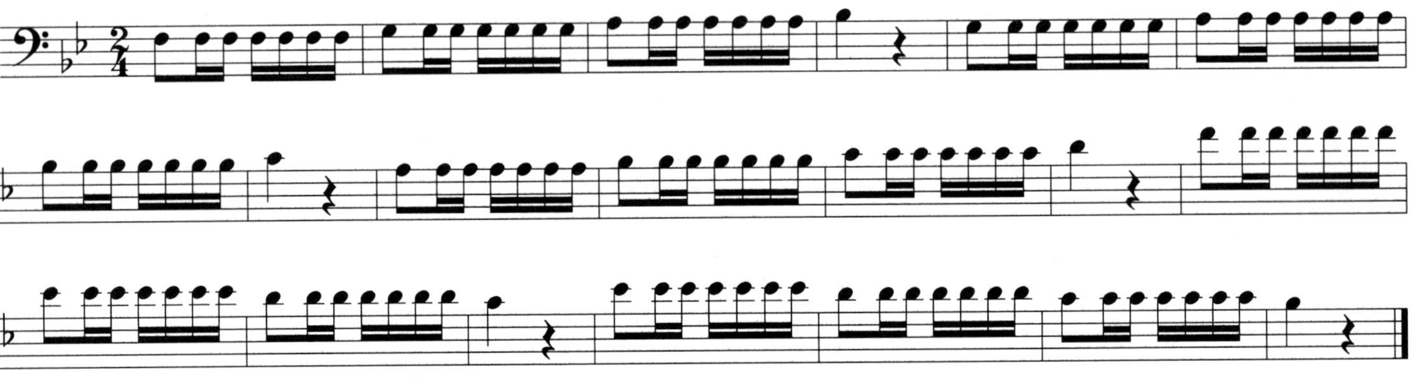

81.

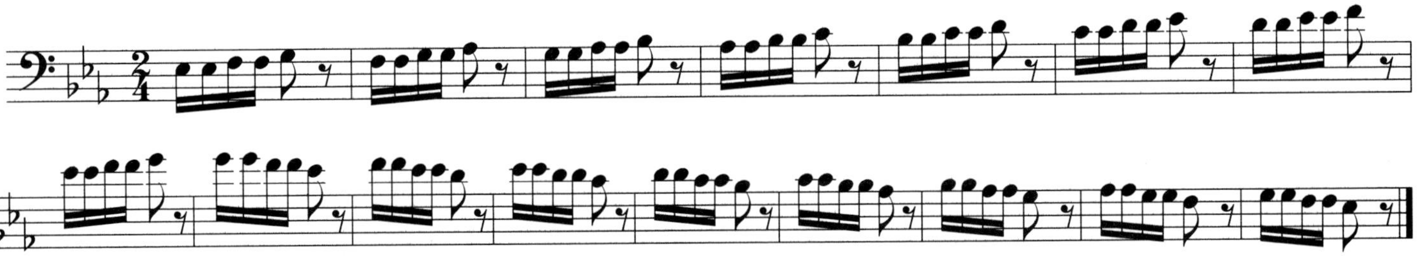

82.

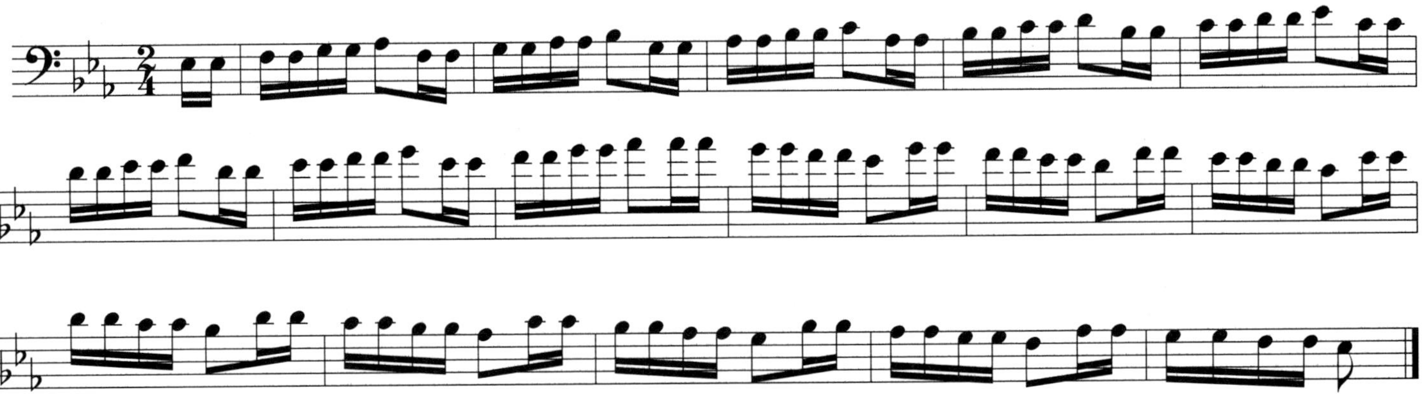

83.

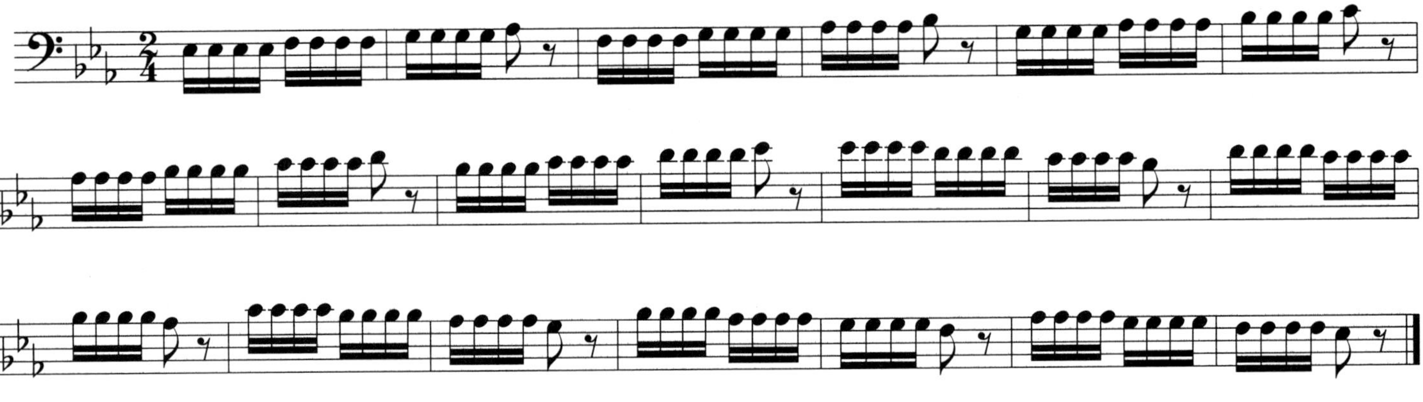

84.

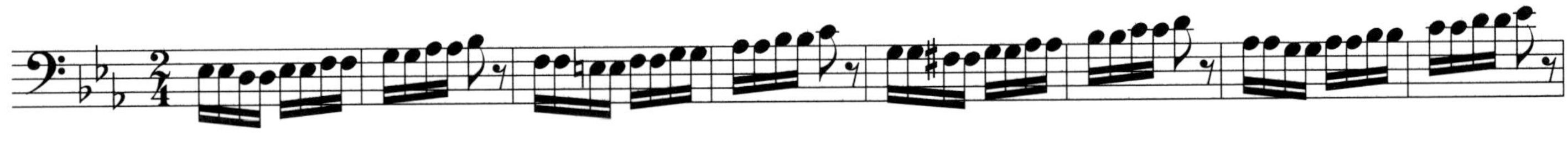

MULTIPLE TONGUING Arban • 199

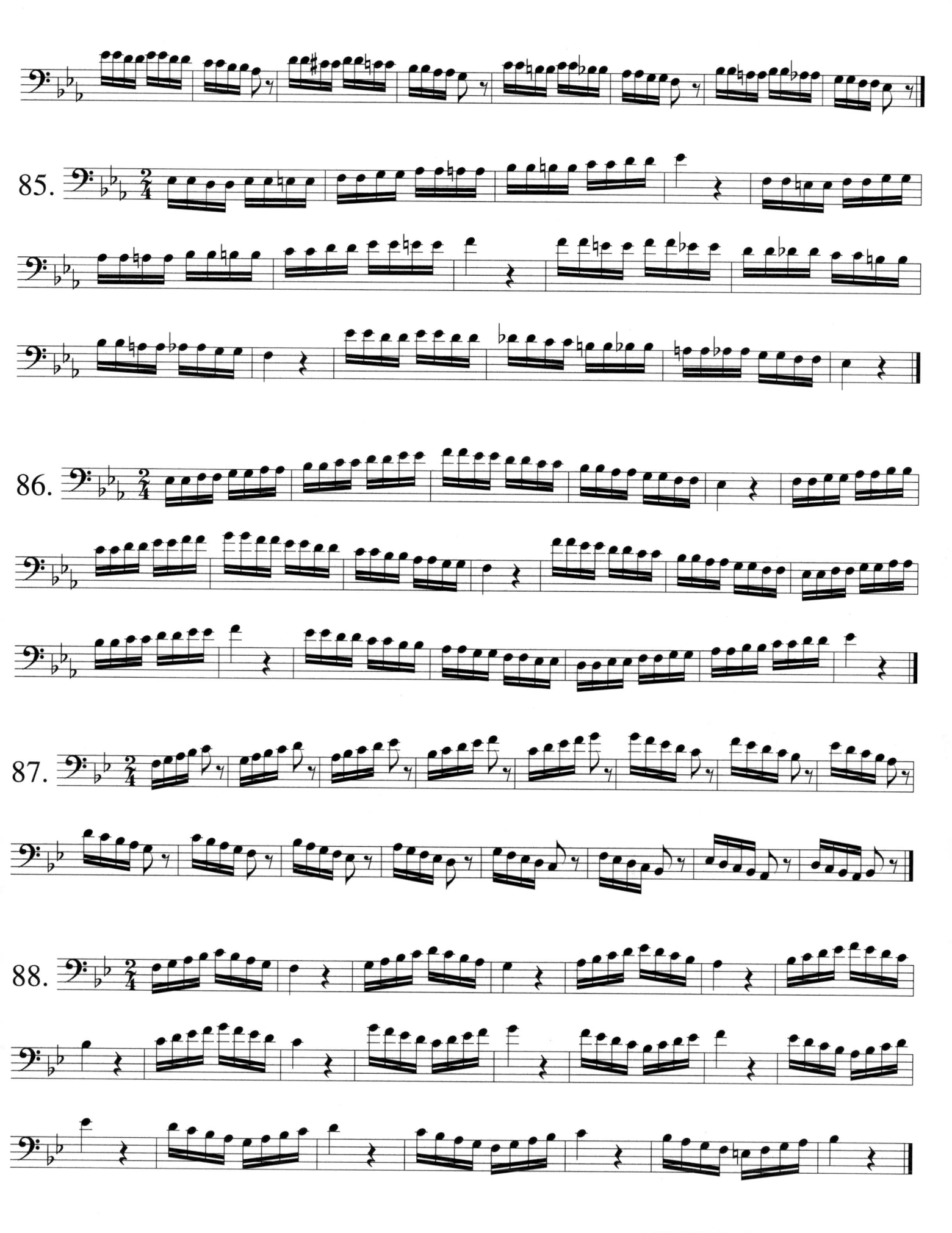

200 • Arban MULTIPLE TONGUING

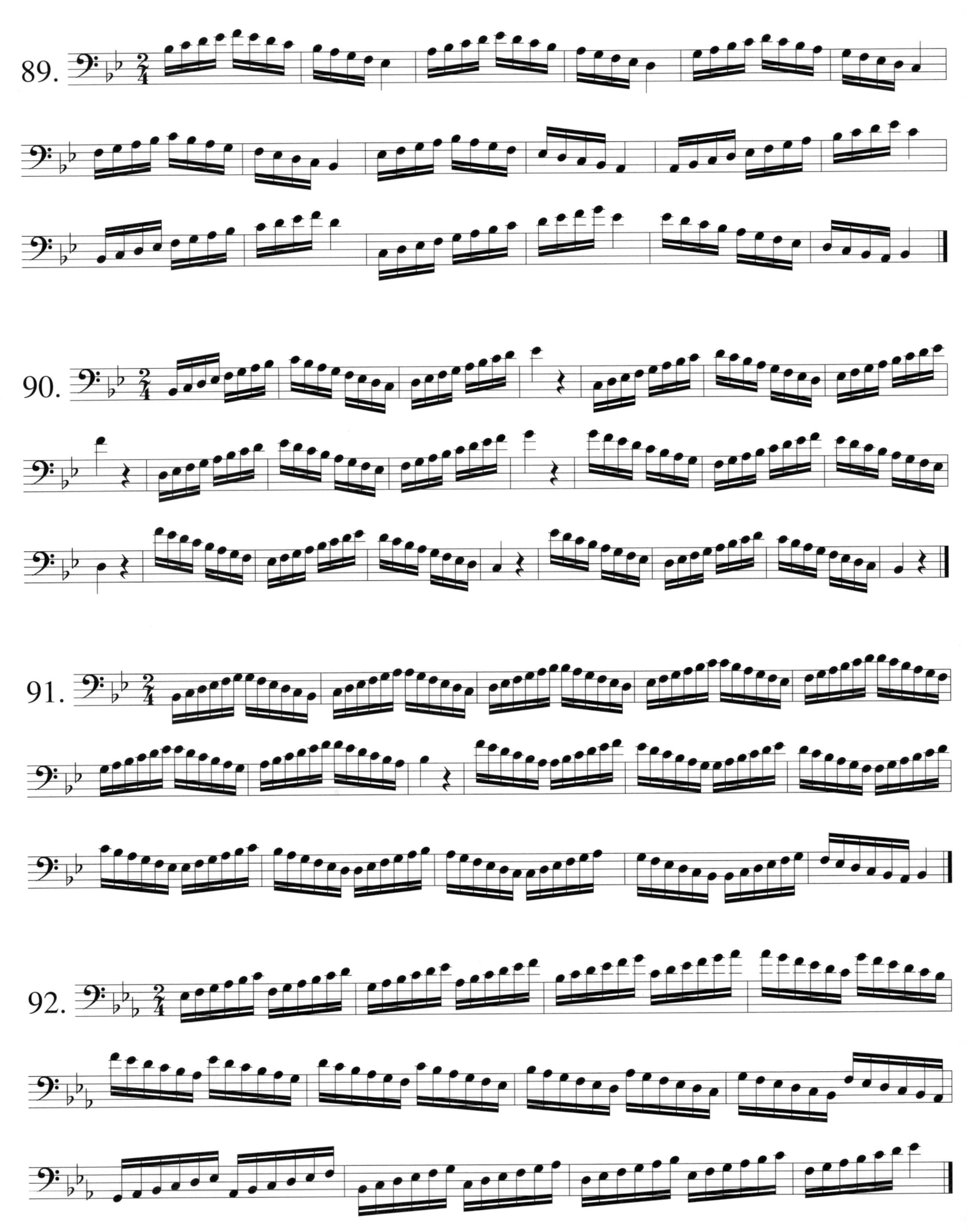

*MULTIPLE TONGUING* Arban • 201

202 • Arban MULTIPLE TONGUING

MULTIPLE TONGUING Arban • 203

204 • Arban MULTIPLE TONGUING

112.

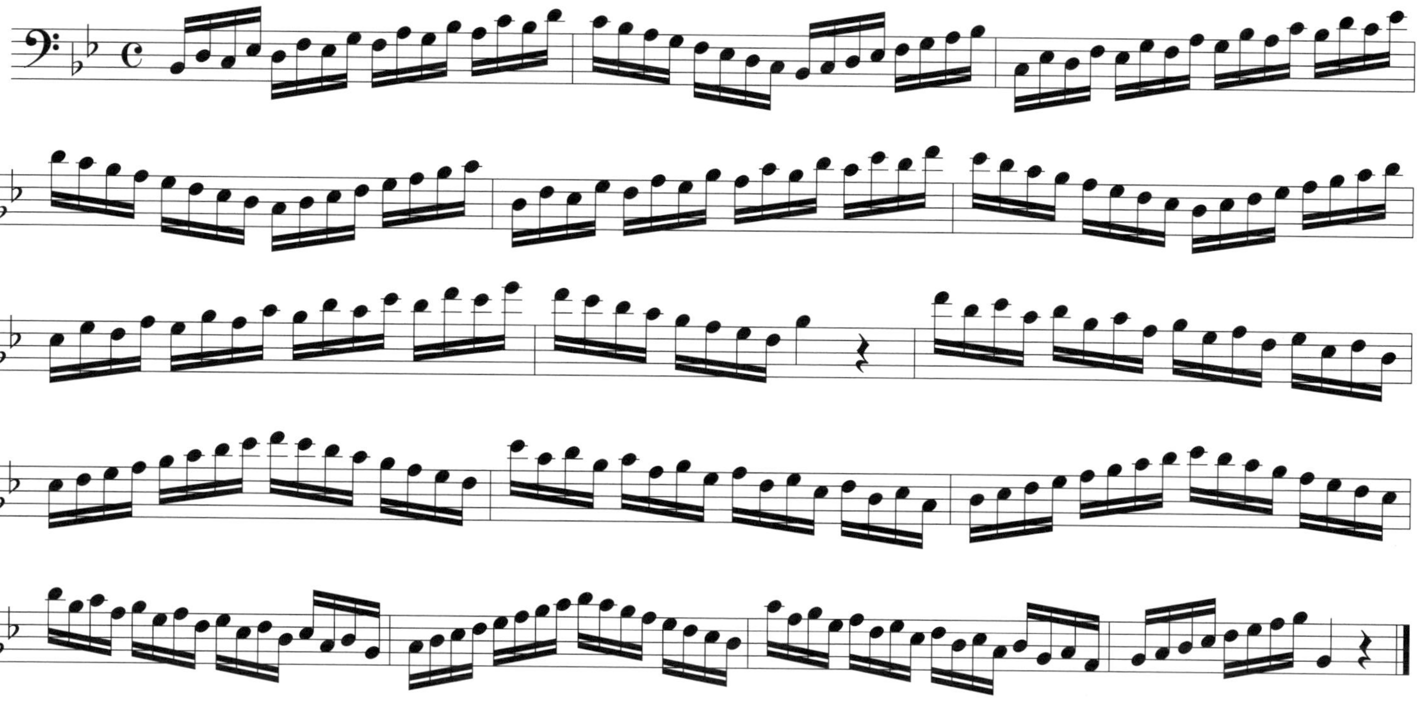

113.

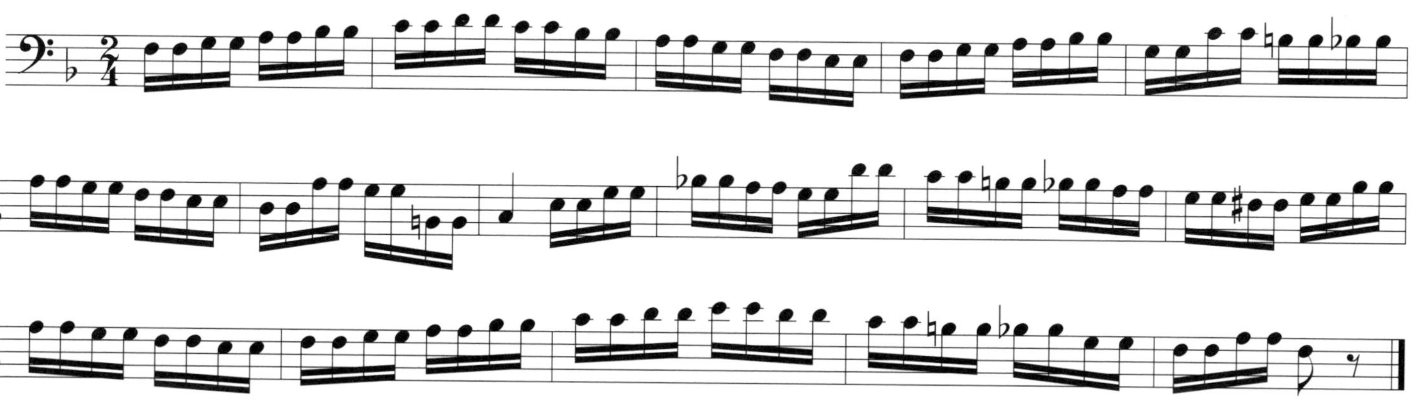

114.

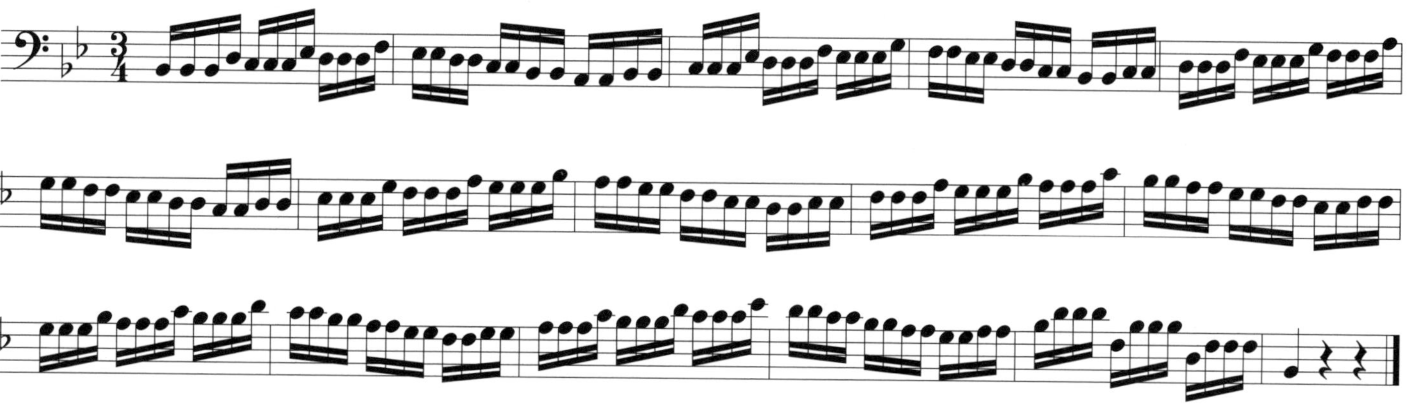

115.

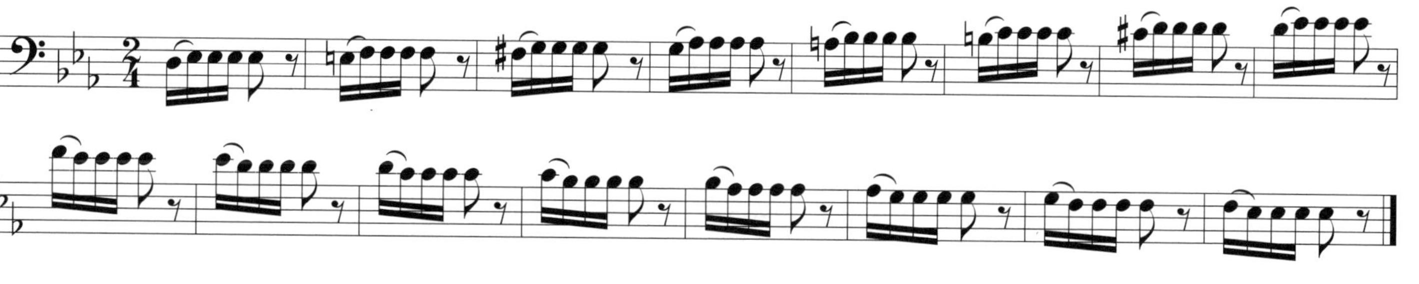

116.

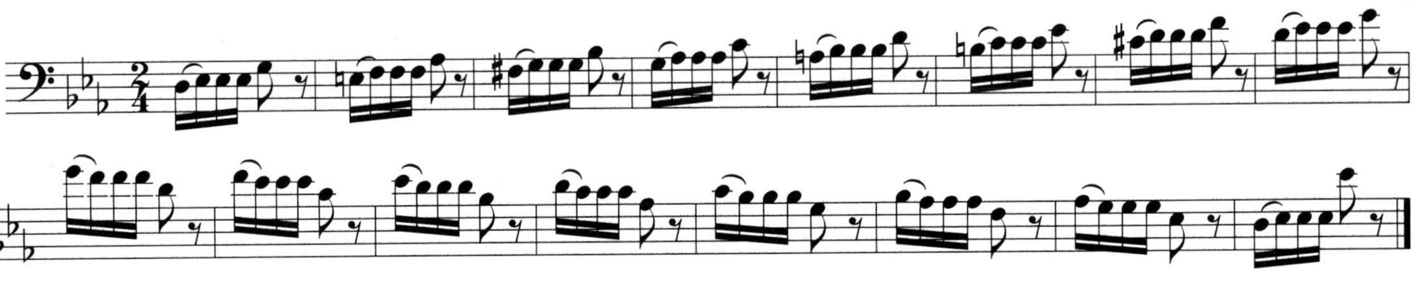

117.

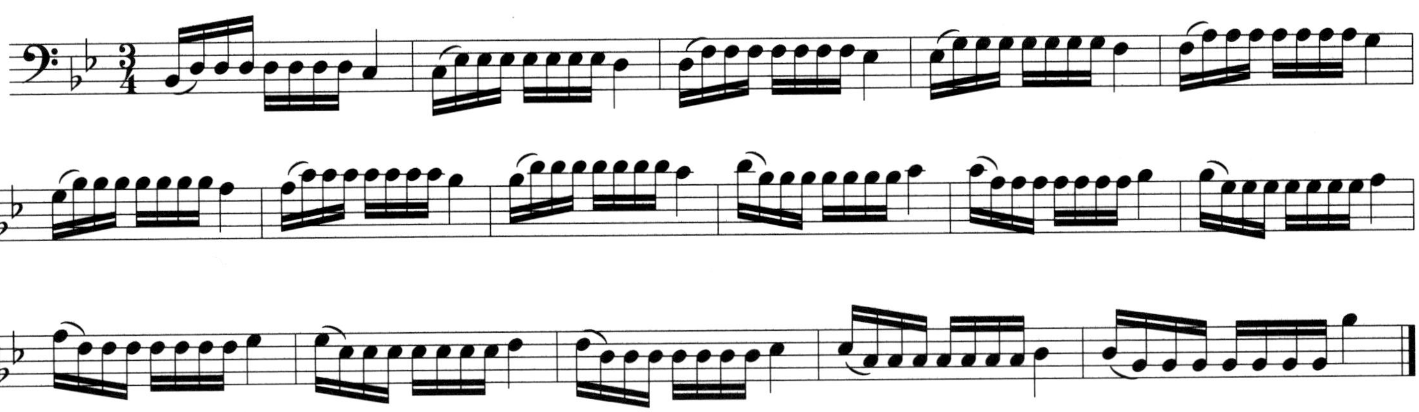

118.

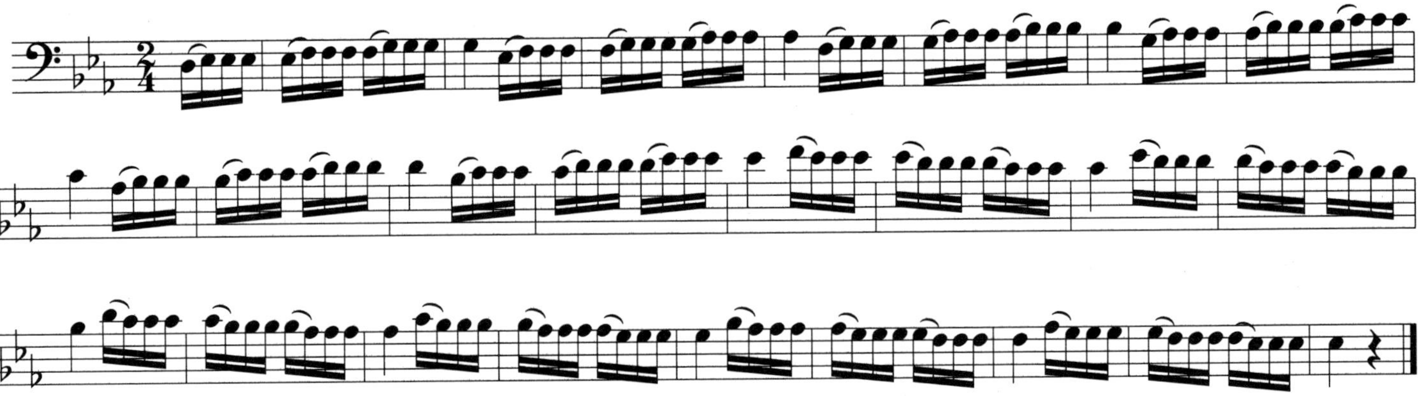

119.

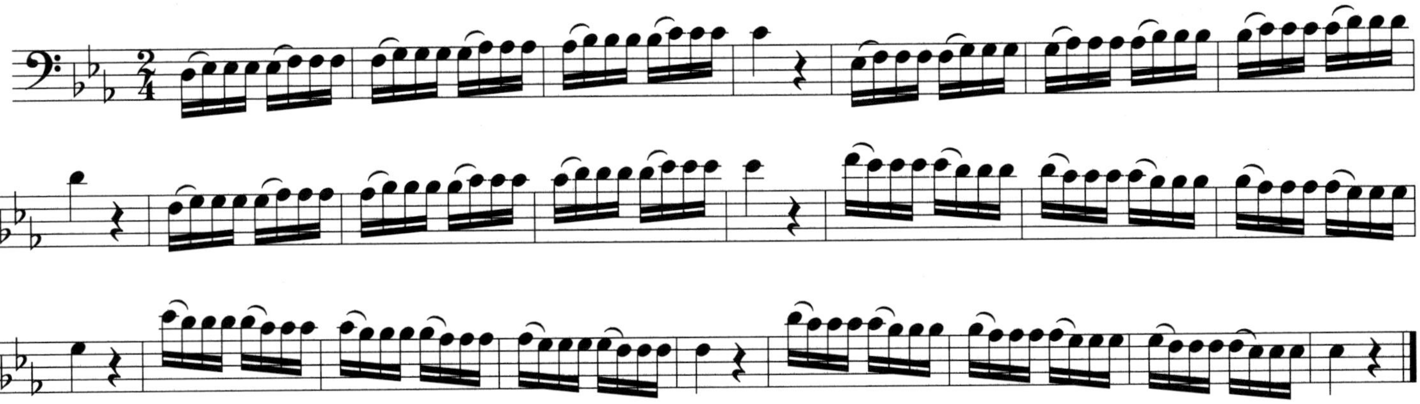

120.

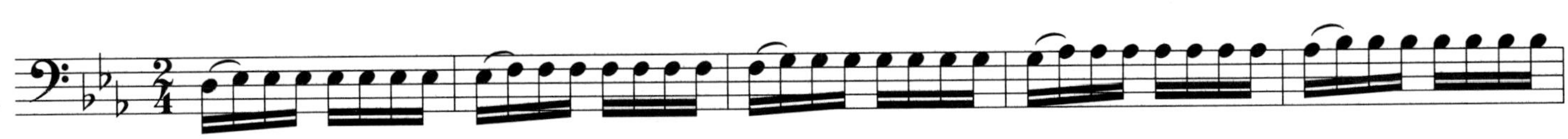

**MULTIPLE TONGUING Arban • 207**

208 • Arban MULTIPLE TONGUING

128.

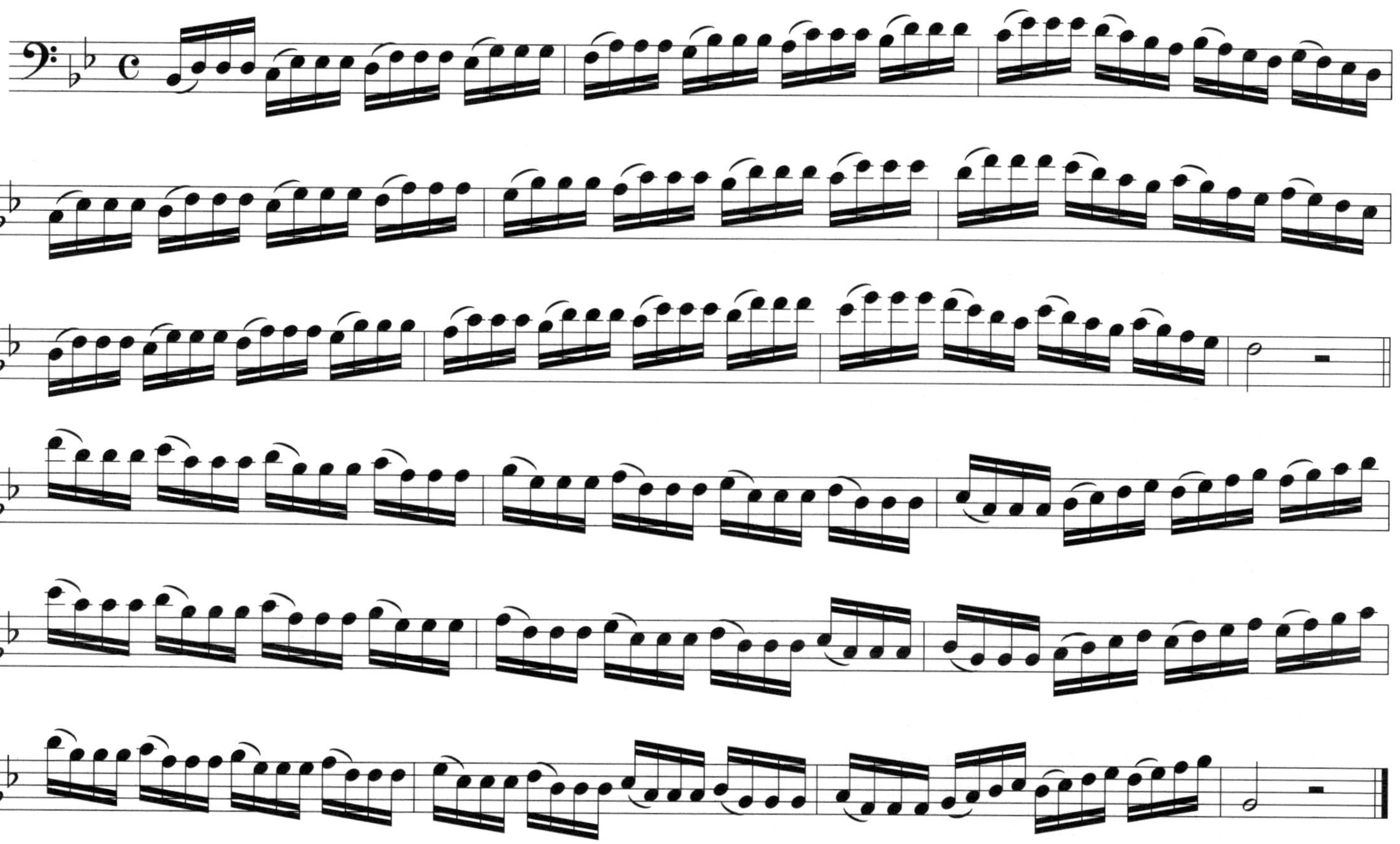

129.

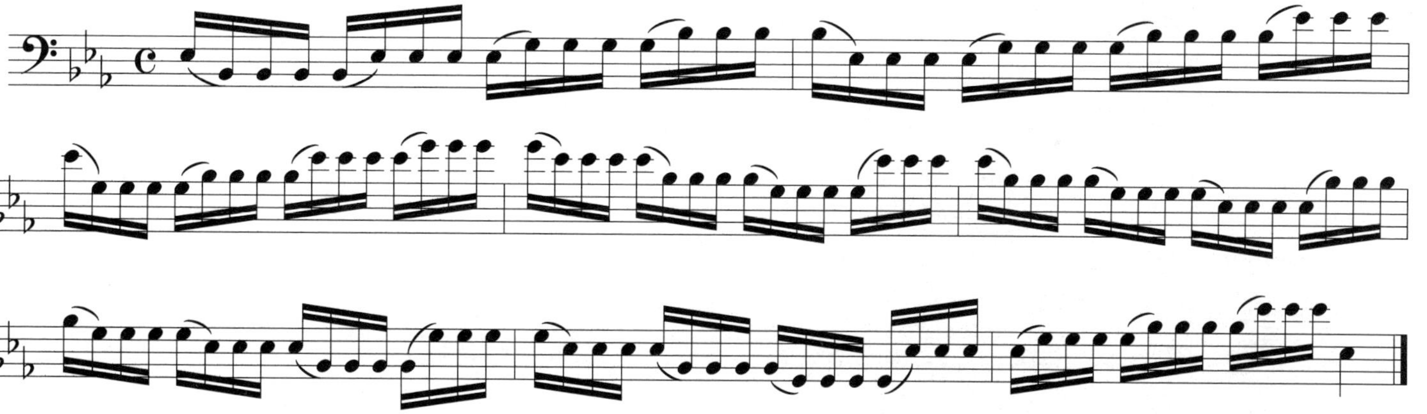

130.

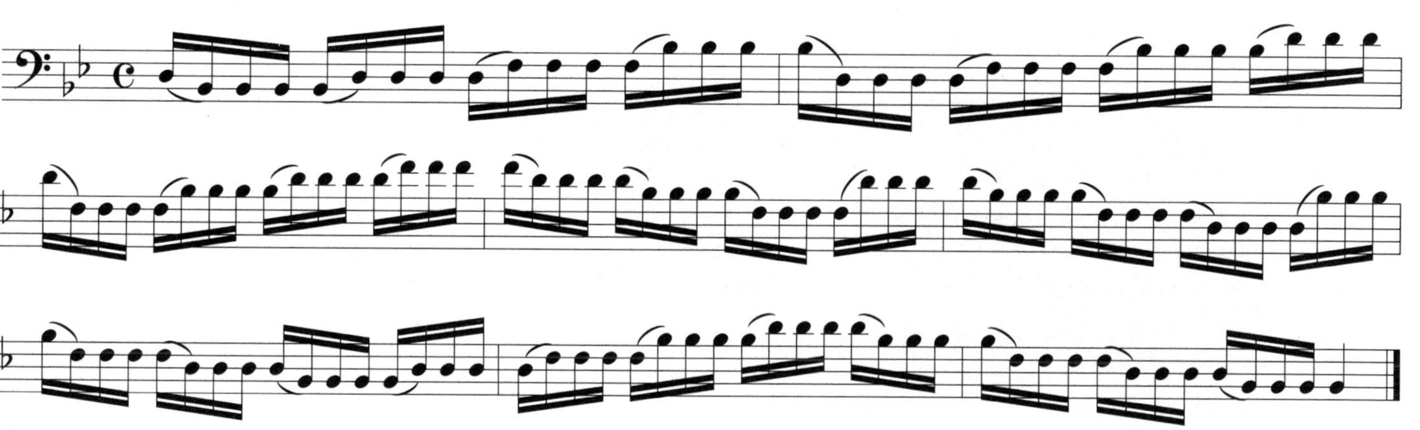

131.

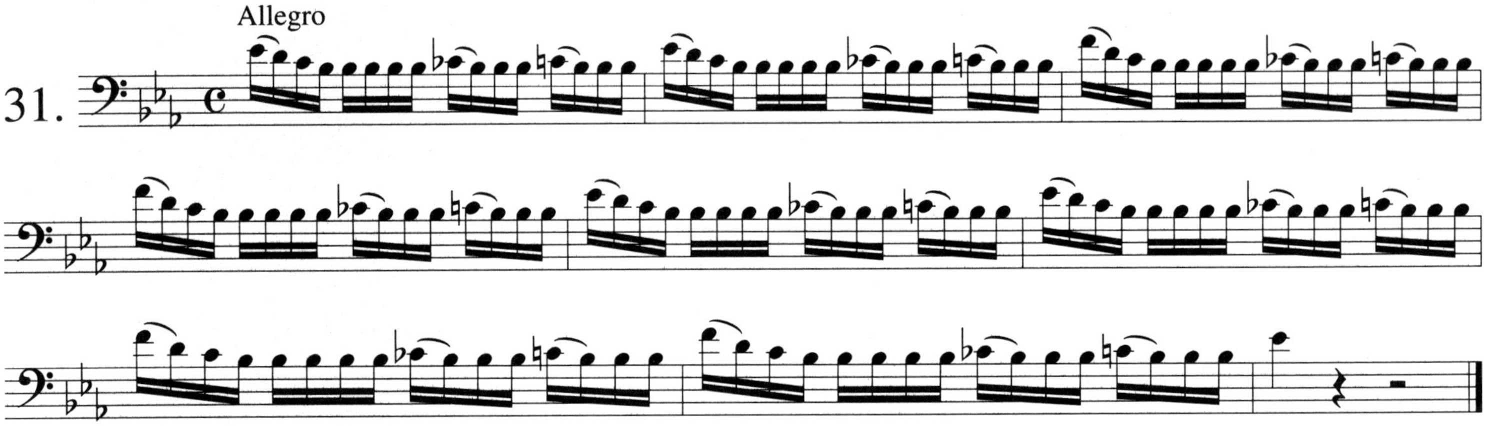


132.

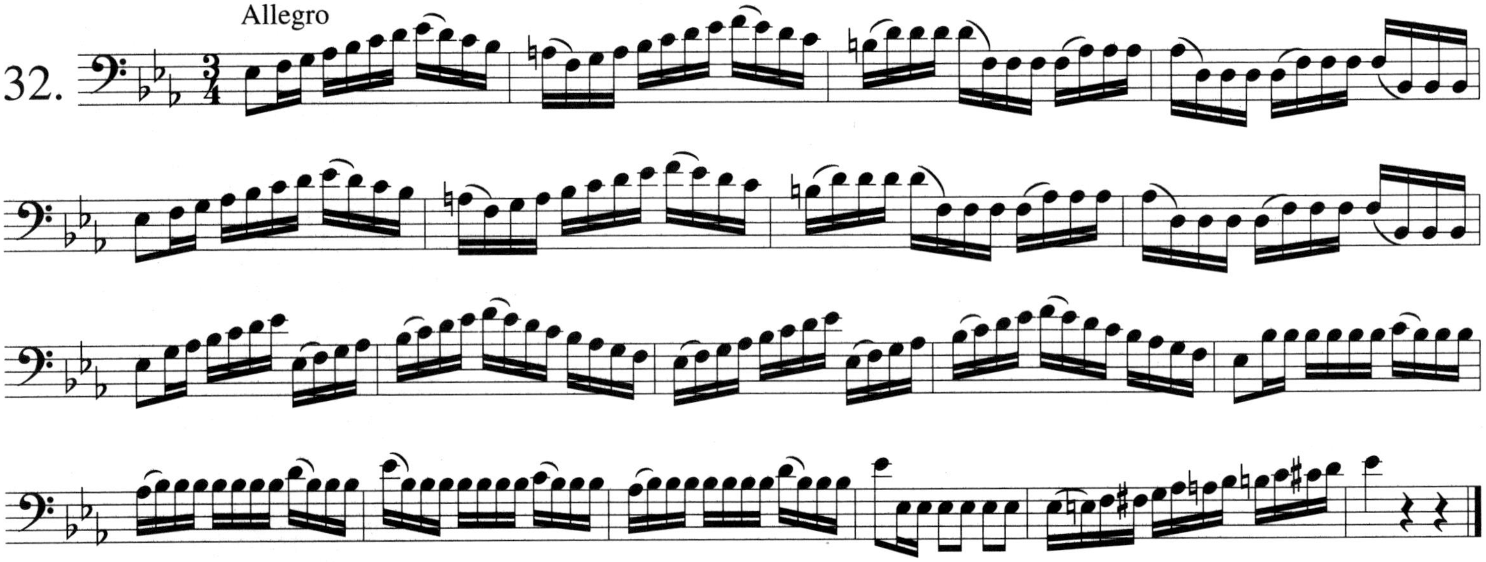


133.

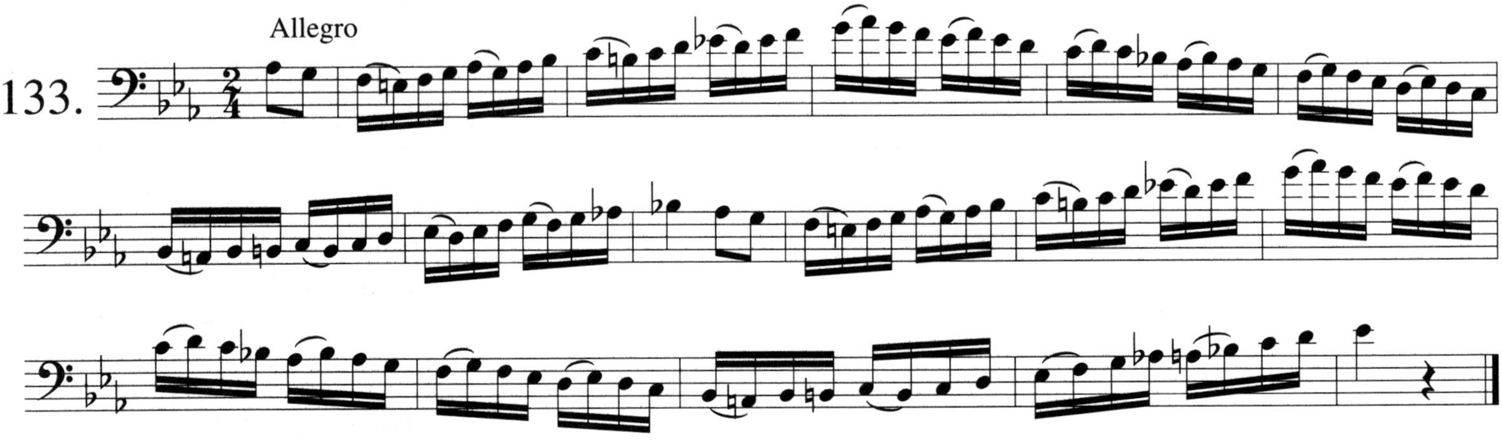


134.

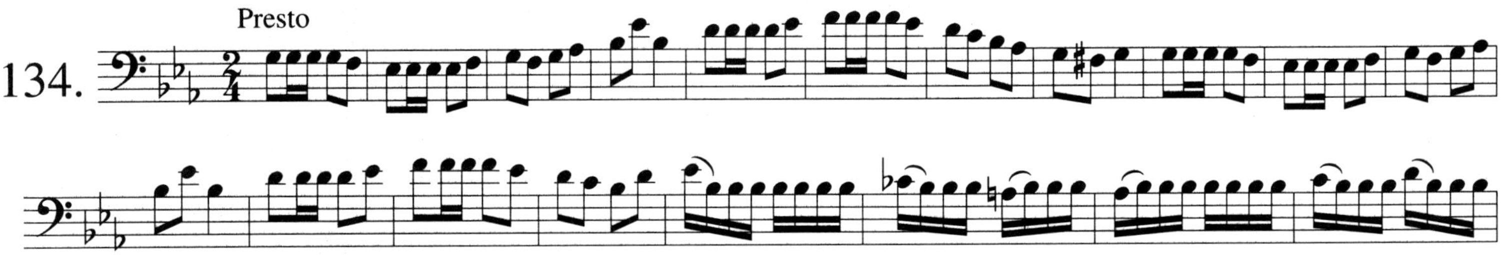

MULTIPLE TONGUING Arban • 211

212 • Arban MULTIPLE TONGUING

## MULTIPLE TONGUING Arban

# Arban's Comments from the Original Edition
## Le Grande Method Complete Pour Cornet à Pistons et de Saxhorn

### On Mouthpiece Position

Some teachers make a point of changing the position of the mouthpiece previously adopted by the pupils who apply to them. I have seldom known this method to succeed. To my own knowledge, several players, already possessed of remarkable talent, have attempted what we call at the Conservatoire, the 'orthopedic system,' which consists in correcting the wrong placing of the mouthpiece. I consider it my duty to say that these artists—after having wasted several years in uselessly trying the system in question—were compelled to return to their original placement of the mouthpiece, not one of them having obtained any advantage, while some of them were no longer able to play at all."

"Always remember that the phrase *coup de langue* (stroke of the tongue) is merely a conventional expression. The tongue does not strike; on the contrary, it performs a retrograde movement, simply behaving like a valve."

"This should be kept in mind before placing the mouthpiece on the lips; the tongue ought to be placed against the teeth of the upper jaw in such a way that the mouth is hermetically sealed. As the tongue recedes, the column of air which was pressing against it is pushed violently into the mouthpiece causing the sound."

"The pronunciation of the syllable 'tu' serves to determine the attack of the sound. This syllable may be pronounced harder or softer, according to the degree of force to be imparted to the note."

### On Faults to be Avoided

"The first matter to which the student should give special attention is the proper production of the tone. This is the basis of all good playing, and a musician whose method of producing tone is faulty will never become a great artist."

"In playing softly as well as loudly, the 'attack' of the sound ought to be free, clear and immediate. In striking the tone it is always necessary to articulate the syllable 'tu' and not 'doua,' as is the habit of many players. This latter articulation causes the tone to be flat, and imparts to it a thick and disagreeable quality."

"After acquiring the proper methods of tone production, the player must strive to attain a good style. By style is meant, not a lofty abstract ideal only achieved by the greatest artists, but a practical musical competence so essential for the student's mastery of his instrument. To be natural, to be correct, to play music as it is written, to phrase according the style and sentiment of the piece performed—these are qualities which should be of constant concern to the student."

# THE ART OF PHRASING

### Dr. Bowman

The production of a beautiful singing tone quality and musical interpretation are the important goals of playing these exercises. Consider the euphonium your voice, and play the melodies as if they were being sung. When practicing, sing them and then play them a similar manner. Listen carefully for tone quality, consistency and accurate intonation. This section affords an excellent opportunity to use appropriate vibrato. For variety of interpretation one can vary the dynamics and expression marks from those printed in this book.

### Mr. Alessi

Phrasing can be easily understood by listening to the inflections of a storyteller or to vocalists such as the great Frank Sinatra. Search for a note in the phrase that feels important to you. Usually this focal note can be approached by using a crescendo to create the feeling of an arrival point in the phrase. In my experience listening to entrance auditions at the Juilliard School, I have noted a large discrepancy between the student who makes no use of phrasing and one who does. The person who does also knows how to taper the ends of phrases and when to use vibrato (usually on longer sustained notes).

When playing repeated phrases or patterns in music, a good "phraser" will add progressively more intensity to make the repeated music more important than the previous. If you will observe etude #1, the first four bars are repeated, with the exception of the ornament. It is important for the performer to make the second four bars more important—or different—than the first four bars. This can be done by changing the dynamic level for the second four bars. The performer can decide whether to make this softer or louder, depending on his or her interpretation.

Furthermore, one must understand when to stress the appoggiatura. Appoggiaturas add tension to the phrase. A good example is found in etude #2 in the second bar on the A-natural. Play the first two bars, but instead of playing the A-natural in the second bar, play a G-natural for three beats with a rest on the fourth beat. Continue on to the third bar. Notice how the etude still makes sense harmonically. This is a good method for identifying appoggiaturas. Now play the etude as written, and when playing the A-natural appoggiatura, use a bit of vibrato and stress this note with a little more sound. When resolving to the G-natural, release this tension a bit. This is an example of good phrasing. Remember, just playing the notes is not enough.

**ROBIN ADAIR**

# LOVING, I THINK OF THEE

Krebs

# MY PRETTY JANE

# HOW FAIR THOU ART

H. Weidt

# AMERICA

## LAST ROSE OF SUMMER

## MY OWN, MY GUIDING STAR

## WHY DO I WEEP FOR THEE?

*W. V. Wallace*

## BLUE BELLS OF SCOTLAND

# DUTCH AIR

10.

# NOW THE SWALLOWS ARE RETURNING
Fr. Abt.

11.

# WHO SHALL BE FAIREST?

12.

# RUSSIAN HYMN

13.

218 • Arban ART OF PHRASING

# O, YE TEARS

**14.** *Fr. Abt.*

# PURITAN'S DAUGHTER

**15.** *Balfe*

# WOODMAN SPARE THAT TREE

**16.** *H. Russell*

# LOVE NOT

**17.** *V. Wallace*

# THEN YOU'LL REMEMBER ME
*Balfe*

# O WERT BUT MINE OWN LOVE
*Fr. Kücken*

# WE MAY BE HAPPY YET
*Balfe*

# CONSTANCE
*G. Linley*

## THE HEART OF THY NORA IS BREAKING FOR THEE

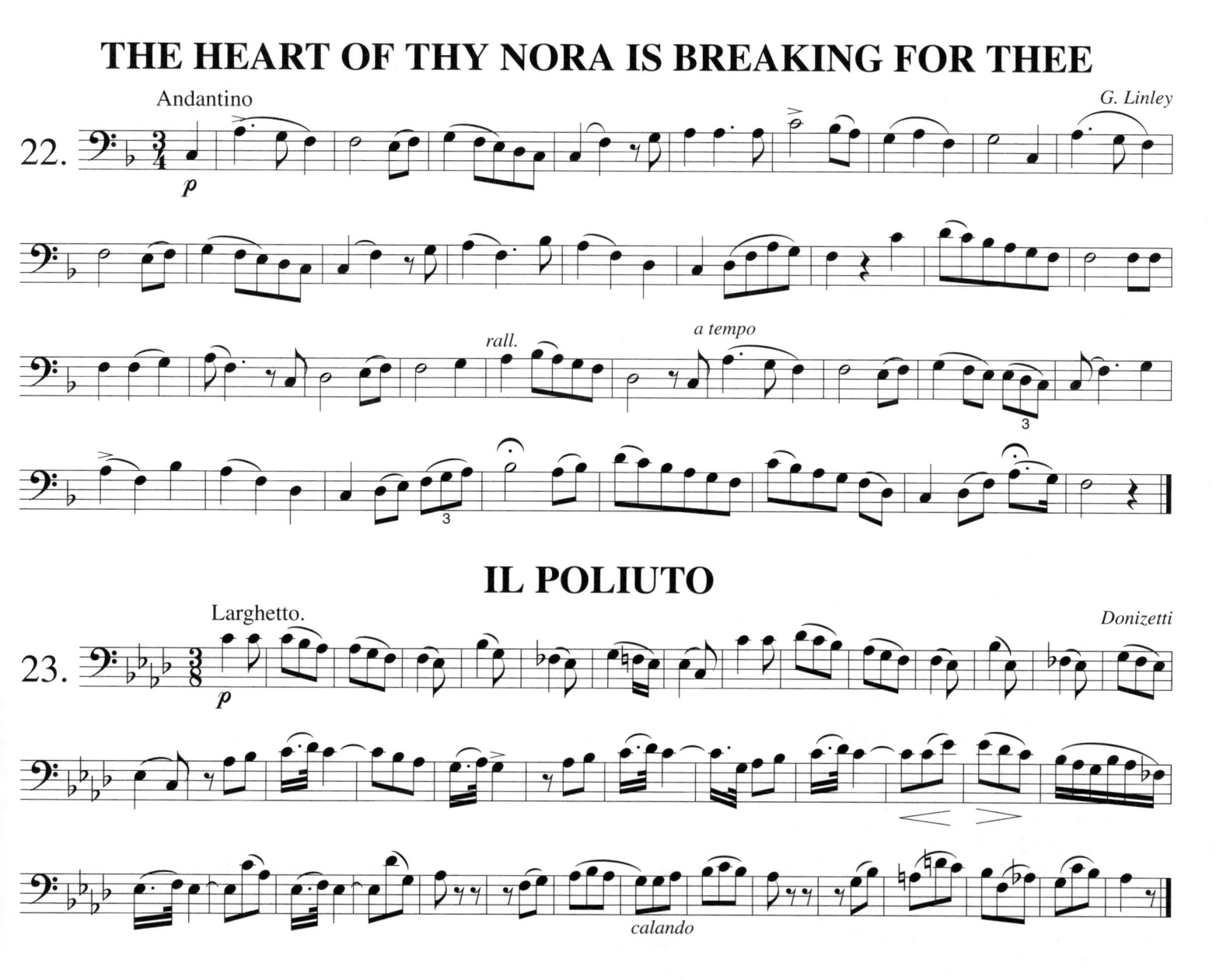

*G. Linley*

22. Andantino

## IL POLIUTO

*Donizetti*

23. Larghetto.

*calando*

## THE HEART BOWED DOWN

*Balfe*

24. Larghetto cantabile.

# WHEN WE MEET AGAIN

*L. Waldman*

**25.** Moderato

# GERMAN SONG

**26.** Andante moderato

# FRIENDS OF MY YOUTH

*G. Barker.*

**27.** Andante

# ROMANCE

**28.** Andantino ma non lento — Chas. Lecocq.

# THERE IS A FLOWER THAT BLOOMETH

**29.** Moderato — V. Wallace

# L'ARA O L'AVELLO APPRESTAMI

**30.** Moderato — Verdi

Più mosso

ART OF PHRASING Arban • 223

# MY BARK WHICH O'ER THE TIDE

31. *Allegretto* — Balfe

# 'TWAS RANK AND FAME

32. *Andante cantabile.* — Balfe

# VIEN, LEONORA

33. *Larghetto* — Donizetti

## SICILIAN VESPERS

34. Largo cantabile. — Verdi

## BLACK EYED SUSAN

35. Andante

## I'M LEAVING THEE IN SORROW

36. Andante — G. Barker.

# GOOD-BYE, SWEETHEART

*Hatton*

**37.** Andante con moto

# FAREWELL TO THEE, MARY

*F.N. Grouch*

**38.** Andante

# IN HAPPY MOMENTS

*W.V. Wallace.*

**39.** Moderato

226 • Arban ART OF PHRASING

# CALL ME THINE OWN

*Halevy*

40. Andantino espressivo

# KATHLEEN MAVOUREEN

41. Andante

# SLUMBER ON

*Fr. Abt.*

42. Moderato

## BRIGHTEST EYES

*G. Stigelli*

43.

## BALLAD "LOVE'S OWN TEAR"

*T. Crampton*

44.

## RESTORE THOSE VISIONS BRIGHT

*Spohr*

45.

# IL FURIOSO

*Donizetti*

46. Andante

# ROMANCE

*Donizetti*

47. Moderato

# ROMANZETTA

*Bellini*

48. Andante cantabile

## BE STILL, MY HEART
*Henrion*

49.

## JESSIE
*G. Linley*

50.

## PIETA RISPETTO
**from Macbeth**
*Verdi*

51.

230 • Arban ART OF PHRASING

# THE EXILE'S LAMENT

Rich. Albert.

**52.** Con espressione

# SICILIAN VESPERS

Verdi.

**53.** Allegro agitto espress.

# I THINK OF THEE

F. Abt.

**54.** Andantino

# BEATRICE DI TENDA

*Bellini*

**55.** Andante amoroso

## LA GAZZA LADRA

58. Andante con brio — Rossini

## LA GAZZA LADRA

59. Allegro — Rossini

## LA DONNA DEL LAGO

*Rossini*

## LA CENERENTOLA

*Rossini*

## QUANDO LE SERE AL PLACIDO

*Verdi*

## ALLA VITA CHE T'ARRIDE

*Verdi*

63.

## THE IRISH IMMIGRANT

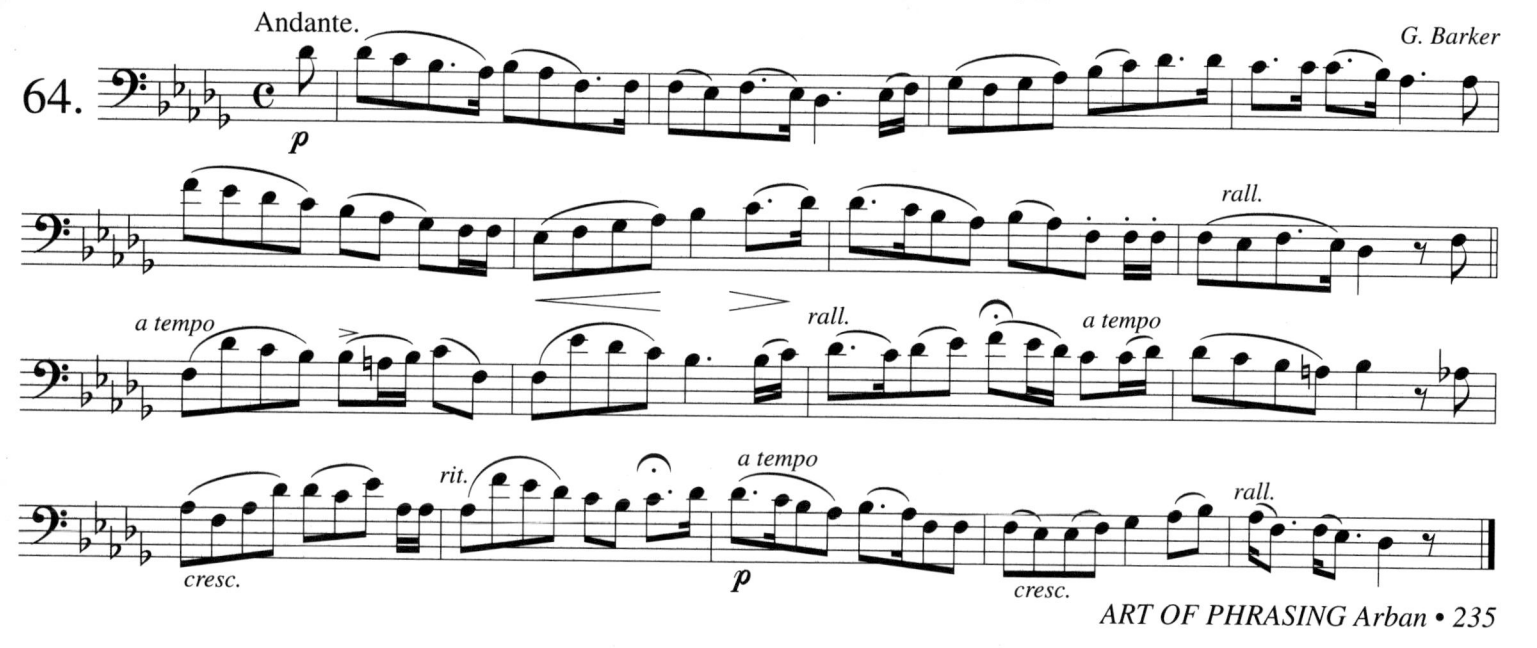

*G. Barker*

64.

ART OF PHRASING Arban • 235

# DON JUAN
*Mozart*

**65.** Andante

# CAN I BE DREAMING?
*from "The Talisman"*

*Balfe*

**66.** Larghetto.

*p dolce*

# LE DESIR
*Beethoven*

**67.** Moderato

## ANDANTE FROM A MAJOR SYMPHONY

*Mendelssohn*

68.

## AL BEN DE' TUOI QUAL VITTIMA

69.

# FUNERAL MARCH

Chopin

**70.** Lento

# ANNA BOLENA

Donizetti

**71.** Moderato

# ANNA BOLENA

Donizetti

**72.** Cantabile

## ARIETTE
*Weber*

73. Andante con moto

## SONG OF THE MER MAIDS
*Weber*

74. Andante con moto
*dolce*

*rall.*

## L'AMOR FUNESTO
*Donizetti*

**75.** Andante — *p espressivo* — *dolce* — *accel. avec chaleur.* — *p* — *cresc.* — *dolce* — *rall.*

## ROMEO
*Bellini*

**76.** Moderato — *f* — *rit.* — *a tempo*

## ROMEO
*Bellini*

**77.** Andante — *f dim.*

240 • Arban ART OF PHRASING

## FREISCHÜTZ

Weber

78. Adagio

## ADIEU

Schubert

79. Andante

*con espressione*

ART OF PHRASING Arban • 241

# EULOGY OF TEARS

*Schubert*

80. Andante

# ANNA BOLENA

*Donizetti*

81. Larghetto

# SERENADE

*Schubert*

82. Moderato

242 • Arban ART OF PHRASING

## ERNANI
*Verdi*

83. Moderato

## ERNANI
*Verdi*

84. Andante

ART OF PHRASING Arban • 243

# "L'ADIEU"

**85.** Andantino

# ORANGE AND BLUE JIG

**86.** Allegro

# LANCASHIRE CLOG DANCE

**87.**

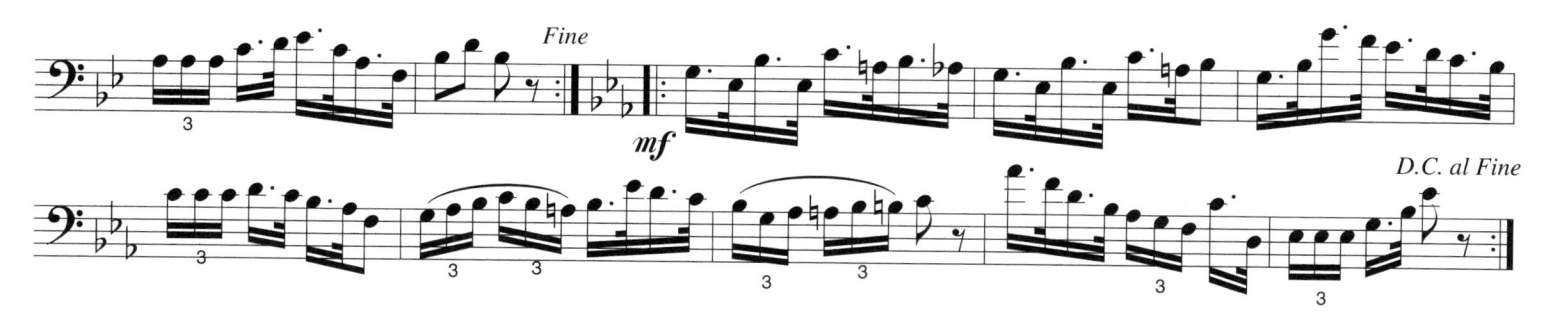

## "L'AMOUR"

88.

## TRAVIATA

89. *Verdi*

# TRAVIATA

*Verdi*

**90.** Allegro brillante

# RIGOLETTO

*Verdi*

**91.** Allegretto

# RIGOLETTO

*Verdi*

**92.** Allegro

246 • Arban ART OF PHRASING

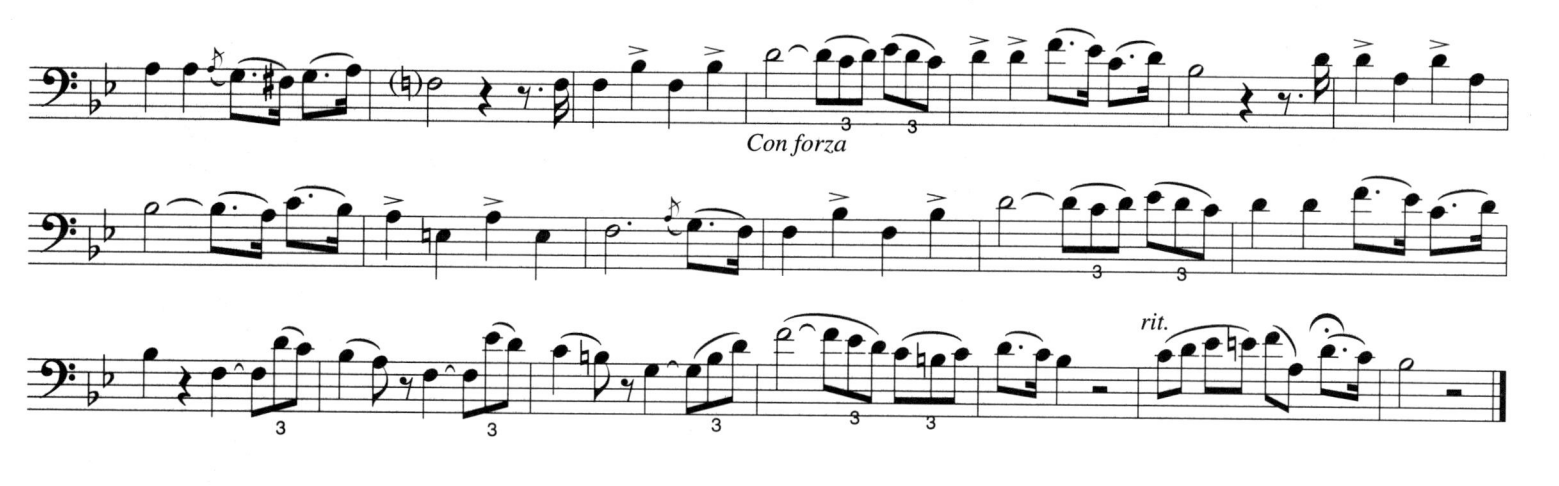

## IL TROVATORE

93. Largo — Verdi

# IL TROVATORE

Verdi

94. Andante

# IL TROVATORE

Verdi

95. Allegro

# IL TROVATORE

Verdi

96. Adagio
*p con espress.*

# IL TROVATORE

*Verdi*

97.

# IL TROVATORE
Verdi

98. Allegretto.

# IL TROVATORE
Verdi

99. Allegro brillante

## IL TROVATORE

*Verdi.*

100.

## O SALUTARIS

**Mozart**

101.

## "MACBETH"

*Verdi.*

102.

*ART OF PHRASING Arban • 251*

# LE PORTE ETENDARD

*Lindpaintner*

103.

# SERENADE

*Grètry*

104.

# THE TEAR

*Kücken*

105.

## MELODY
*Mendelssohn*

106. Andantino

## LA PARISINA
*Donizetti*

107. Andante

# NORMA

*Bellini*

**108.** Allegro moderato

# DAUGHTER OF THE REGIMENT

*Donizetti*

**109.** Andante con moto

# NEAPOLITAN SONG

**110.** Andante animato

## LA SOMNAMBULA

111. Andante — Bellini

## CAPULETTI

112. Allegro maestoso — Bellini

# DOPO DUE LUSTRI

*Mercadante*

**113.**

# IL CROCIATO

*Meyerbeer*

**114.**

# EURYANTHE

*Weber*

**115.**

# ABSENCE

*Beethoven*

**116.**

## THE CAPTIVE
*Kuchen*

117. Lento Con dolore

## OTELLO
*Rossini*

118. Moderato

# SEMIRAMIDE

Rossini.

**119.** Allegro

# L'ELISIRE D'AMORE

Donizetti.

**120.** Andante

# FREISCHUTZ

**121.** Allegro moderato — Weber.

# IL TROVATORE

**122.** Allegro — Verdi.

# THE MAGIC FLUTE
*Mozart*

**123.** Allegretto

# NIOBÉ
*Pacini*

**124.** Allegretto

# SWISS SONG

**125.** Moderato

# DON JUAN

**126.** Andante — Mozart — Fine — D.C. al Fine

# AUSTRIAN HYMN

**127.** Maestoso

# LA SOMNAMBULE

**128.** Allegro — Bellini

*ART OF PHRASING Arban • 261*

## LA PARISINA ROMANZA

*Donizetti*

**129.** Moderato

## LA SOMNAMBULE

*Bellini*

**130.** Allegro moderato

## J'AIMERAI TOUTE MA VIE

*Dalairac*

**131.** Andantino

## NEAPOLITAN SONG

132. Allegretto

## ANDANTE FROM "A MAJOR" SYMPHONY

*Mendelssohn*

133. Adagio

# THE ALPINE HORN

134.

## TRAVIATA

135.

# IN MIA MAN ALFIN TU SEI

**136.** Andante

# IL RIVAL SALVAR TU DEI

**137.** Lento

# THOU ART SO NEAR, AND YET SO FAR

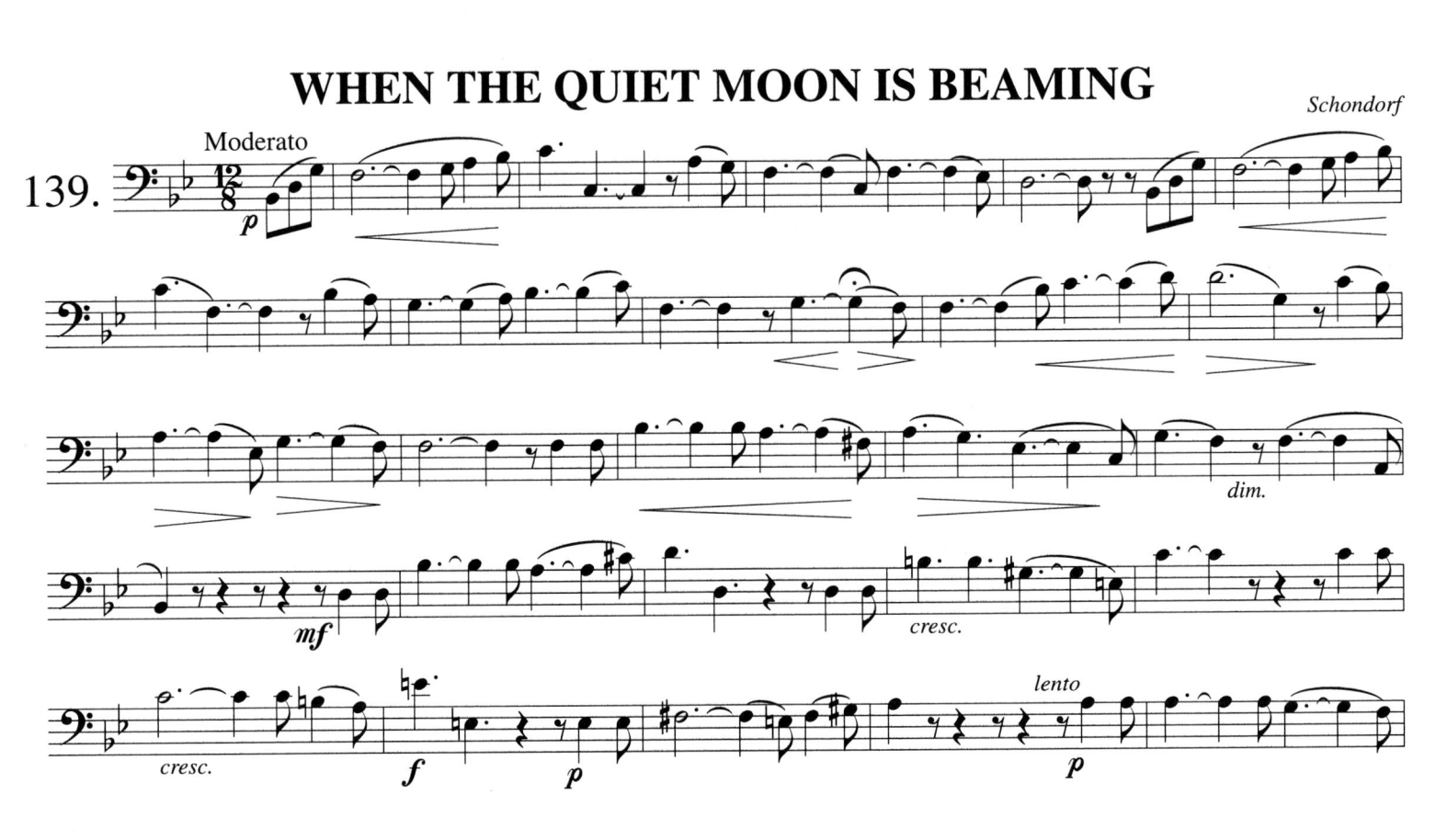

*Reichardt*

138.

## CAVATINA FROM "THE HUGUENOTS"

# BESSONIAN POLKA

141.

# STARS OF PARIS POLKA

142.

# CAVATINA FROM "ERNANI"

Verdi

# THE PILGRIM OF LOVE

144.

# "DEAR LITTLE HEART"

# KEEL ROW

# HOME SWEET HOME

ART OF PHRASING Arban • 275

# BLUE BELLS OF SCOTLAND

148.

ART OF PHRASING Arban • 277

# YANKEE DOODLE

# AMERICA

Var. 3 Vivace

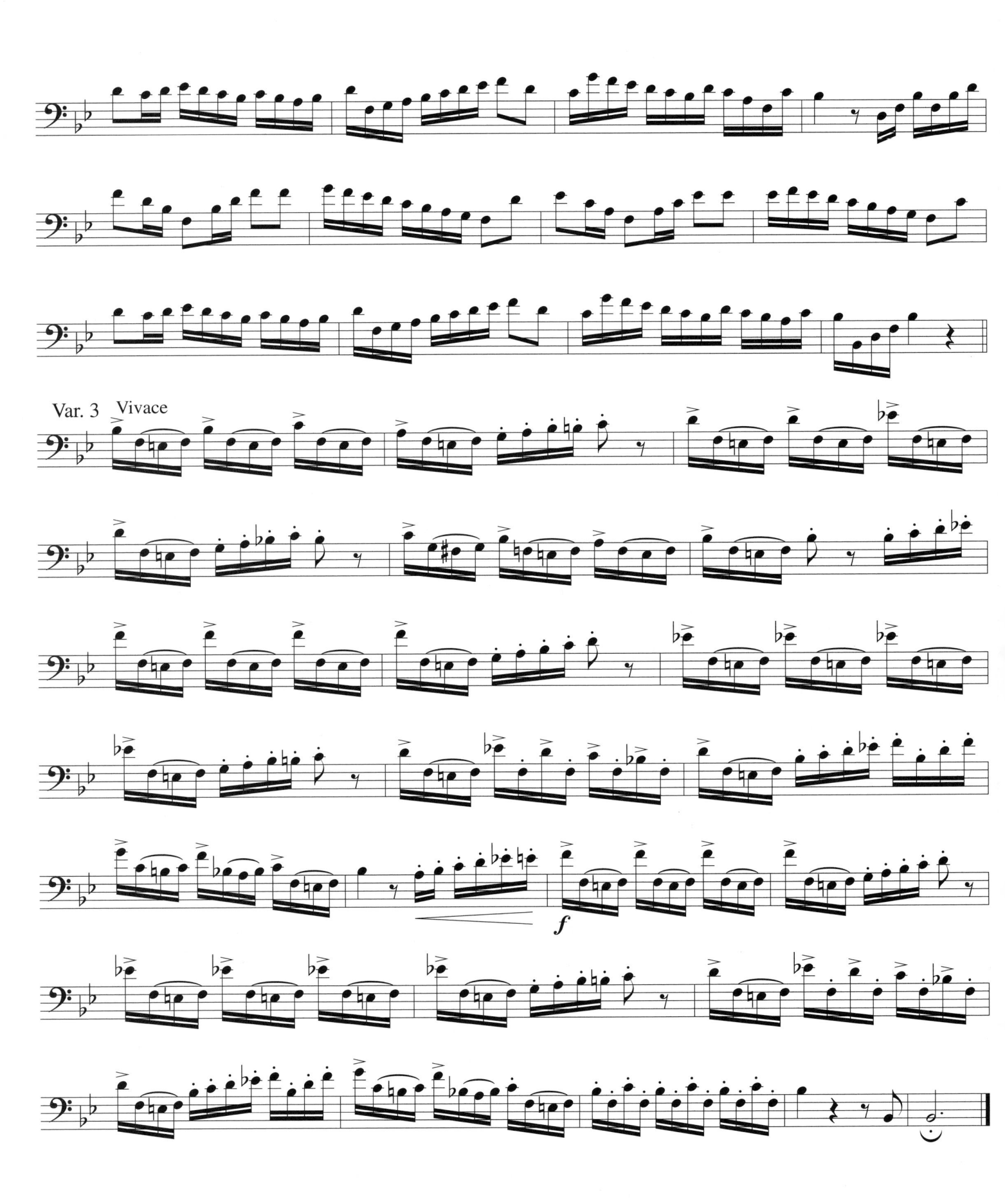

# 68 DUETS

## Dr. Bowman

This section presents an excellent opportunity to learn some basics of chamber music playing. While these duets are not overly challenging technically, they provide a great opportunity for developing rhythmic precision, intonation and tone quality blending.

## Mr. Alessi

This collection of duets is perfect for the study of intonation and harmony. Try recording one voice, then playing it back so that you will be able to play duets with yourself. A very useful method of study!

## SACRED SONG
*Portniansky*

## RUSSIAN HYMN

# CRADLE SONG

C.M. v. Weber

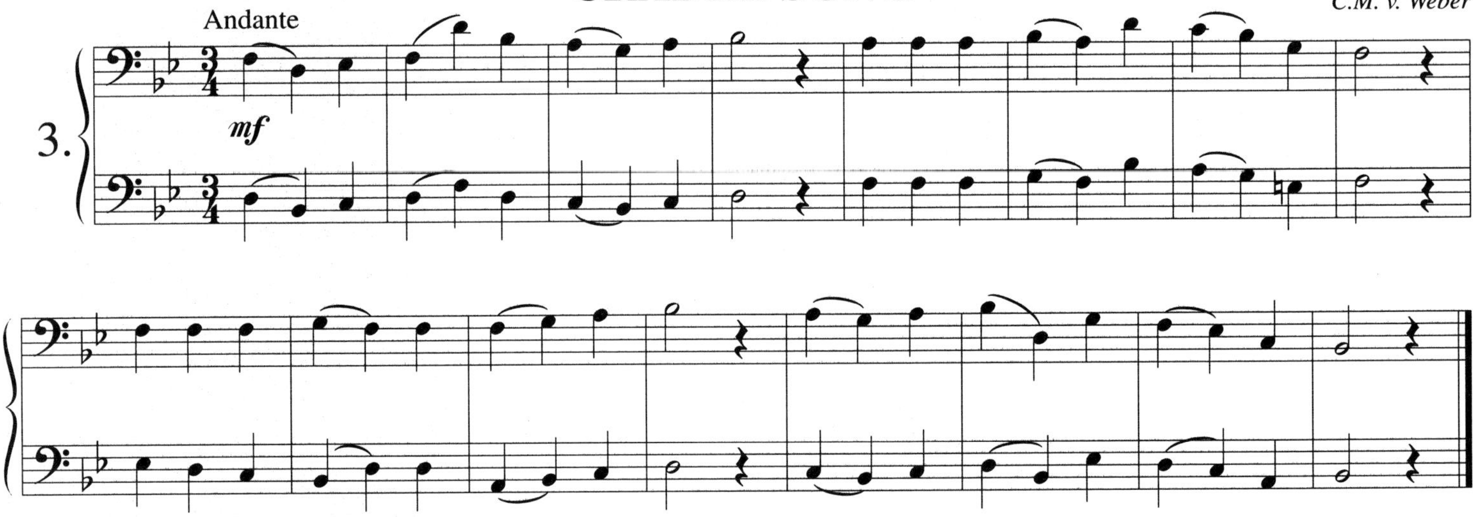


# MELODY

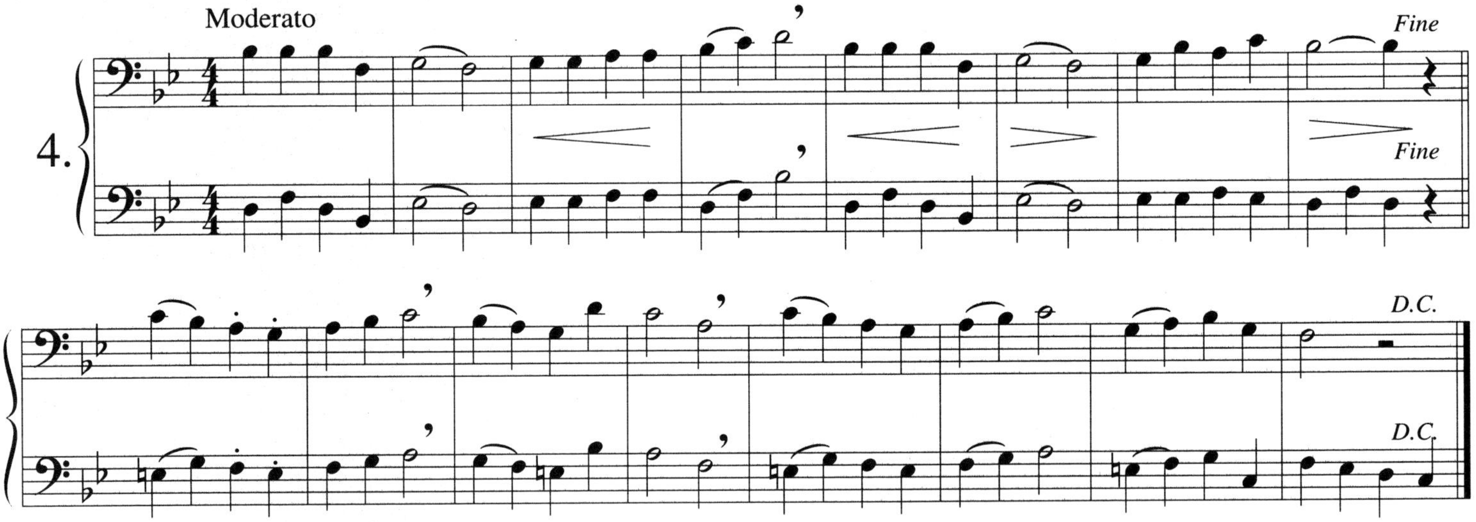


# MELODY

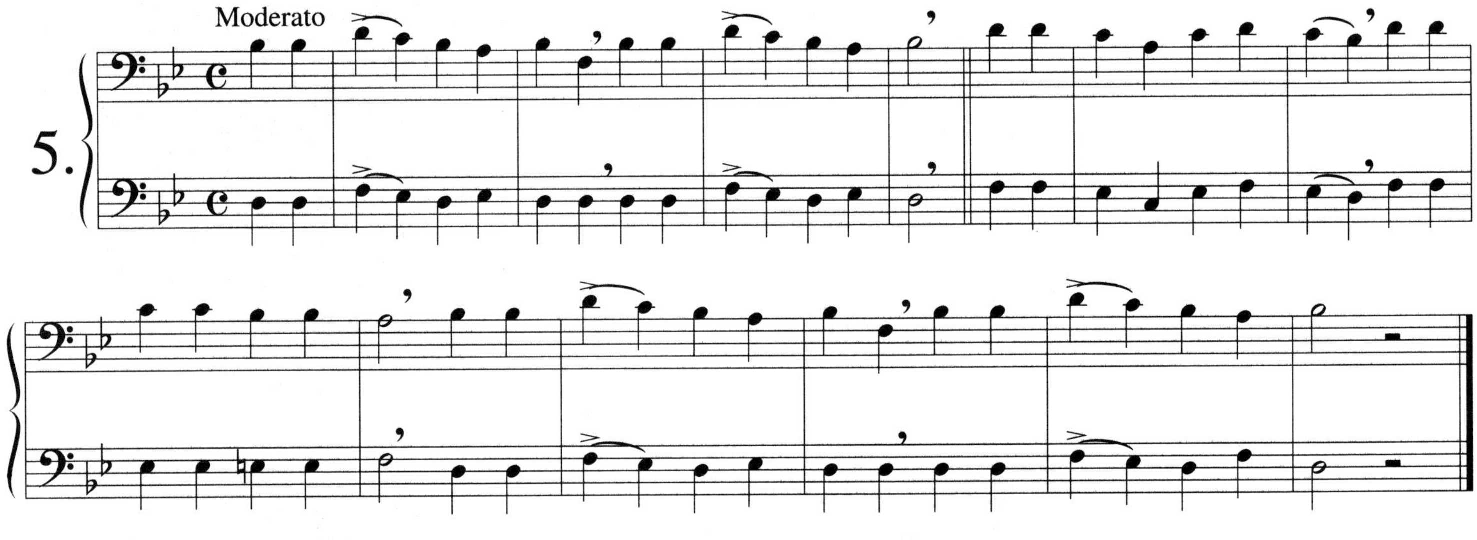

# MELODY

*Saverio*

## ADESTE FIDELES

# AMERICA

# AIR BY MOZART

# AIR BY GRETRY

## NOEL ANCIEN

## AIR BY BEETHOVEN

## ARABIAN SONG

## SERENADE

*Gretry*

286 • Arban DUETS

## LA ROMANESCA

## ROMANCE FROM "JOSEPH"

Mehul

## ROMANCE

De Gouy

288 • Arban DUETS

# NOEL ANCIEN

**18.** Allegretto

# MARCH

**19.** Con energia

*De Gouy*

## SONG OF MASTER ADAM

## LE SOUVENIR

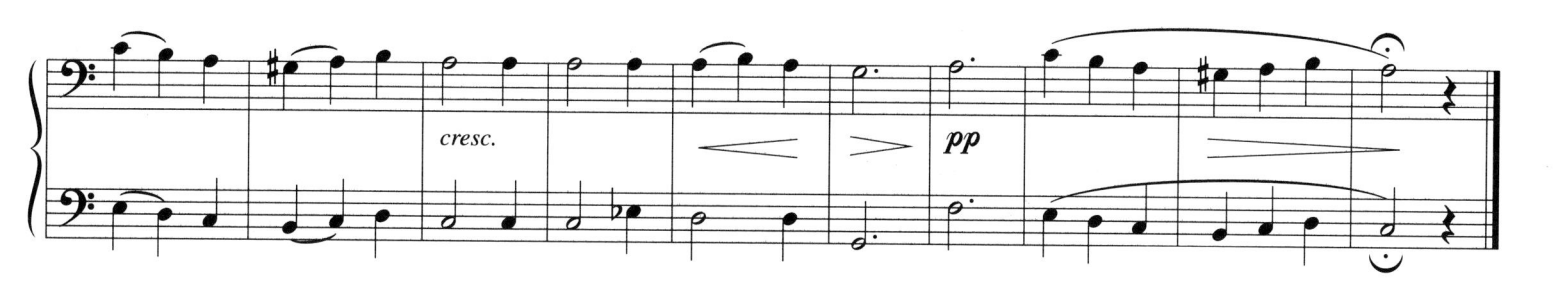

## RICHARD OF THE LION HEART

*Gretry*

22.

## THE TWO SAVOYARDS

23.

## SILENT SORROW
Webbe

**24.** Andante

## MELODY

**25.** Allegro Moderato

## THE LION HUNT

*Allegretto*                                           *Saverio*

26.

## ELESIRE D'AMORE

*Lento*                                               *Donizetti*

27.

## I WOULD THAT MY LOVE

*Mendelssohn*

28.

## PRAYER TO THE VIRGIN

*Saverio*

29.

294 • Arban DUETS

## SPANISH ROYAL MARCH

30.

# MARCH OF TWO MISERS

**31.** Moderato

# MELODY

**32.** Allegro moderato

## COUNTRY WEDDING

**33.** Allegro vivo

DUETS Arban • 297

# BIVOUAC SONG

# BIRTHDAY FESTIVAL

# MELODY

# GERMAN SONG

*Kücken*

# RICHARD OF THE LION HEART

*Gretry*

## MARCH

*De Gouy*

**39.** Allegro moderato

# TIC E TIC E TOC

40.

# CARNIVAL OF VENICE

41.

# NEL COR PIU

*Pæsiello*

42.

## BOLERO

De Guoy

43.

302 • Arban DUETS

## NORMA

Bellini

## MELODY

## LAST ROSE OF SUMMER

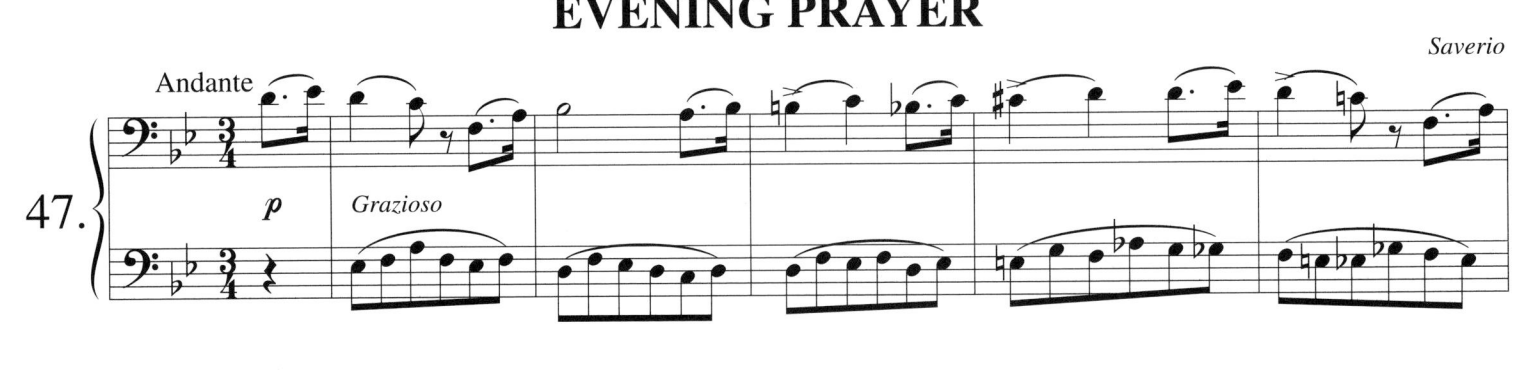

## EVENING PRAYER

*Saverio*

## CAVATINA FROM "SOMNAMBULA"

Bellini

48. Andante moderato

# AUSTRIAN NATIONAL HYMN

*Haydn*

**49.**

# "FREISCHUTZ"

*Weber*

**50.**

# FRENCH AIR

**51.** Allegretto

# BURNING FEVER

*Gretry*

**52.** Andante assai

## ELESIRE D'AMORE

Donizetti

# AIR FROM "SOMNAMBULA"

Bellini

# WIND AND WAVE

## TYROLIENNE

**56.** Moderato

## ITALIAN AIR

**57.** Andante

310 • Arban DUETS

## ALPINE HORN

Proch

# THE HERMIT

Lambert

Allegro poco Andante

59.

# FREISCHÜTZ

# WALTZ: "FLOWER OF DAMASCUS"

*Saverio*

# WALTZ FROM "PURITANI"

Bellini

# PRAYER FROM "MOSES"

*Rossini*

63.

# SIÉGE OF ROCHELLE

Balfe

# HAIL! STAR OF MARY

Proch

# THE TWO FRIENDS

# MARTHA

*Flotow*

# THE FOX HUNTERS

# FOURTEEN CHARACTERISTIC STUDIES

### Dr. Bowman

These fourteen etudes represent the culmination of study in the Arban book. They have become standard material for testing musician's abilities and have been required in auditions for high school all-state band, solo competitions and the professional military bands. The mastery of these etudes is a requirement for the complete preparation of the euphonium player. Each of these etudes has been carefully edited and marked with tempi and dynamics. Breath marks have been added—although these may have to be altered depending upon the player's ability.

### Mr. Alessi

These wonderful etudes are some of my favorites of all time. It is time to put to the test all of the technique that you have studied up to this point. Here are a few points to keep in mind:

- Play these etudes at a comfortable tempo—not at a frantic pace.

- If necessary, take time for breathing, although work on taking breaths without destroying the tempo. To accomplish this, practice taking the auxiliary breath in the middle of the phrase. This type of breath is not a full one, but a small sip of air to support you to the end of the phrase or to a natural breathing point.

- Make good use of alternate positions.

- Make a recording of etude #2. The goal is to play back the recording at half-speed to check your legato and slide technique. There are several recording devices available with this function. When listening to the playback, you should sound ideally like a fantastic tuba player with a great command of the airstream.

I have made notations for suggested alternate positions in these etudes. These suggestions will suit the player who mainly uses natural slurs—as opposed to players who use the legato tongue exclusively.

When there are repeated phrases within each etude, one should also apply the pattern of these alternate positions to the repeated phrase. There are several situations where the fourth position D is used consistently—especially when D is surrounded by C and E♭. Be certain that this fourth position D is a slightly elongated fourth position, and F in fourth position is a slightly shortened fourth position. The fifth position B♭, the fifth position D♭ and the sixth position F are used frequently when playing in keys with five flats or more. This facilitates passages in the key of D♭ and G♭. The use of the F attachment in an elongated third position when playing low B♭ is also a helpful aid in these awkward keys.

My recommendation is to omit etudes 13 and 14 as they are primarily designed for the euphonium player, therefore, alternate positions are not noted for these exercises.

**Allegro moderato**

1.

324 • Arban CHARACTERISTIC STUDIES

2. Legato

**3.** Moderato

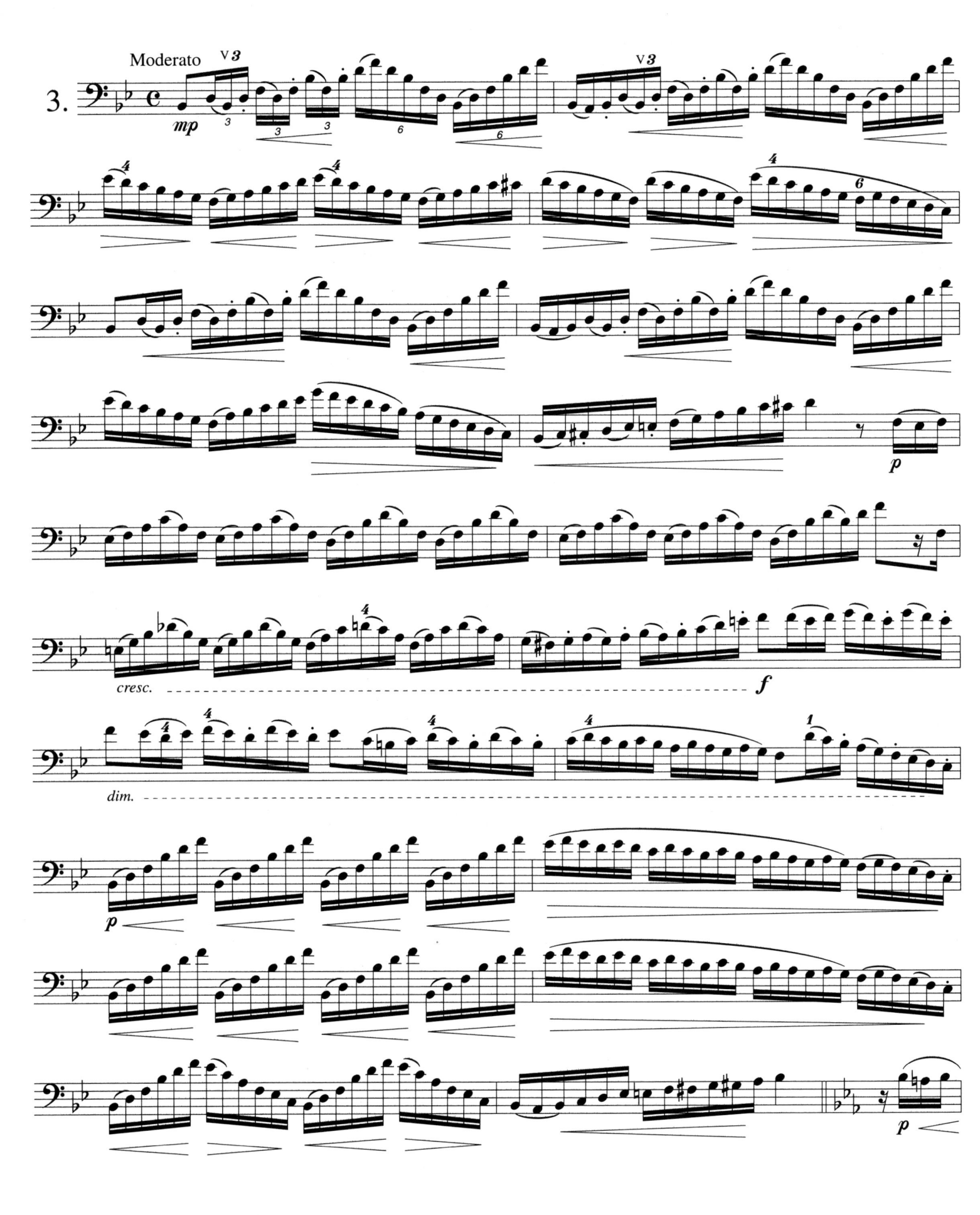

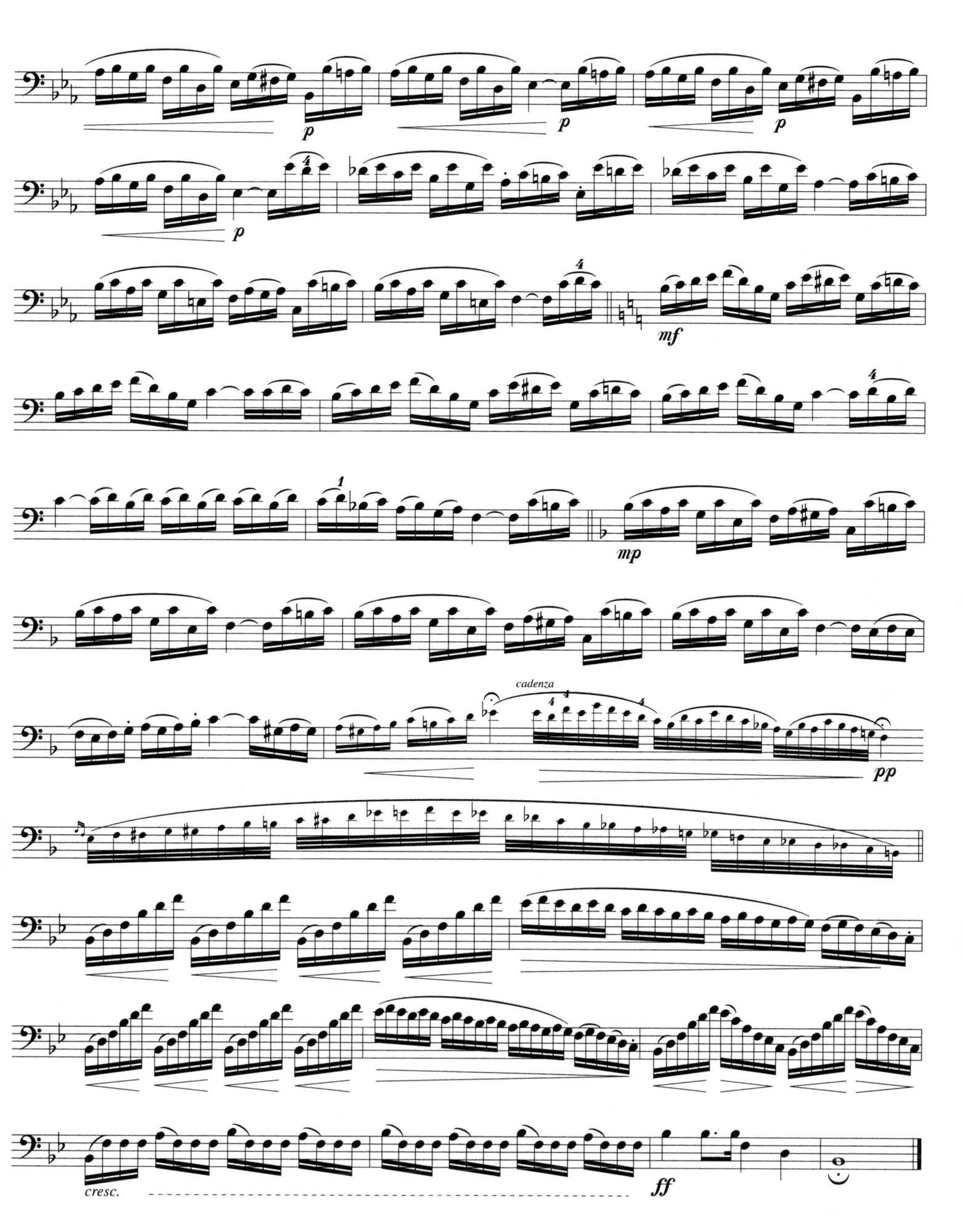

CHARACTERISTIC STUDIES Arban • 327

4.

CHARACTERISTIC STUDIES Arban • 329

# 5.

*Allegro*

**6.**

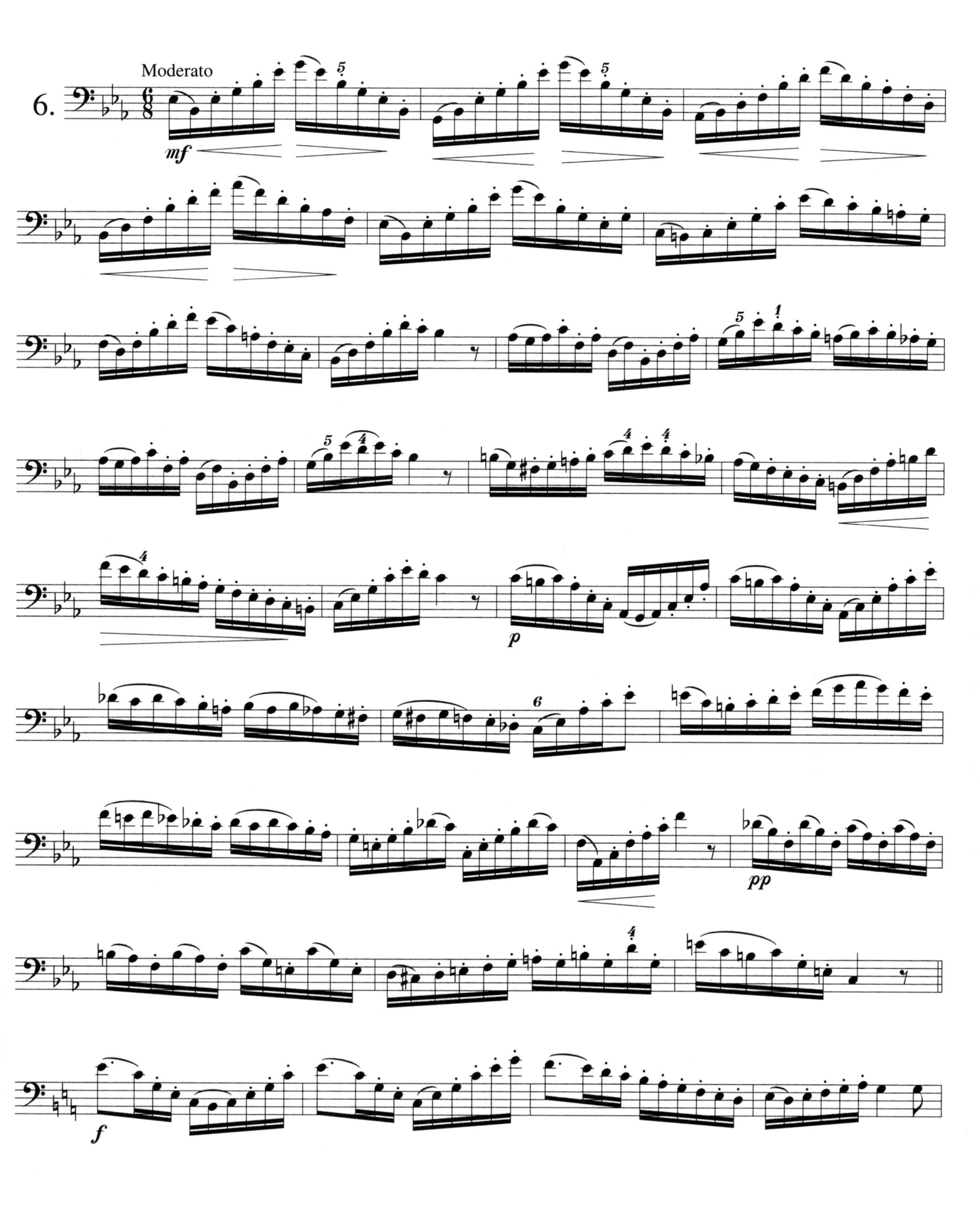

332 • Arban CHARACTERISTIC STUDIES

CHARACTERISTIC STUDIES Arban • 333

Allegro moderato
8.
mp
simile
p
tr
cresc.
f
p cantabile
a tempo
mf

CHARACTERISTIC STUDIES Arban

# 9. Allegro

CHARACTERISTIC STUDIES Arban

338 • Arban CHARACTERISTIC STUDIES

CHARACTERISTIC STUDIES Arban • 339

340 • Arban CHARACTERISTIC STUDIES

CHARACTERISTIC STUDIES Arban • 341

## 12.

**Allegro moderato**

CHARACTERISTIC STUDIES Arban

13. Allegro moderato

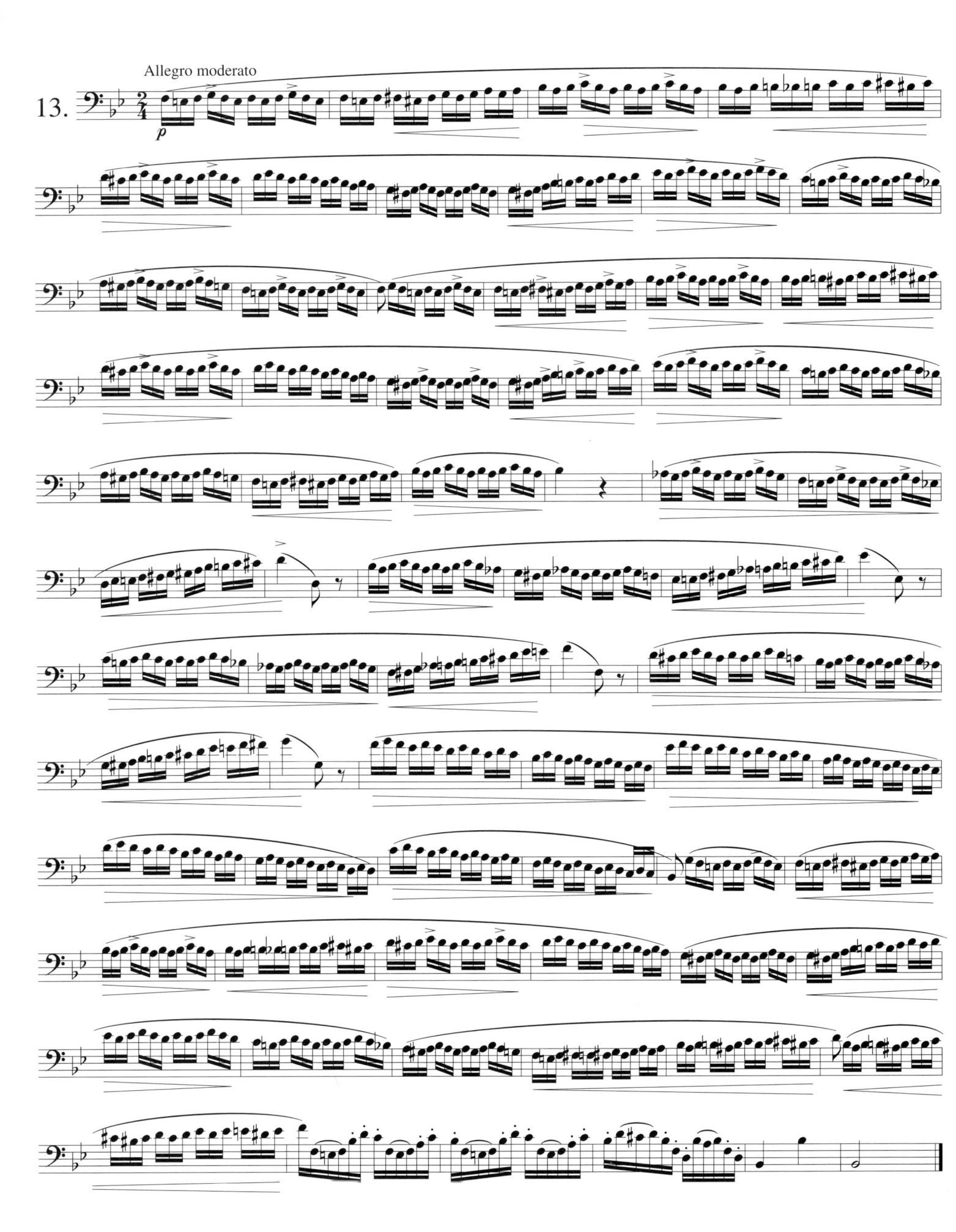

## 14. Legato chromatique

*CHARACTERISTIC STUDIES Arban • 345*

346 • Arban CHARACTERISTIC STUDIES

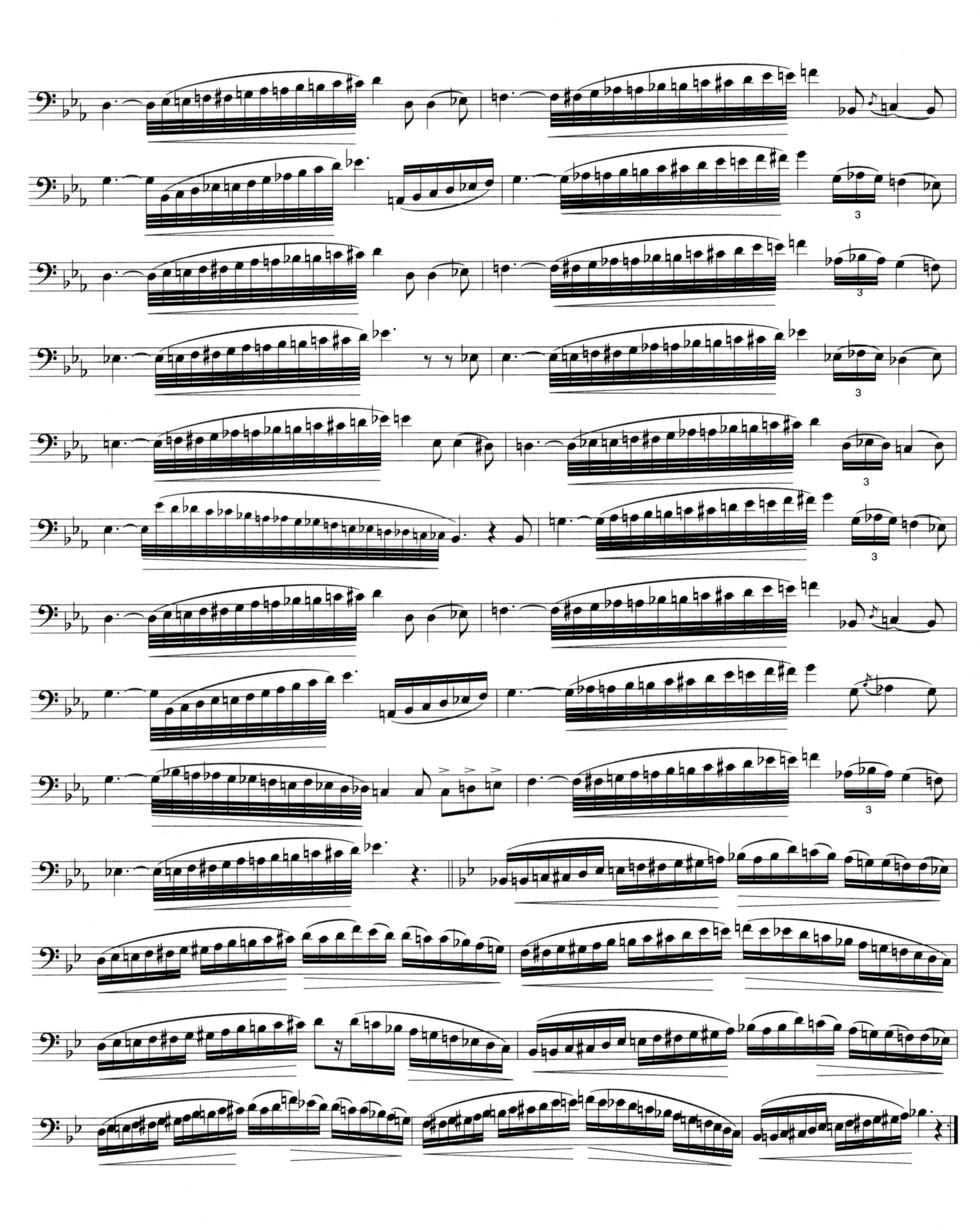

# No. 1
# Fantasie and Variations
## on a Cavatina
### from *Beatrice di Tenda* by V. Bellini

J.B. Arban

**Introduction**
**Andante** ♩= 76

**Theme** ♩= 88

348 • Arban SOLOS

**Var.III and Finale I** ♩= 112
*Triple tonguing*

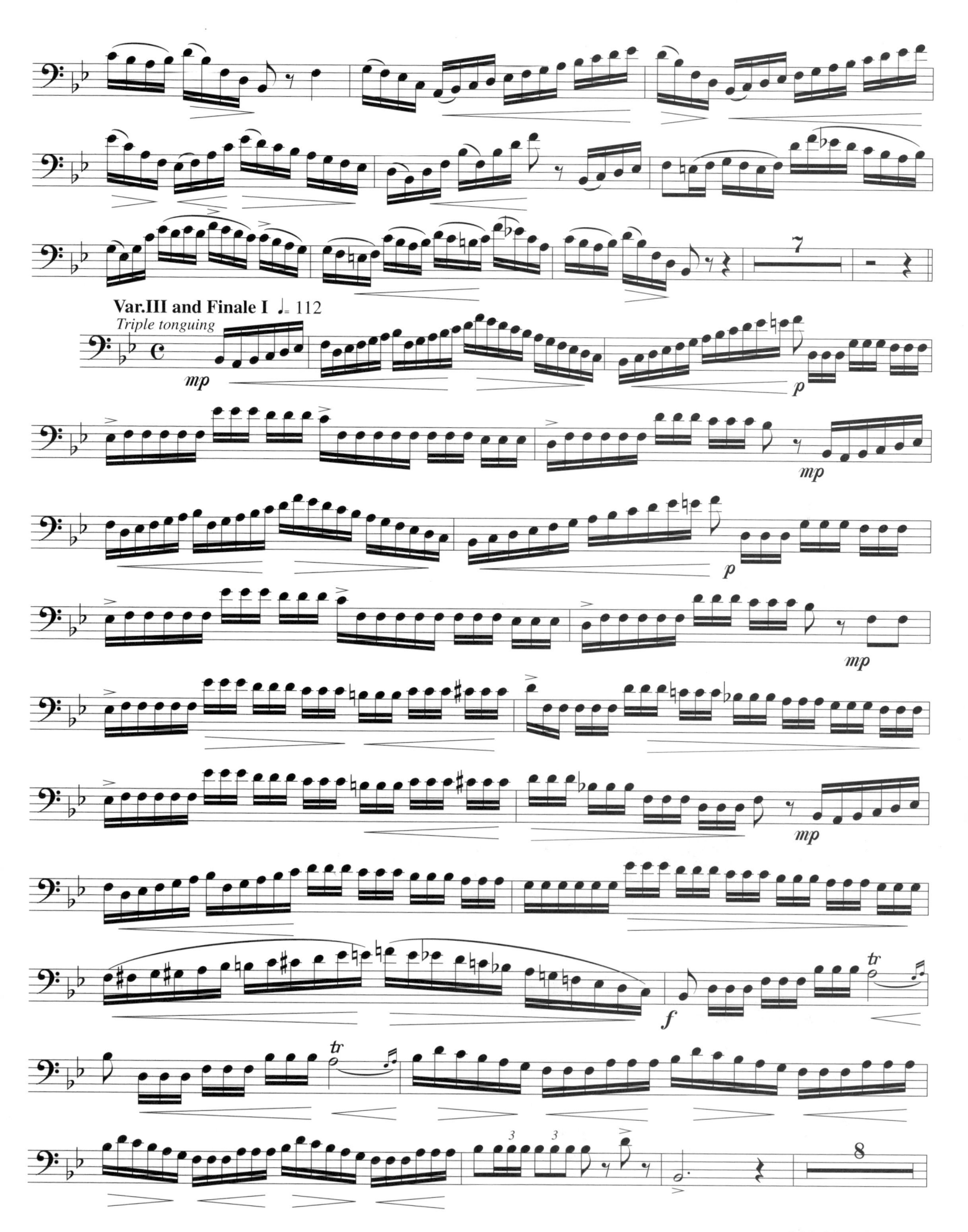

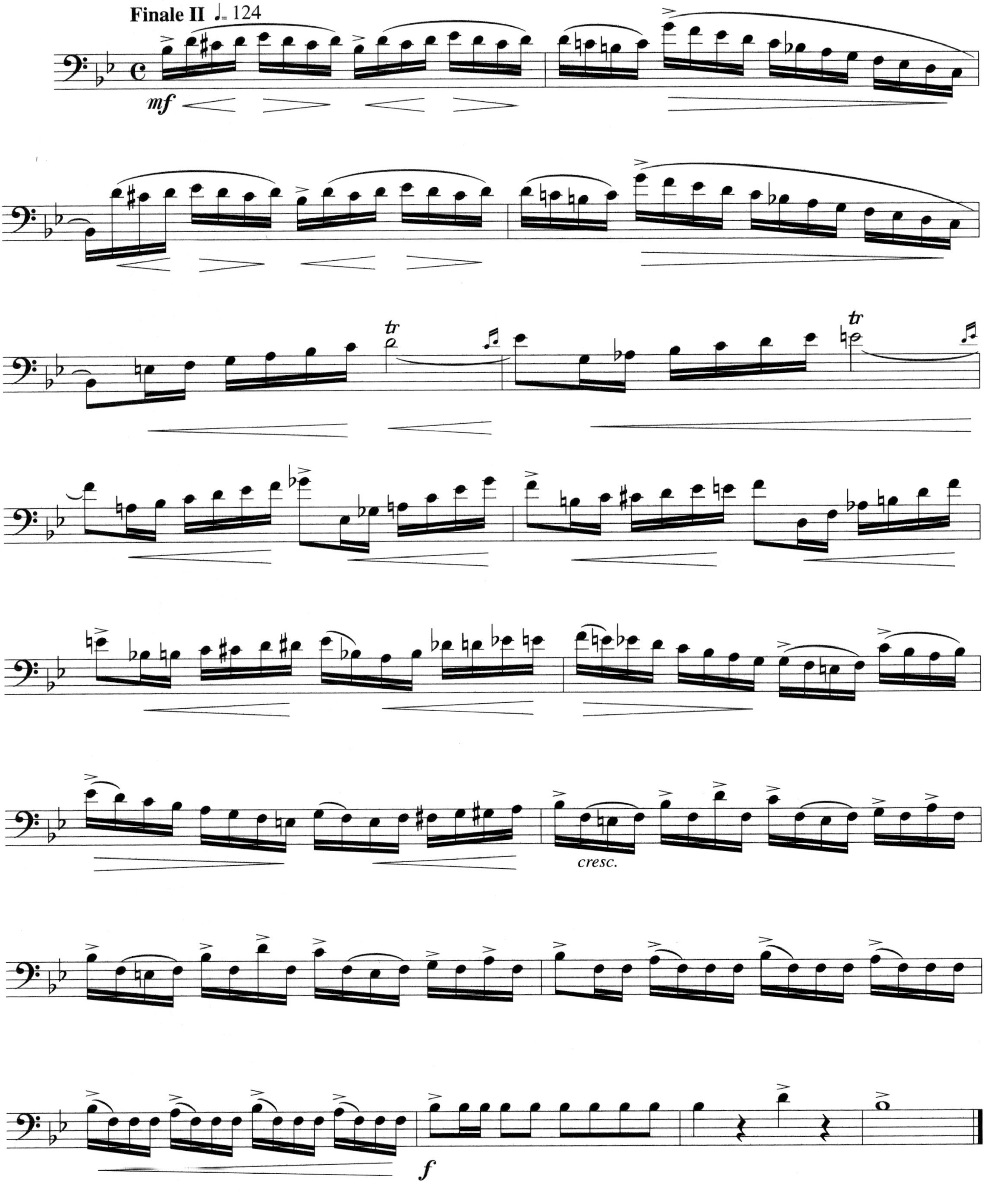
Finale II ♩= 124
mf
tr
tr
cresc.
f

# No. 2
# Fantasie and Variations
## on
## *Acteon*

**Introduction**
**Andante**

*J.B. Arban*

Theme
Allegretto
p
tr
più lento
a tempo
f
veloce
a tempo
p
ad. lib.
16
Var.I
Vivace
p
più lento
mf
a tempo
p
cresc.
f
f
rall.
Tempo I
mp

16
Piu moderato
mf
a tempo
3
rall.
tu ku tu tu ku
tu ku tu tu ku
tr
mf
ad. lib.
rall.
tu ku tu tu ku
Allegro
16

354 • Arban SOLOS

# No. 3
# Fantasie Brillante

*J.B. Arban*

**Introduction**
**Allegro maestoso**

356 • Arban SOLOS

*(Double tonguing may be used ad lib.)*      *ad lib.*

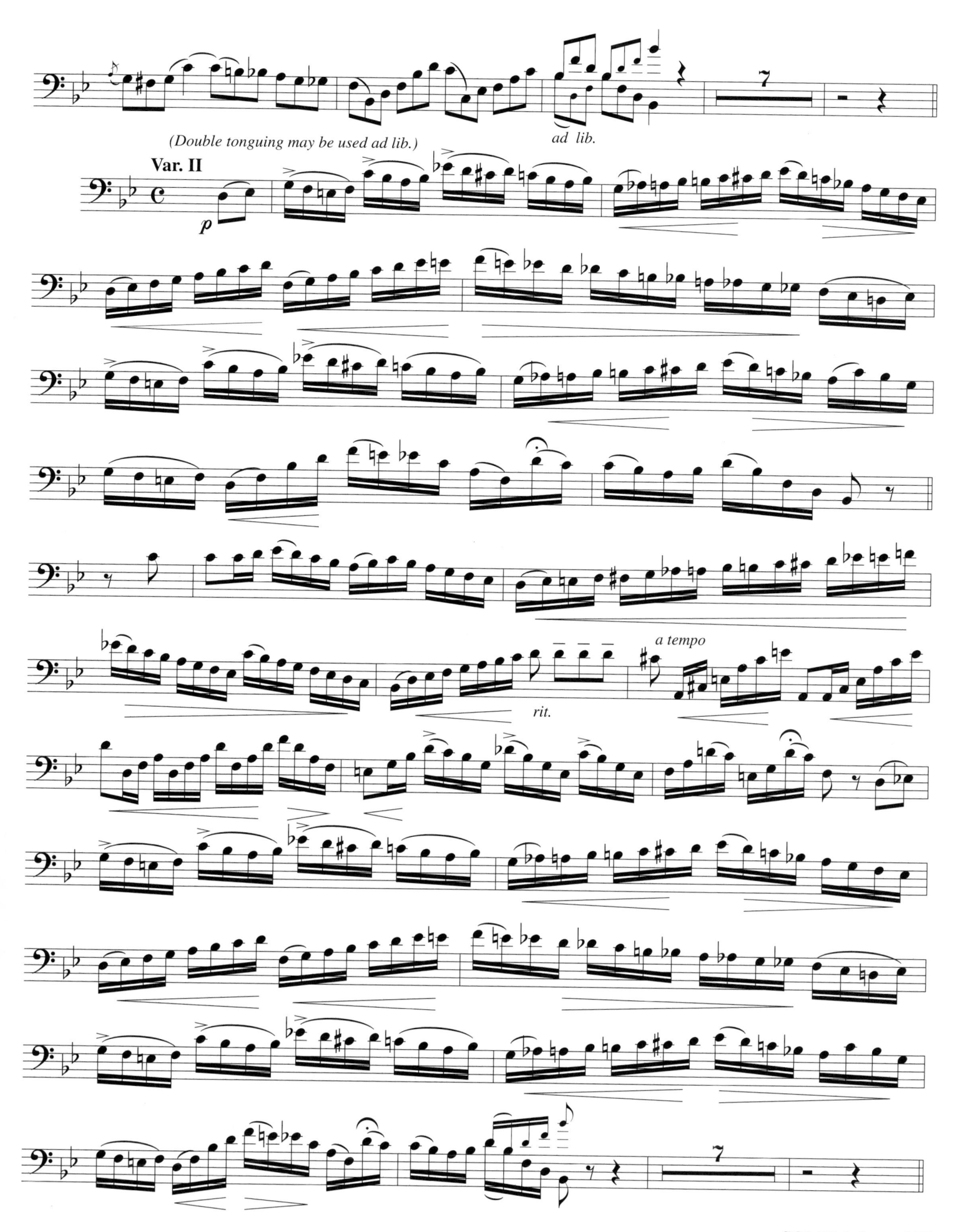

**Var. II**

*p*

*a tempo*

*rit.*

SOLOS Arban • 357

358 • Arban SOLOS

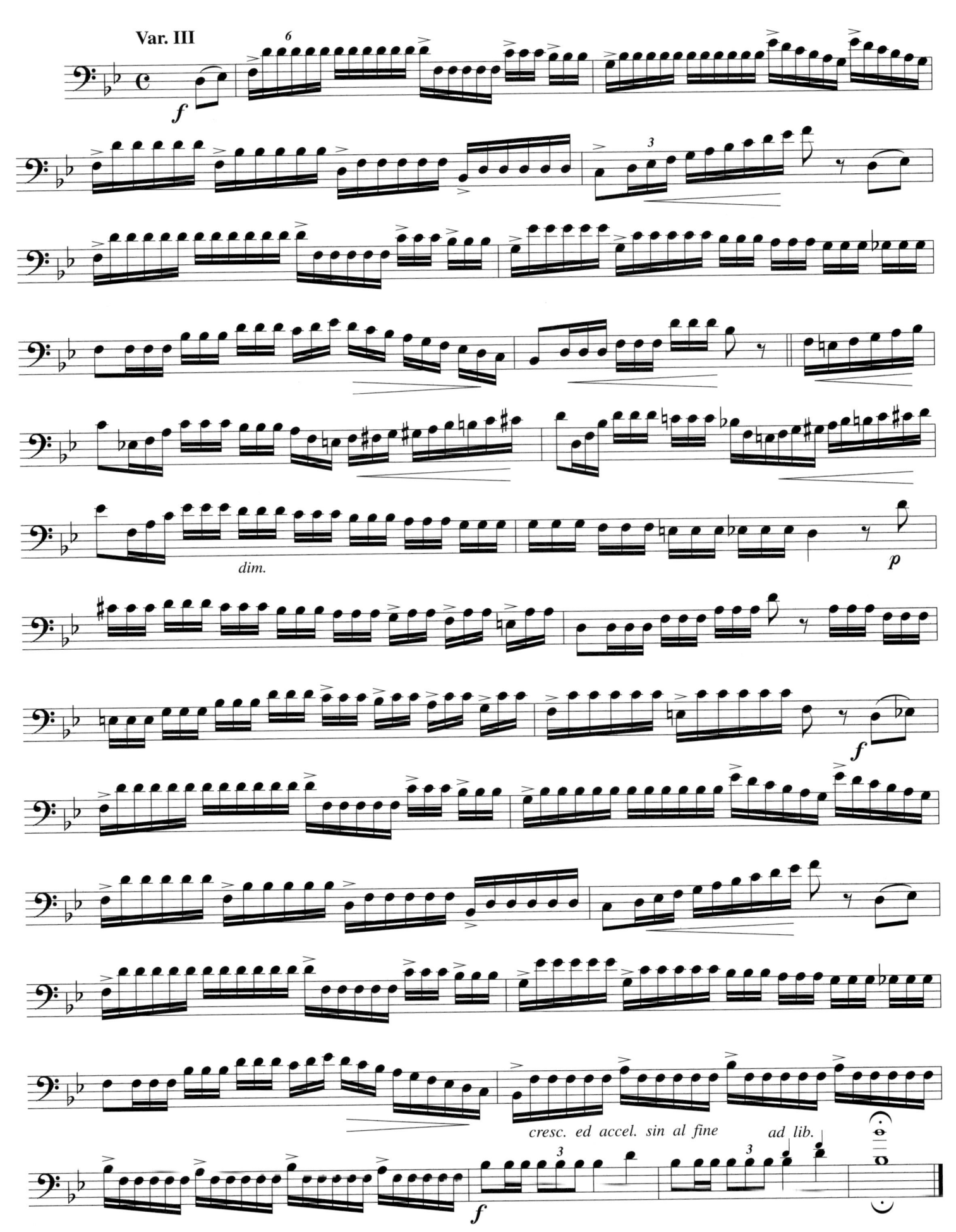

# No. 4
# Variations
## on a
## *Tyrolienne*

*J.B. Arban*

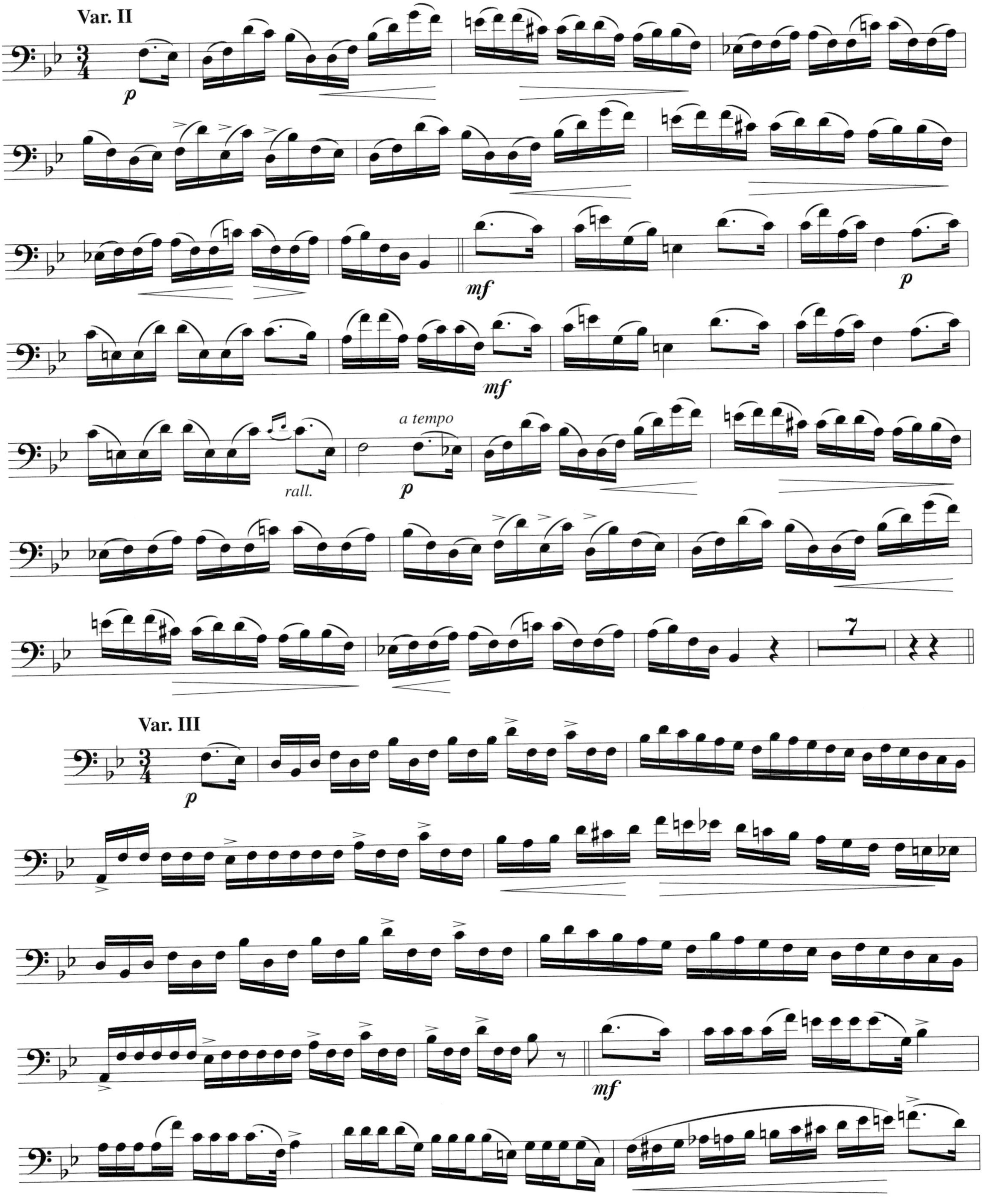
Var. II
p
mf
p
mf
a tempo
rall.
p
7
Var. III
p
mf

SOLOS Arban • 361

Rondo
Allegro
p
mf
For speed brilliant effect, use double tonguing
mf
p
mf
pp
f

# No. 5
## Variations
on a song
*Voise-tu la neigre qui brille*
*(The Beautiful Snow)*

J.B. Arban

364 • Arban SOLOS

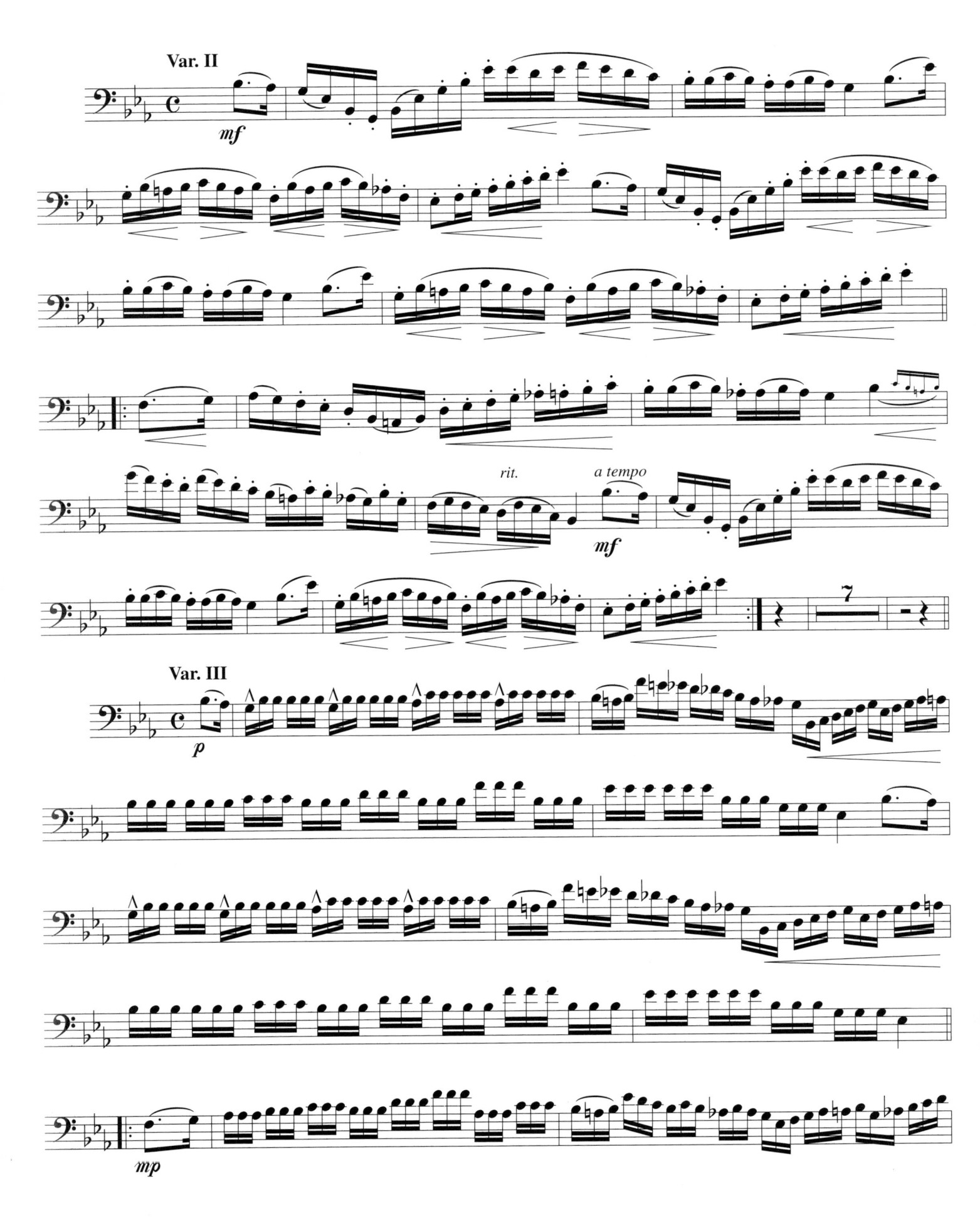

**Finale**
**Lento**

**Allegro** *(Use double tonguing ad lib.)*

# No. 6
## Cavatina and Variations

J.B. Arban

**Var. I**

*sempre stacc.*

**Var. II**

*a tempo*

**Var. III**

368 • Arban SOLOS

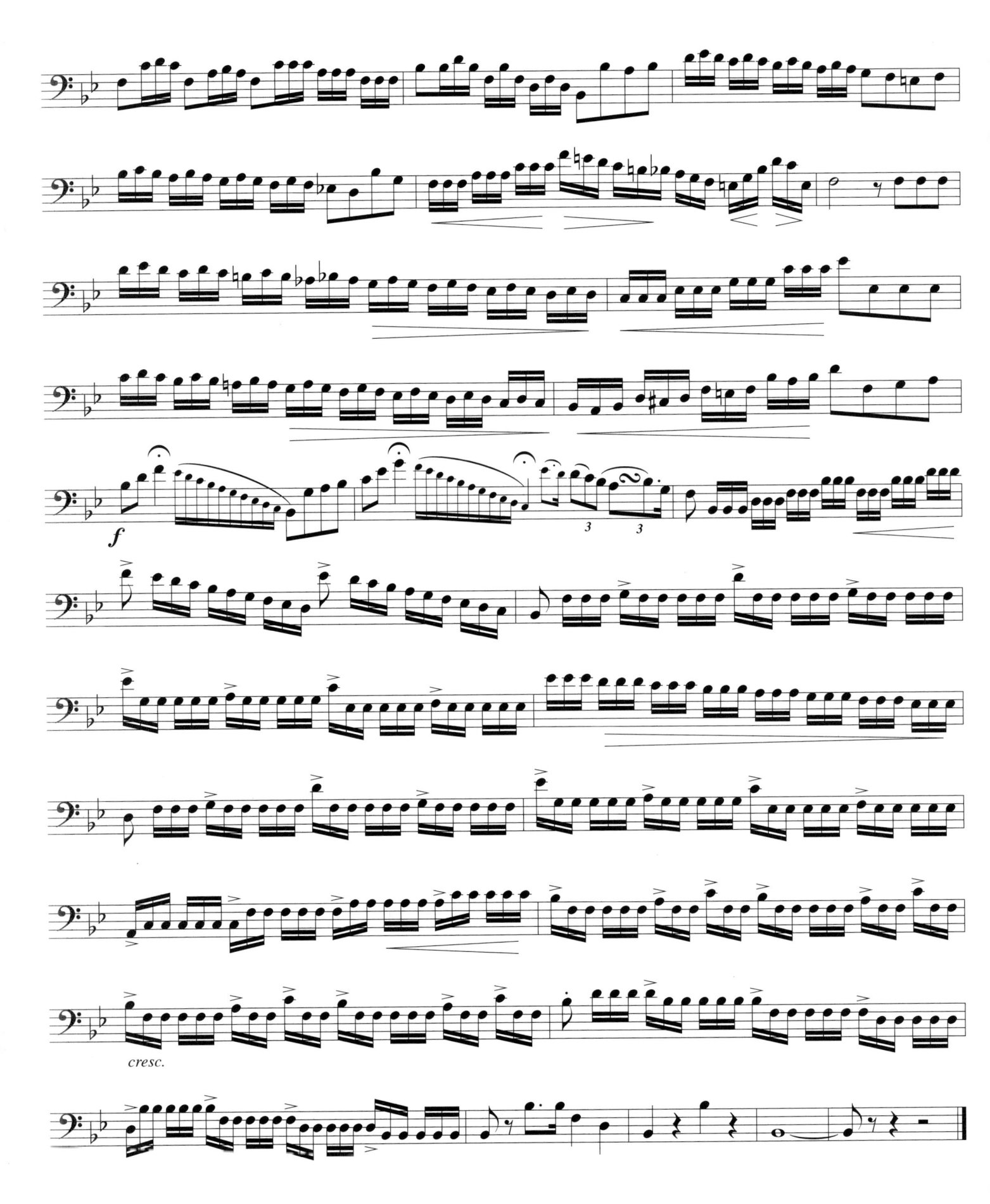

# No. 7
# Air Varie
## on a Folk Song
### *The Little Swiss Boy*

J.B. Arban

**Introduction Andante** ♩= 72

Theme
Andante (♪) =100
p
mf
rall.
a tempo
p
cresc.
a tempo
rall.
7
Var. I ♩= 50
ff
p
f
rall.
a tempo
p
rall.
a tempo
ff
p
f
a tempo
rall.
p
rall.
a tempo
f
p
ff
a tempo
p
f
rall.
p
rall.
a tempo
7

Var. II
mf
tu ku tu ku tu ku
p
tu ku tu ku tu ku
cresc.
(Triple tonguing)
7
Var. III
Adagio ♩= 52
p
mf
tr

**Var. IV et Finale**
Allegro ♩= 104

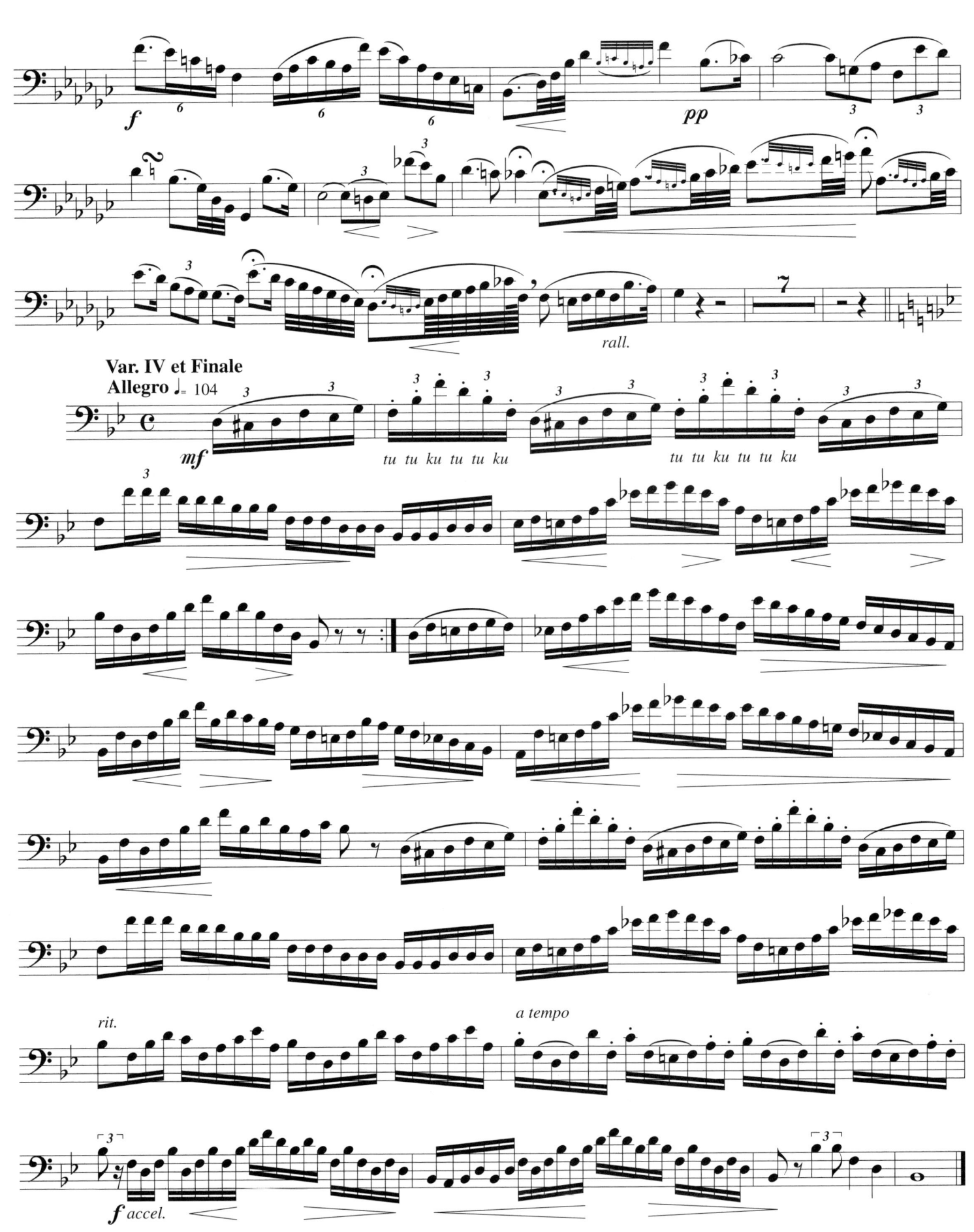

*tu tu ku tu tu ku    tu tu ku tu tu ku*

*rit.*    *a tempo*

*f accel.*

# No. 8
# Caprice and Variations

*J.B. Arban*

374 • Arban SOLOS

**Var. II**

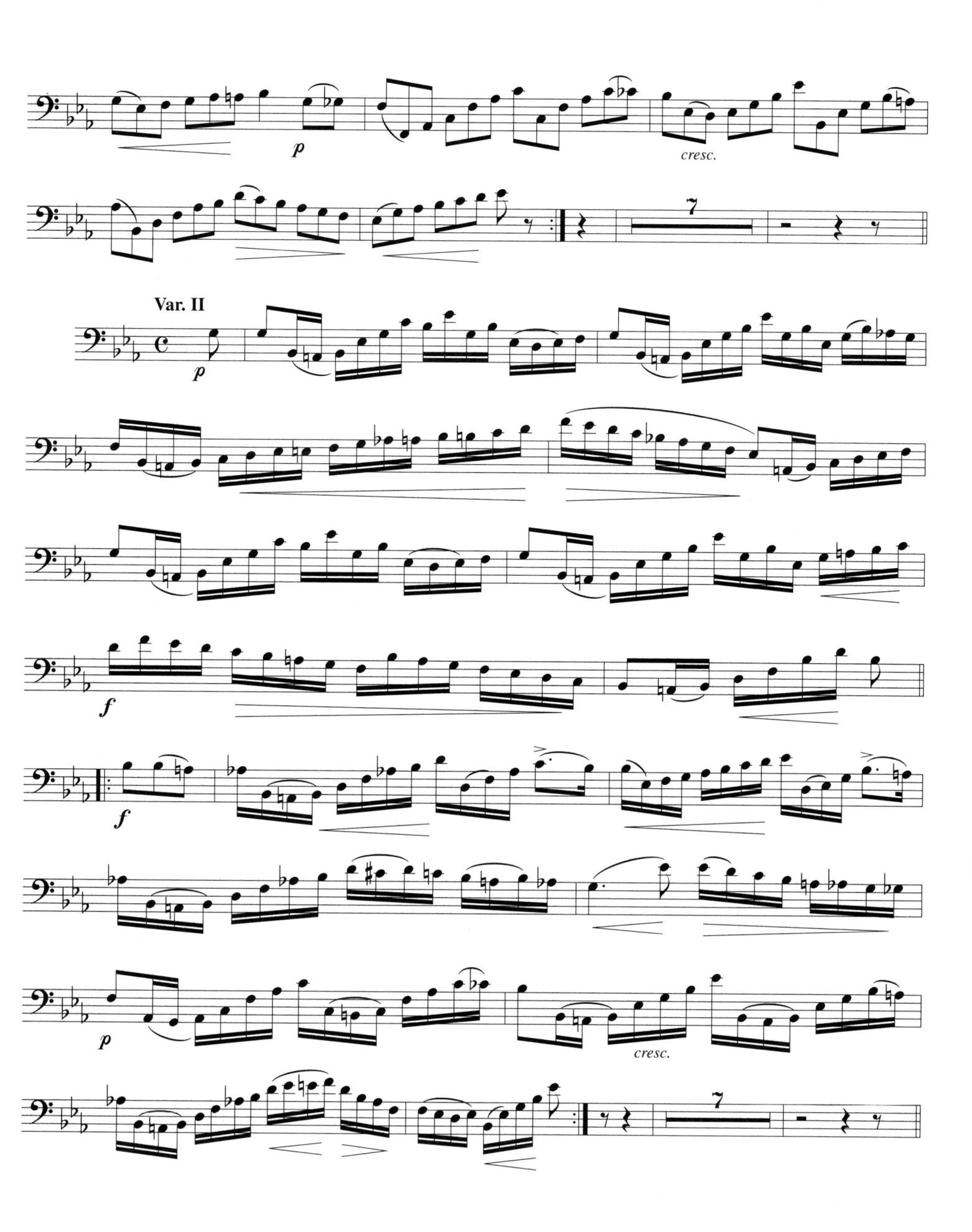

SOLOS Arban • 375

**Var. III**
**Più lento**

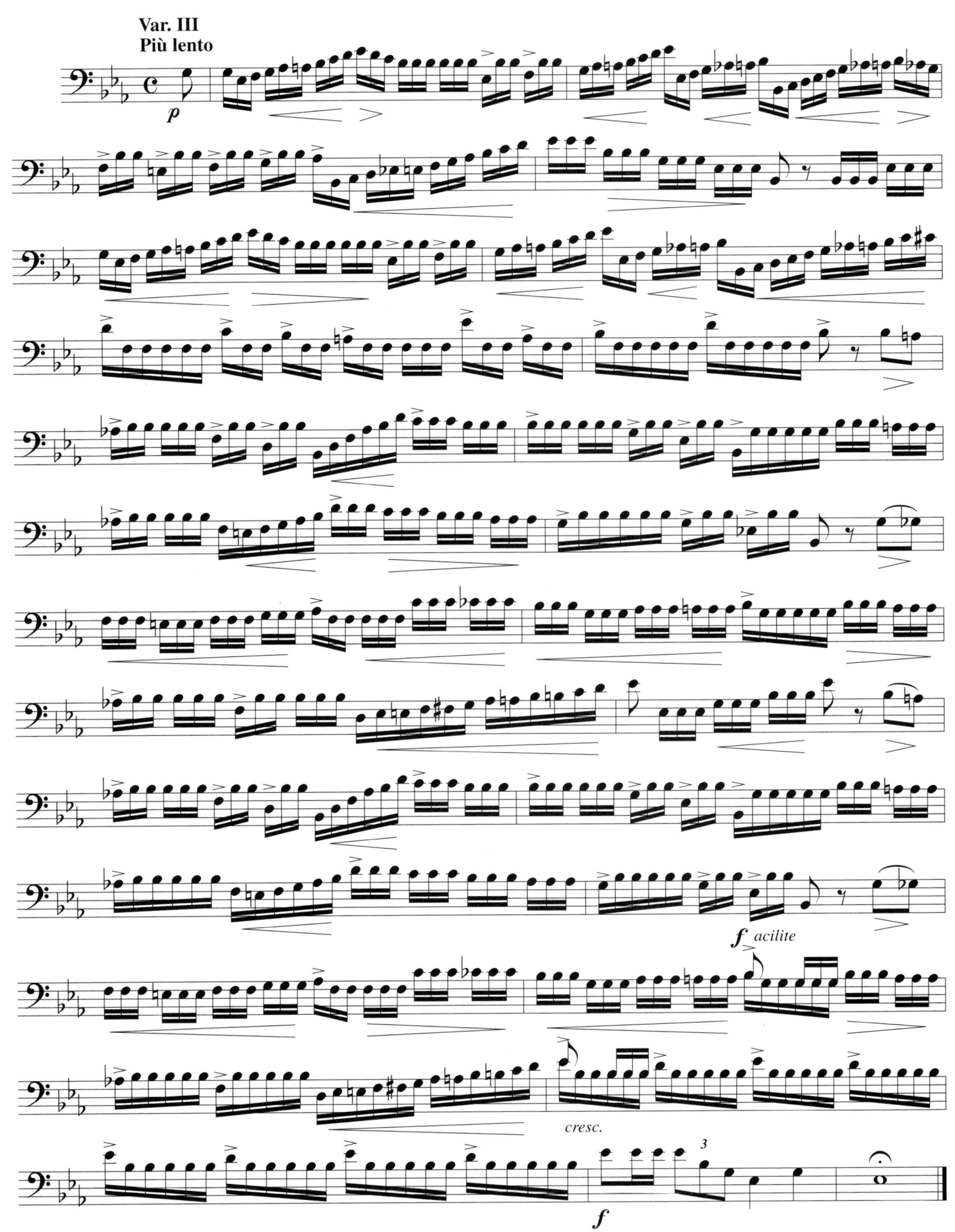

# No. 9
## Fantaisie and Variations
on a German Theme

J.B. Arban

**Allegro moderato** ♩= 112

378 • Arban SOLOS

### Var. III

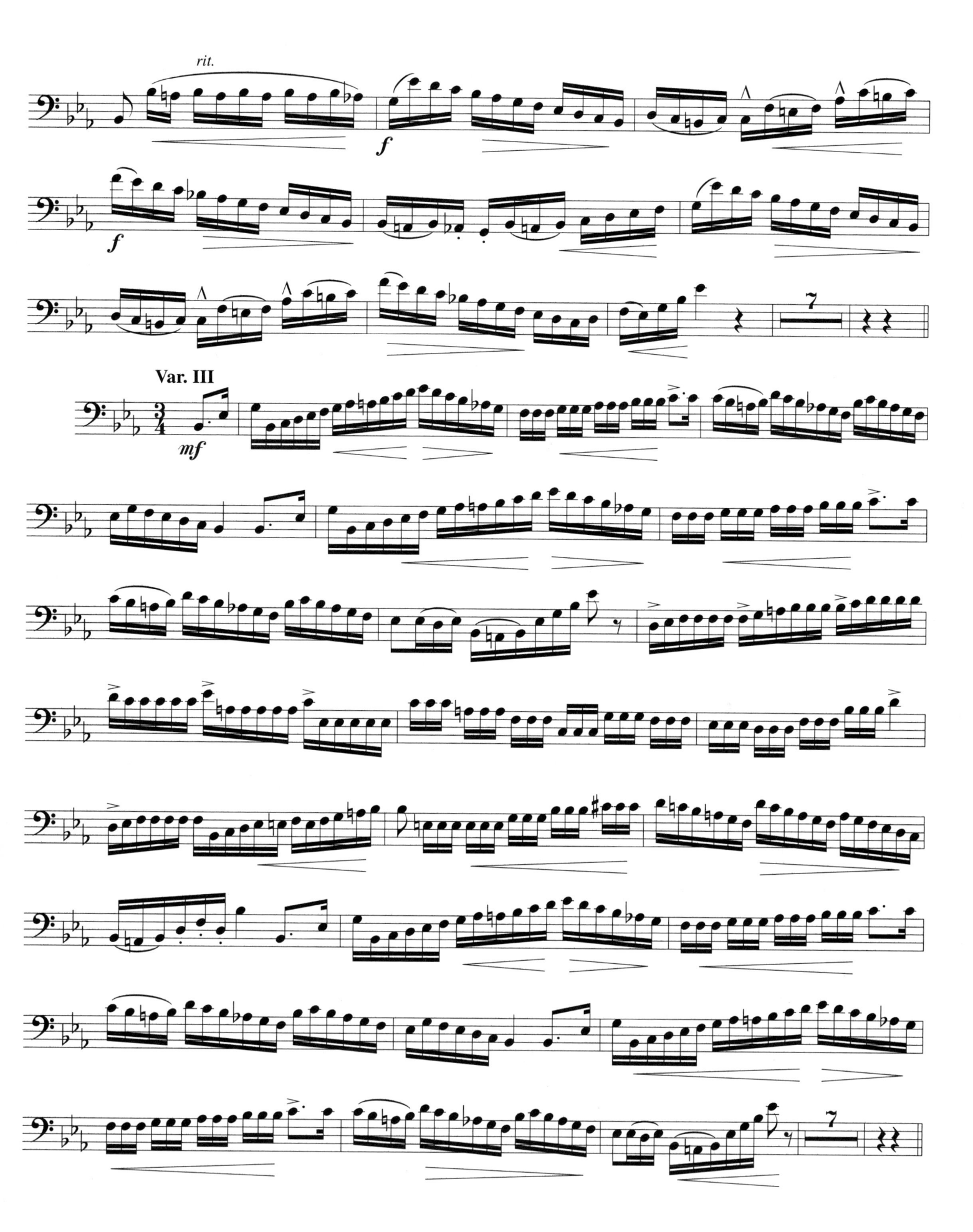

Finale

# No. 10
# Variations
## on a favorite theme
## by
## C. M. von Weber

J.B. Arban

**Introduction**
**Allegro moderato** ♩= 108

*Più lento*

*mf*

**Tempo I**

*f*

**Theme**
**Andante non troppo**

**Var. I**

**Var. II**

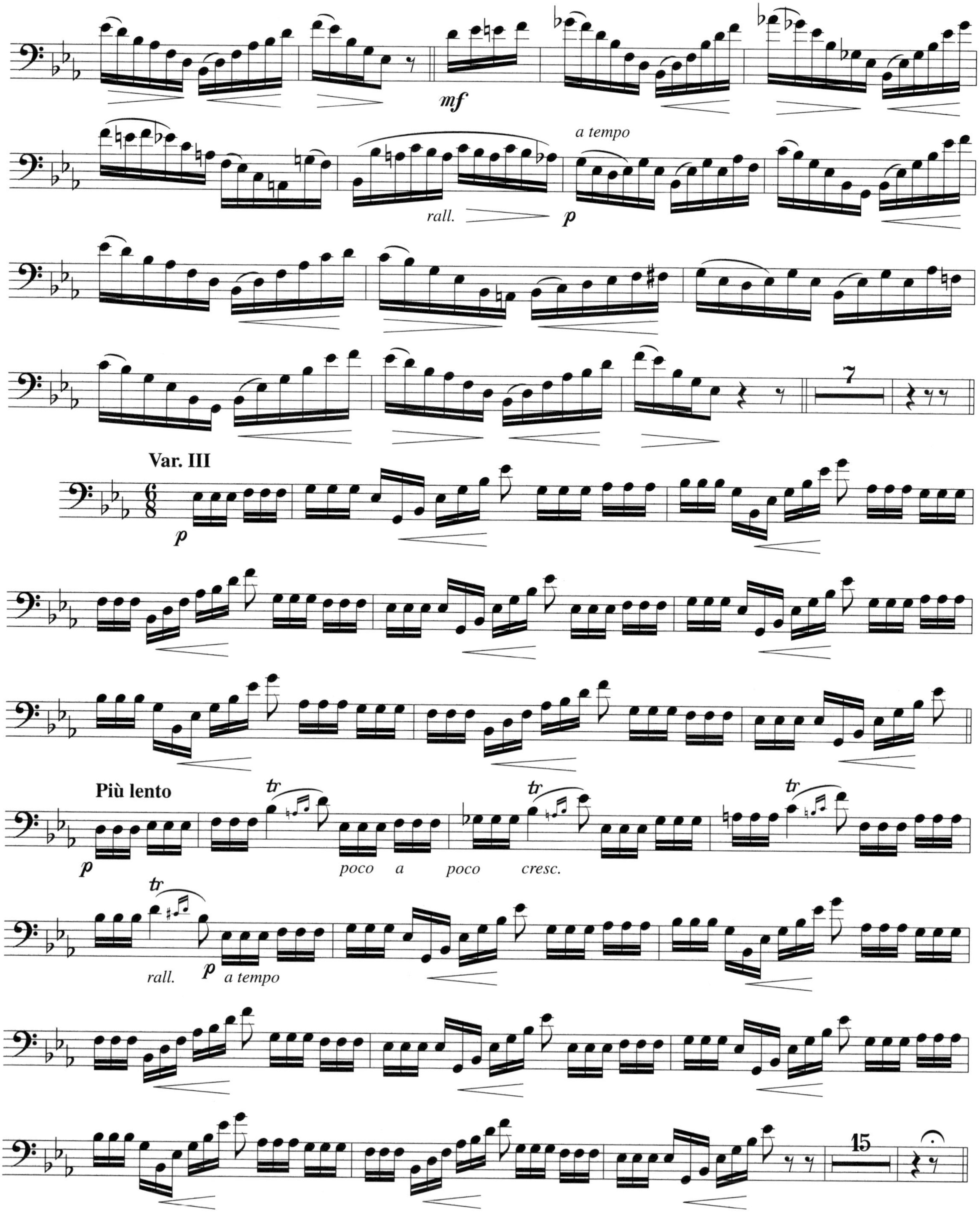
mf
a tempo
rall.
p
7
Var. III
p
Più lento
p
tr
poco a poco cresc.
tr
rall.
p a tempo
15

**Var. IV**

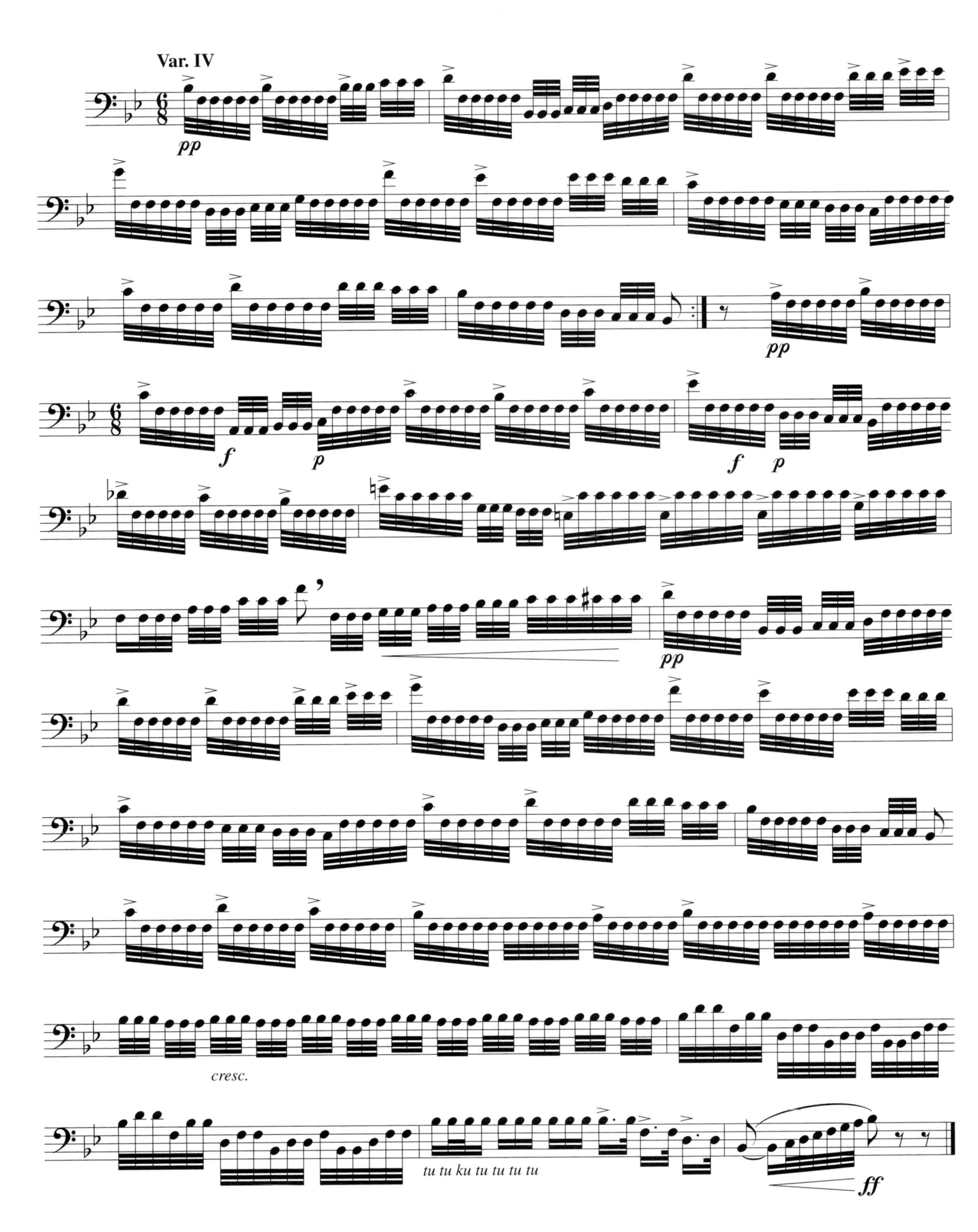

# No. 11
# Fantaisie Variations
## on
## *The Carnival of Venice*

*J.B. Arban*

**Introduction**
**Allegretto** ♩= 84

**Var. I**

*(Double tonguing)*

**Var. II** *poco più mosso*

**Var. III**
**Andante**

**Var. IV**

*mf*

**Coda**

*f*  *tu ku tu ku tu ku*

*tu tu ku tu tu tu tu*

# No. 12
# Variations
## on a theme from
## *Norma*
## by V. Bellini

*J.B. Arban*

**Var.I**

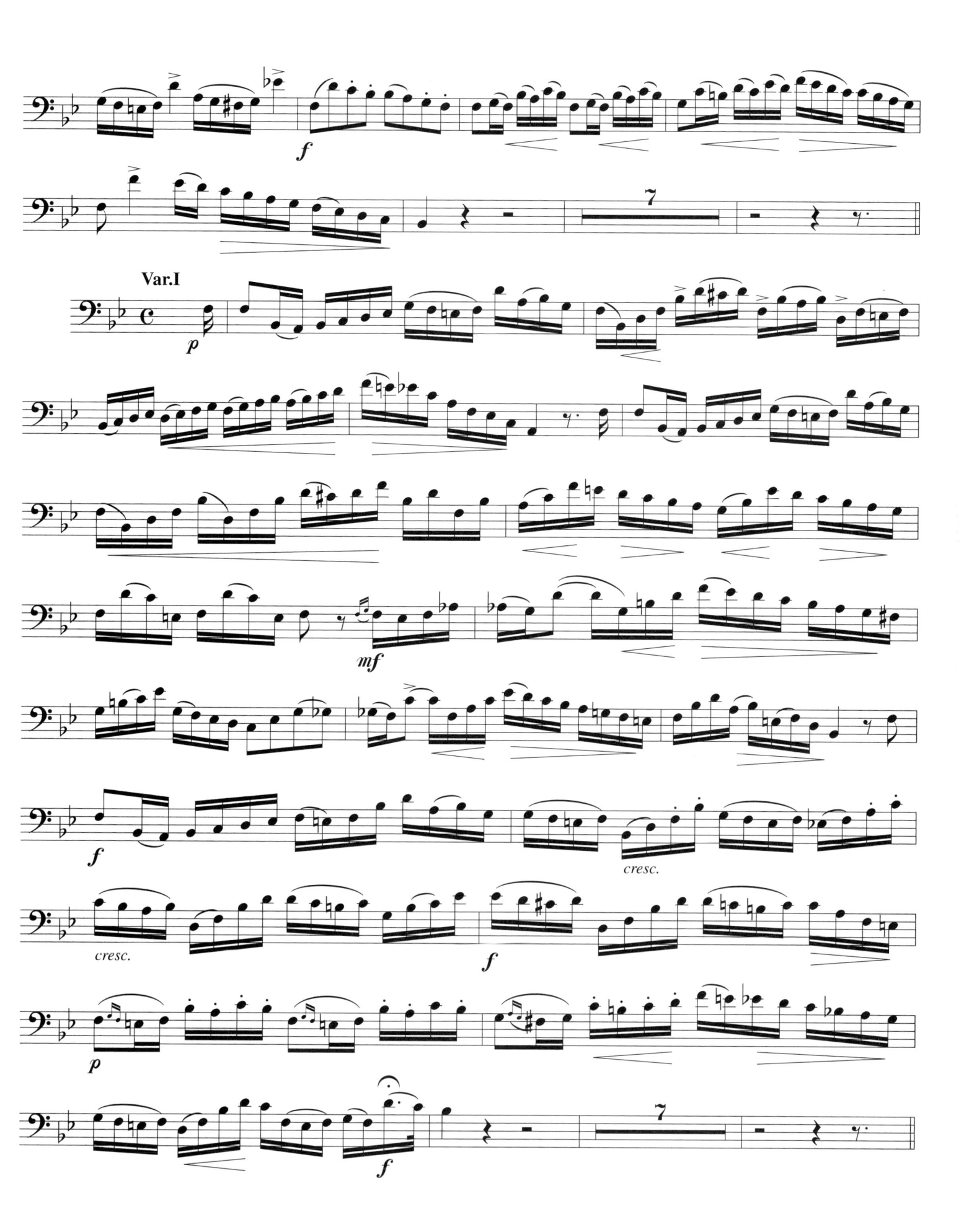

*SOLOS Arban • 391*

**Var.II**

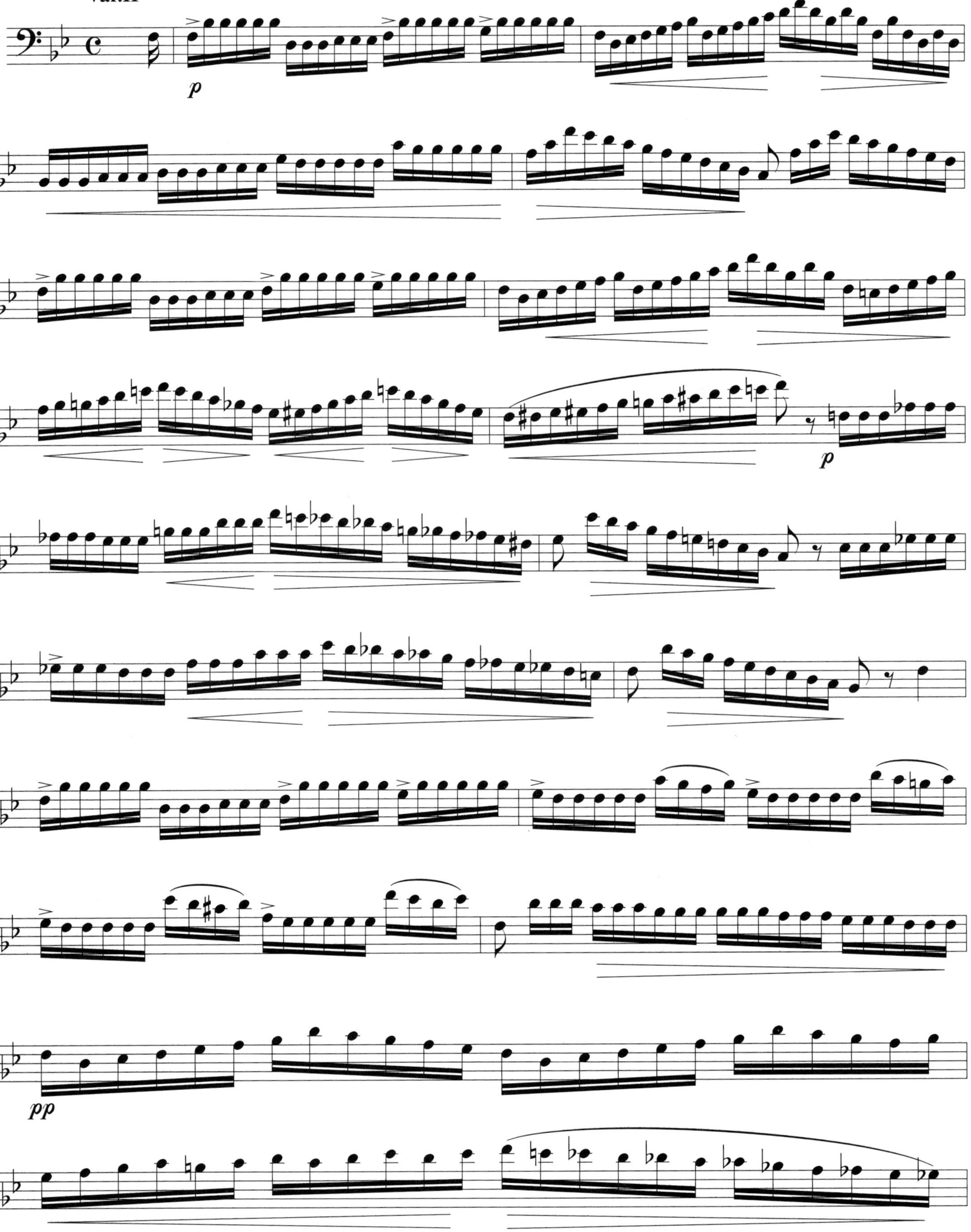

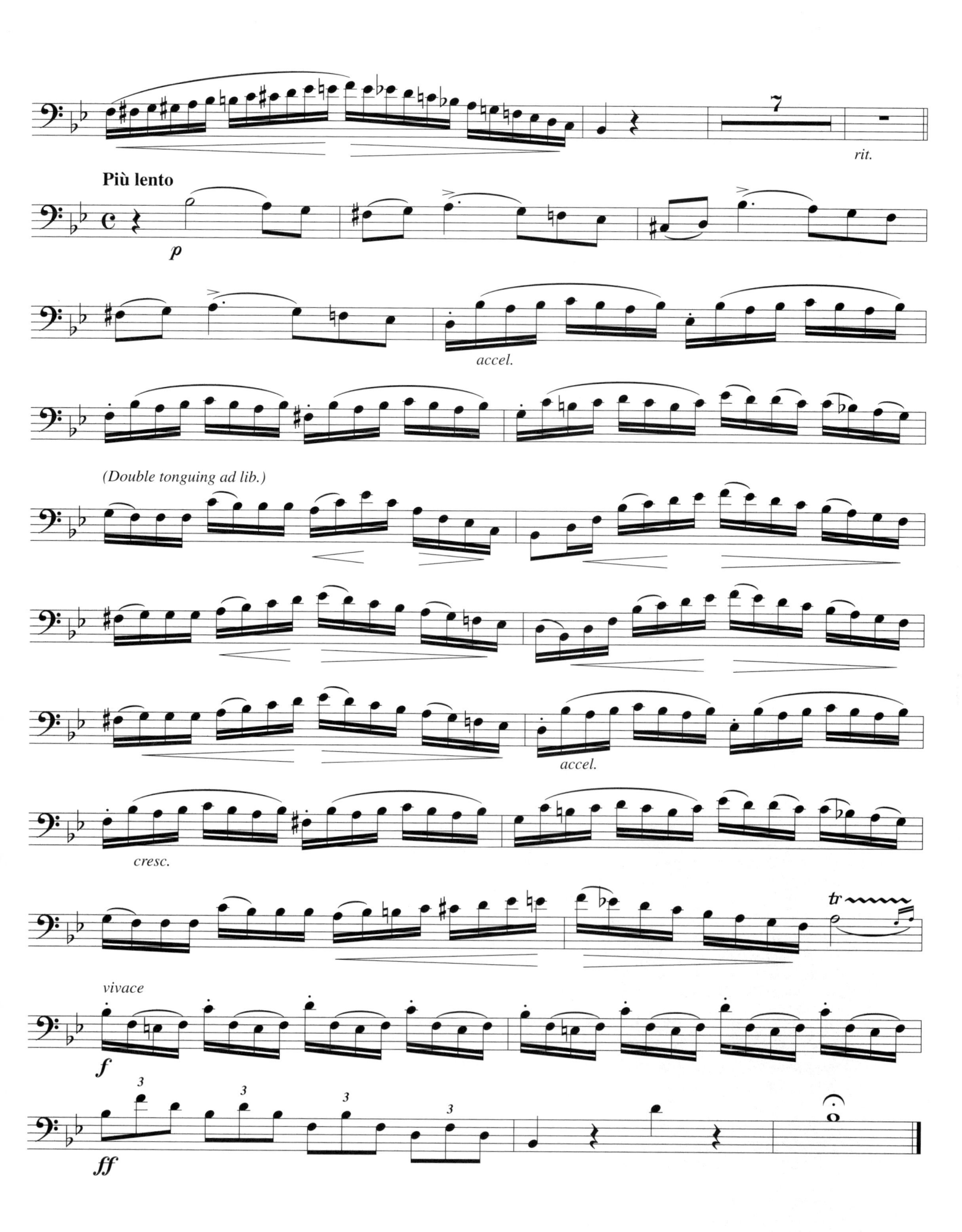

SOLOS Arban • 393

# Fingering Chart
## Four valve compensating (non compensating) euphonium
Each fingering may also be used for the note one octave above.

# Progress Notes

# Progress Notes

# Progress Notes

# Progress Notes

# Progress Notes

# Progress Notes